MASTERING THE MARKET CYCLE

MASTERING
THE
MARKET CYCLE

GETTING THE ODDS
ON YOUR SIDE

Howard Marks

Houghton Mifflin Harcourt
Boston   New York
2018

This book presents the ideas of its author. It is not intended to be a substitute for consultation with a financial professional. The publisher and the author disclaim liability for any adverse effects resulting directly or indirectly from information contained in this book.

For information about permission to reproduce selections from this book, write to trade.permissions@hmhco.com or to Permissions, Houghton Mifflin Harcourt Publishing Company, 3 Park Avenue, 19th Floor, New York, New York 10016.

hmhco.com

Library of Congress Cataloging-in-Publication Data
Names: Marks, Howard S., author.
Title: Mastering the market cycle : getting the odds on your side / Howard S. Marks.
Description: Boston : Houghton Mifflin Harcourt, 2018. | Includes index. | Identifiers: LCCN 2018006867 (print) | LCCN 2018008133 (ebook) | ISBN 9781328480569 (ebook) | ISBN 9781328479259 (hardback)
Subjects: LCSH: Investments. | Finance, Personal. | BISAC: BUSINESS & ECONOMICS / Personal Finance / Investing.
Classification: LCC HG4521 (ebook) | LCC HG4521 .M3214 2018 (print) | DDC 332.6 — dc23
LC record available at https://lccn.loc.gov/2018006867

All graphs courtesy of the author

Printed in the United States of America
DOC 10 9 8 7 6 5 4 3 2 1

With All My Love
to Nancy
Jane, Justin, Rosie and Sam
Andrew and Rachel

CONTENTS

Introduction   1

I. Why Study Cycles?   9

II. The Nature of Cycles   22

III. The Regularity of Cycles   39

IV. The Economic Cycle   46

V. Government Involvement with the Economic Cycle   67

VI. The Cycle in Profits   74

VII. The Pendulum of Investor Psychology   82

VIII. The Cycle in Attitudes Toward Risk   101

IX. The Credit Cycle   136

X. The Distressed Debt Cycle   161

XI. The Real Estate Cycle   169

XII. Putting It All Together — The Market Cycle   185

XIII.   How to Cope with Market Cycles   207

XIV.   Cycle Positioning   246

XV.   Limits on Coping   262

XVI.   The Cycle in Success   270

XVII.   The Future of Cycles   285

XVIII. The Essence of Cycles   294

        Index   317

MASTERING THE MARKET CYCLE

INTRODUCTION

Seven years ago I wrote a book called *The Most Important Thing: Uncommon Sense for the Thoughtful Investor,* regarding where investors should direct their greatest attention. In it I said "the most important thing is being attentive to cycles." The truth, however, is that I applied the label "the most important thing" to nineteen other things as well. There is no single most important thing in investing. Every one of the twenty elements I discussed in *The Most Important Thing* is absolutely essential for anyone who wishes to be a successful investor.

Vince Lombardi, the legendary coach of the Green Bay Packers, is famous for having said, "winning isn't everything, it's the only thing." I've never been able to figure out what Lombardi actually meant by that statement, but there's no doubt he considered winning the most important thing. Likewise, I can't say an understanding of cycles is everything in investing, or the only thing, but for me it's certainly right near the top of the list.

Most of the great investors I've known over the years have had an exceptional sense for how cycles work in general and where we stand in the current one. That sense permits them to do a superior job of positioning portfolios for what lies ahead. Good cycle timing — combined with an effective investment approach and the involvement of exceptional people —

has accounted for the vast bulk of the success of my firm, Oaktree Capital Management.

It's for that reason — and because I find something particularly intriguing about the fluctuations of cycles — and because where we stand in the cycle is one of the things my clients ask about most — and finally because so little has been written about the essential nature of cycles — that I decided to follow *The Most Important Thing* with a book devoted entirely to an exploration of cycles. I hope you'll find it of use.

∾

Some patterns and events recur regularly in our environment, influencing our behavior and our lives. The winter is colder and snowier than the summer, and the daytime is lighter than the night. Thus we plan ski trips for the winter and sailing trips for the summer, and our work and recreation for the daytime and our sleeping at night. We turn on the lights as evening draws nigh and turn them off when we go to bed. We unpack our warm coats as the winter approaches and our bathing suits for the summer. While some people swim in the ocean in winter for exhilaration and some elect to work the night shift to free up their days, the vast majority of us follow the normal circadian patterns, making everyday life easier.

We humans use our ability to recognize and understand patterns to make our decisions easier, increase benefits and avoid pain. Importantly, we depend on our knowledge of recurring patterns so we won't have to reconsider every decision from scratch. We know hurricanes are more likely in September, so we avoid the Caribbean at that time of year. We New Yorkers schedule our visits to Miami and Phoenix for the winter months, when the temperature differential is a positive, not a negative. And we don't have to wake each day in January and decide anew whether to dress for warmth or cold.

Economies, companies and markets also operate pursuant to patterns. Some of these patterns are commonly called cycles. They arise from naturally occurring phenomena but, importantly, also from the ups and downs of human psychology and from the resultant human behavior. Because human psychology and behavior play such a big part in creating them, these cycles aren't as regular as the cycles of clock and calendar, but they still give rise to better and worse times for certain actions. And they can profoundly affect investors. If we pay attention to cycles, we can come out ahead. If we study past cycles, understand their origins and import, and keep alert for the next one, we don't have to reinvent the wheel in order to understand every investment environment anew. And we have less of a chance of being blindsided by events. We can master these recurring patterns for our betterment.

∾

It's my primary message that we should pay attention to cycles; perhaps I should say "listen to them." Dictionary.com supplies two closely related but distinct definitions for the word "listen." The first is "to attend closely for the purpose of hearing." The second is "to heed." Both definitions are relevant to what I'm writing about.

In order to properly position a portfolio for what's going on in the environment — and for what that implies regarding the future of the markets — the investor has to maintain a high level of attention. Events happen equally to everyone who is operating in a given environment. But not everyone listens to them equally in the sense of paying attention, being aware of them, and thus potentially figuring out their import.

And certainly not everyone heeds equally. By "heed" I mean "obey, bear in mind, be guided by or take to heart." Or, in other words, "to absorb a lesson and follow its dictates." Perhaps I can better convey this "heeding"

sense for listening by listing its antonyms: ignore, disregard, discount, reject, overlook, neglect, shun, flout, disobey, tune out, turn a deaf ear to, or
be inattentive to. Invariably, investors who disregard where they stand in
cycles are bound to suffer serious consequences.

In order to get the most out of this book — and do the best job of dealing
with cycles — an investor has to learn to recognize cycles, assess them, look
for the instructions they imply, and do what they tell him to do. (See the
author's note below regarding my use of male pronouns.) If an investor listens in this sense, he will be able to convert cycles from a wild, uncontrol-
lable force that wreaks havoc, into a phenomenon that can be understood
and taken advantage of: a vein that can be mined for significant outperformance.

∾

A winning investment philosophy can be created only through the combination of a number of essential elements:

- A technical education in accounting, finance and economics provides the foundation: necessary but far from sufficient.
- A view on how markets work is important — you should have one
  before you set out to invest, but it must be added to, questioned,
  refined and reshaped as you proceed.
- Some of your initial views will come from what you've read, so
  reading is an essential building block. Continuing to read will enable you to increase the efficacy of your approach — both embrac-
  ing those ideas you find appealing and discarding those you don't.
  Importantly, it's great to read outside the strict boundaries of investing. Legendary investor Charlie Munger often points to the

benefits of reading broadly; history and processes in other fields can add greatly to effective investment approaches and decisions.

- Exchanging ideas with fellow investors can be an invaluable source of growth. Given the non-scientific nature of investing, there's no such thing as being finished with your learning, and no individual has a monopoly on insight. Investing can be solitary, but I think those who practice it in solitude are missing a lot, both intellectually and interpersonally.

- Finally, there really is no substitute for experience. Every year I have come to view investing differently, and every cycle I've lived through has taught me something about how to cope with the next one. I recommend a long career and see no reason to stop any time soon.

Writing my books has given me a wonderful vehicle for acknowledging the people who have contributed to my investment insight and the texture of my working life.

- I've gained a great deal from reading the work of Peter Bernstein, John Kenneth Galbraith, Nassim Nicholas Taleb and Charlie Ellis.
- I've continued to pick up pointers from the people I cited in *The Most Important Thing* and others, including Seth Klarman, Charlie Munger, Warren Buffett, Bruce Newberg, Michael Milken, Jacob Rothschild, Todd Combs, Roger Altman, Joel Greenblatt, Peter Kaufman and Doug Kass. And since Nancy and I moved to New York in 2013 to follow our kids, I've been fortunate to add Oscar Schafer, Jim Tisch and Ajit Jain to this circle. Each of these people's way of looking at things has added to mine.

- Finally I want to return to the most important collaborators, my
  Oaktree co-founders: Bruce Karsh, Sheldon Stone, Richard Masson and Larry Keele. They honored me by adopting my philosophy as the foundation for Oaktree's investment approach; applied
  it skillfully (and thus gained recognition for it); and helped me
  add to it over the thirty-plus years we've been associated. As indicated in what follows, Bruce and I have exchanged ideas and
  backed each other up almost daily over that period, and my give-
  and-take with him — especially in the most difficult of times — has
  played a particularly indispensable part in the development of the
  approach to cycles on which this book is based.

I also want to thank the people who played important parts in this
book's creation: my talented editor at HMH, Rick Wolff; my resourceful
agent, Jim Levine, who brought me to Rick; my great friend Karen Mack
Goldsmith, who pushed me at every turn to make the book more appealing; and my highly supportive long-time assistant, Caroline Heald. I particularly want to cite Prof. Randy Kroszner of the University of Chicago's
Booth School, who helped out by reviewing the chapters on the economic
cycle and government intervention with it.

≈

Since knowledge is cumulative but we never know it all, I look forward to
learning more in the years ahead. In investing, there is nothing that always
works, since the environment is always changing, and investors' efforts
to respond to the environment cause it to change further. Thus I hope to
know things in the future that I don't know now, and I look forward to
sharing them in memos and books yet to come.

Author's notes:

1. As I did in *The Most Important Thing,* I want to issue up front a blanket apology for my consistent use of male pronouns. It can be force of habit for someone who started to write more than sixty years ago. I find it much easier and more attractive to write "he" than "he/she." Alternating between "he" and "she" seems forced. And I dislike the use of "they" when the subject is a single person. The exceptional women I've been privileged to work with over the course of my career know I absolutely think every bit as much of them as professionals and investors as I do their male counterparts.

2. Also as in *The Most Important Thing,* in order to make my points here I will borrow from time to time from the client memos I've written over the years starting in 1990. I will also borrow from my first book. I could go to the trouble of reinventing the wheel and writing on these subjects anew, but I won't. Instead, I'll lift key passages from my book and memos that I think make their point clearly. I hope my doing so won't make those who buy this book feel they've received less than their money's worth.

   In order to advance the purposes of this book, I will occasionally add a few words to or delete a few from the passages I cite, or present paragraphs in an order different from that in which they appeared in the original. Since they're my passages, I think it's okay to do so without noting it in every case. But I do it only to increase their helpfulness, not to alter their meaning or make them more correct with the benefit of hindsight.

3. And finally as in *The Most Important Thing,* I'll be dealing here with a topic that—like investing in general—is complex and in-

volves elements that overlap and can't be neatly segregated into discrete chapters. Since some of those elements are touched on in multiple places, you'll likewise find some instances of repetition where I include noteworthy quotations from others or citations from my book and memos that I can't resist using more than once.

4.   Please note that when I talk about "investing," I'll assume the investor is buying, holding or, as we say, "being long" in the expectation that certain assets will appreciate. This is as opposed to selling short securities that one doesn't own in the hope they'll decline. Investors aren't always "long" rather than "short," but most of the time they are. The number of people who sell stocks short or ever get "net short" — that is, whose short positions have a total value exceeding that of the stocks they own — is tiny relative to those who don't. Thus, in this book I'm going to speak exclusively about investing in things because they're expected to rise, not selling assets short in the hope they'll fall.

5.   Lastly, whereas I first conceived of this book as being just about cycles, as I wrote I came up with ideas on lots of other topics, such as asset selection and "catching falling knives." Rather than discard them, I've included them, too. I hope you'll be glad they're here: providing a bonus rather than straying from the mission.

I

WHY STUDY CYCLES?

===

The odds change as our position in the cycles changes. If we don't change our investment stance as these things change, we're being passive regarding cycles; in other words, we're ignoring the chance to tilt the odds in our favor. But if we apply some insight regarding cycles, we can increase our bets and place them on more aggressive investments when the odds are in our favor, and we can take money off the table and increase our defensiveness when the odds are against us.

Investing is a matter of preparing for the financial future. It's simple to define the task: we assemble portfolios today that we hope will benefit from the events that unfold in the years ahead.

For professional investors, success consists of doing this better than the average investor, or outperforming an assigned market benchmark (the performance of which is determined by the actions of all the other investors). But achieving that kind of success is no small challenge: although it's very easy to generate average investment performance, it's quite hard to perform above average.

One of the most important foundational elements of my investment philosophy is my conviction that we can't know what the "macro future" has in store for us in terms of things like economies, markets or geopolitics. Or, to put it more precisely, few people are able on balance to know more about the macro future than others. And it's only if we know more than others (whether that consists of having better data; doing a superior job of interpreting the data we have; knowing what actions to take on the basis of or our interpretation; or having the emotional fortitude required to take those actions) that our forecasts will lead to outperformance.

In short, if we have the same information as others, analyze it the same way, reach the same conclusions and implement them the same way, we shouldn't expect that process to result in outperformance. And it's very difficult to be consistently superior in those regards as relates to the macro.

So, in my view, trying to predict what the macro future holds is unlikely to help investors achieve superior investment performance. Very few investors are known for having outperformed through macro forecasting.

Warren Buffett once told me about his two criteria for a desirable piece of information: it has to be important, and it has to be knowable. Although "everyone knows" that macro developments play a dominant role in determining the performance of markets these days, "macro investors" as a whole have shown rather unimpressive results. It's not that the macro doesn't matter, but rather that very few people can master it. For most, it's just not knowable (or not knowable well enough and consistently enough for it to lead to outperformance).

Thus I dismiss macro prediction as something that will bring investment success for the vast majority of investors, and I certainly include myself in that group. If that's so, what's left? While there are lots of details and nuances, I think we can most gainfully spend our time in three general areas:

- trying to know more than others about what I call "the knowable": the fundamentals of industries, companies and securities,
- being disciplined as to the appropriate price to pay for a participation in those fundamentals, and
- understanding the investment environment we're in and deciding how to strategically position our portfolios for it.

A great deal has been written on the first two topics. Together, these constitute the key ingredients in "security analysis" and "value investing": judgments regarding what an asset can produce in the future — usually in terms of earnings or cash flow — and what those prospects make the asset worth today.

What do value investors do? They strive to take advantage of discrepancies between "price" and "value." In order to do that successfully, they have to (a) quantify an asset's intrinsic value and how it's likely to change over time and (b) assess how the current market price compares with the asset's intrinsic value, past prices for the asset, the prices of other assets, and "theoretically fair" prices for assets in general.

Then they use that information to assemble portfolios. Most of the time, it's their immediate goal to hold investments offering the best available value propositions: the assets with the greatest upside potential and/or the best ratio of upside potential to downside risk. You might argue that assembling a portfolio should consist of nothing more than identifying the assets with the highest value and the ones whose prices most understate their value. That may be true in general and in the long term, but I think another element can profitably enter into the process: properly positioning a portfolio for what's likely to happen in the market in the years immediately ahead.

In my view, the greatest way to optimize the positioning of a portfolio at a given point in time is through deciding what balance it should strike between aggressiveness and defensiveness. And I believe the aggressiveness/ defensiveness balance should be adjusted over time in response to changes in the state of the investment environment and where a number of elements stand in their cycles.

> The key word is "calibrate." The amount you have invested, your allocation of capital among the various possibilities, and the riskiness of the things you own all should be calibrated along a continuum that runs from aggressive to defensive.... When we're getting value cheap, we should be aggressive; when we're getting value expensive, we should pull back. ("Yet Again?," September 2017)

Calibrating one's portfolio position is what this book is mostly about.

∾

One of the key words required if one is to understand the reasons for studying cycles is "tendencies."

If the factors that influence investing were regular and predictable — for example, if macro forecasting worked — we would be able to talk about what "will happen." Yet the fact that that's not the case doesn't mean we're helpless in contemplating the future. Rather, we can talk about the things that might happen or should happen, and how likely they are to happen. Those things are what I call "tendencies."

In the investment world, we talk about risk all the time, but there's no universal agreement about what risk is or what it should imply for investors' behavior. Some people think risk is the likelihood of losing money, and others (including many finance academics) think risk is the volatility of asset prices or returns. And there are many other kinds of risk — too many to cover here.

I lean heavily toward the first definition: in my view, risk is primarily the likelihood of permanent capital loss. But there's also such a thing as opportunity risk: the likelihood of missing out on potential gains. Put the two together and we see that risk is the possibility of things not going the way we want.

What is the origin of risk? One of my favorite investment philosophers, the late Peter Bernstein, said in an issue of his *Economics and Portfolio Strategy* newsletter titled "Can We Measure Risk with a Number?" (June 2007):

> Essentially risk says we don't know what's going to happen. . . . We walk every moment into the unknown. There's a range of outcomes, and we don't know where [the actual outcome is] going to fall within the range. Often we don't know what the range is.

You'll find below a few ideas (summarized very briefly from the full treatment provided in my memo "Risk Revisited Again" of June 2015) that I think follow directly from the starting point provided by Bernstein. They might help you understand and cope with risk.

As retired London Business School professor Elroy Dimson said, "Risk means more things can happen than will happen." For each event in economics, business and markets (among other things), if only one thing could happen — if there could be only one outcome — and if it was predictable, there would, of course, be no uncertainty or risk. And with no uncertainty regarding what was going to happen, in theory we could know exactly how to position our portfolios to avoid loss and garner maximum gains. But in life and in investing, since there can be many different outcomes, uncertainty and risk are inescapable.

As a consequence of the above, the future should be viewed not as a single fixed outcome that's destined to happen and capable of being predicted, but as a range of possibilities and — hopefully on the basis of insight into their respective likelihoods — as a probability distribution. Probability distributions reflect one's view of tendencies.

Investors — or anyone hoping to deal successfully with the future — have to form probability distributions, either explicitly or informally. If it's done well, those probabilities will be helpful in determining one's proper course of action. But it's still essential to bear in mind that even if we know the probabilities, that doesn't mean we know what's going to happen.

Outcomes regarding a given matter may be governed by a probability distribution in the long run, but with regard to the outcome of a single event there can be great uncertainty. Any of the outcomes included in a distribution can occur, albeit with varying probabilities, since the process through which the outcome is chosen will be affected not only by the merits, but also by randomness. To invert Dimson's statement, even though many things can happen, only one will. We may know what to expect "on average," but that may have no connection with what actually will happen.

In my way of thinking about it, investment success is like the choosing of a lottery winner. Both are determined by one ticket (the outcome) being pulled from a bowlful (the full range of possible outcomes). In each case, one outcome is chosen from among the many possibilities.

Superior investors are people who have a better sense for what tickets are in the bowl, and thus for whether it's worth participating in the lottery. In other words, while superior investors — like everyone else — don't know exactly what the future holds, they do have an above-average understanding of future tendencies.

As an aside, I want to add a thought here. Most people think the way to deal with the future is by formulating an opinion as to what's going to happen, perhaps via a probability distribution. I think there are actually two requirements, not one. In addition to an opinion regarding what's going to happen, people should have a view on the likelihood that their opinion will prove correct. Some events can be predicted with substantial confidence (e.g., will a given investment grade bond pay the interest it promises?), some are uncertain (will Amazon still be the leader in online retailing in ten years?) and some are entirely unpredictable (will the stock market go up or down next month?) It's my point here that not all predictions should be treated as equally likely to be correct, and thus they shouldn't be relied on equally. I don't think most people are as aware of this as they should be.

~

A good way to think about the superior investor described above is as someone whose insight into tendencies permits him to tilt the odds in his favor.

Let's say there are 100 balls in a jar, some black and some white. Which color should you bet will come up?

- If you don't know anything about the contents of the jar, betting would be just a matter of guessing: uninformed speculation. The situation is similar if you know there are 50 black and 50 white. You can just as wisely bet on black as white, but doing either wouldn't give you more than a 50:50 chance of being right. Thus betting would be dumb unless you're offered odds that are at least even — and unless you're able to avoid paying an admission charge (in investing, a commission or bid-asked spread) to play. Betting on black or white at even odds wouldn't very profitable other than if you got lucky, and luck isn't something you can count on. Betting in the absence of a knowledge edge regarding the contents of the jar wouldn't be dependably profitable.

- But what if you do have special insight regarding the contents of the jar? Let's say you know there are 70 black balls and 30 white. That could allow you to win more often than you lose. If you can bet $10 on black against someone who gives you even odds, you'll win $10 70% of the time and lose $10 only 30% of the time, for an expected profit of $40 per 10 picks. (Note: these will be the outcomes on average over a large number of trials, but they are subject to significant variation in the short run due to randomness.)

- Of course, your betting partner will only give you even odds on a bet on black (a) if he doesn't know the balls are 70% black and 30% white and (b) if he doesn't know that you do know. If he knew as much as you do about the contents of the jar, he would give you only 30:70 odds on a bet on black, and the bet would be back to being profitless.

- In other words, in order to win at this game more often than you lose, you have to have a knowledge advantage. That's what the superior investor has: he knows more than others about the future tendencies.

- Yet it's important to remember what I said earlier: even if you know the probabilities — that is, even if you do have superior insight regarding the tendencies — you still don't know what's going to happen. Even if the ratio of balls in the jar is 70 black to 30 white, you still don't know what color the next one picked will be. Yes, it's more likely to be black than white, but it'll still be white

30% of the time. When there are white balls as well as black in the jar, and especially when random and exogenous forces are at work when the next ball is chosen, there can be no certainty regarding the outcome.

- But all this being said, there doesn't have to be certainty in order for the game to be worth playing. A knowledge advantage regarding the tendencies is enough to create success in the long run.

∼

And that brings us to the payoff from understanding cycles. The average investor doesn't know much about it:

- He doesn't fully understand the nature and importance of cycles.
- He hasn't been around long enough to have lived through many cycles.
- He hasn't read financial history and thus learned the lessons of past cycles.
- He sees the environment primarily in terms of isolated events, rather than taking note of recurring patterns and the reasons behind them.
- Most important, he doesn't understand the significance of cycles and what they can tell him about how to act.

The superior investor is attentive to cycles. He takes note of whether past patterns seem to be repeating, gains a sense for where we stand in the various cycles that matter, and knows those things have implications for his actions. This allows him to make helpful judgments about cycles and where we stand in them. Specifically:

- Are we close to the beginning of an upswing, or in the late stages?
- If a particular cycle has been rising for a while, has it gone so far that we're now in dangerous territory?
- Does investors' behavior suggest they're being driven by greed or by fear?
- Do they seem appropriately risk-averse or foolishly risk-tolerant?
- Is the market overheated (and overpriced), or is it frigid (and thus cheap) because of what's been going on cyclically?
- Taken together, does our current position in the cycle imply that we should emphasize defensiveness or aggressiveness?

Attention to these elements gives the superior investor an edge that allows him to win more often than he loses. He understands the tendencies or odds; thus he knows something that others don't about the color of the balls in the jar. He has a sense for whether the chances of winning exceed the chances of losing; thus he is able to invest more when they are favorable and less when they aren't. Importantly, all these things can be assessed on the basis of observations regarding current conditions. As we'll see in later chapters, they can tell us how to prepare for the future without requiring that we be able to predict the future.

Remember, where we stand in the various cycles has a strong influence on the odds. For example, as we'll see in later chapters, opportunities for investment gains improve when:

- the economy and company profits are more likely to swing upward than down,
- investor psychology is sober rather than buoyant,
- investors are conscious of risk or — even better — overly concerned about risk, and
- market prices haven't moved too high.

There are cycles in all these things (and more), and knowing where we stand within them can help us tilt the odds in our favor. In short, the movement through the cycle repositions the probability distribution governing future events. Perhaps I should illustrate with regard to investment returns:

When our position in the various cycles is neutral, the outlook for returns is "normal."

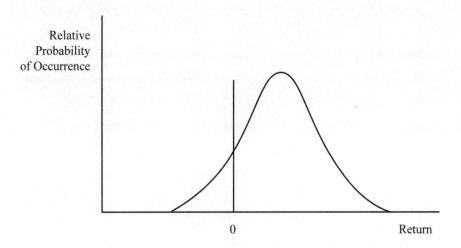

When the cycles are positioned propitiously, the probability distribution shifts to the right, such that the outlook for returns is now tilted in our favor. Our favorable position in the cycles makes gains more likely and losses less so.

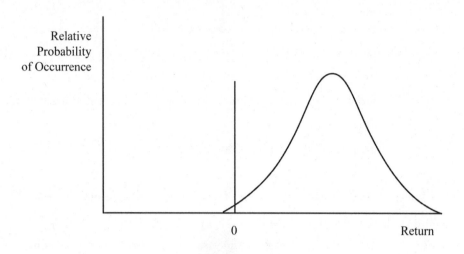

But when the cycles are at dangerous extremes, the odds are against us, meaning the likelihoods are less good. There's less chance of gain and more chance of loss.

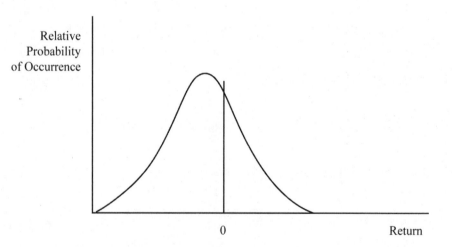

The same is true when our position changes in only a single cycle. For example, regardless of what's going on with regard to the economy and company profits (that is, as the academics say, *ceteris paribus* or "all other things being equal"), the outlook for returns will be better when investors are depressed and fearful (and thus allow asset prices to fall) and worse when they're euphoric and greedy (and drive prices upward).

The odds change as our position in the cycles changes. If we don't change our investment stance as these things change, we're being passive regarding cycles; in other words, we're ignoring the chance to tilt the odds in our favor. But if we apply some insight regarding cycles, we can increase our bets and place them on more aggressive investments when the odds are in our favor, and we can take money off the table and increase our defensiveness when the odds are against us.

The student of cycles doesn't know for a fact what's going to happen next — any more than someone with insight regarding the balls in the jar knows what color ball will come out next. But both have a knowledge advantage regarding what's likely. The student's knowledge of cycles and appreciation for where we stand at a point in time can make a big contribution to the edge that must be present in order for an investor to achieve superior results. The ball-chooser who knows the ratio is 70:30 has an advantage. So does the investor who knows better than others where we stand in the cycle. It's the purpose of this book to help you become that person.

In that interest, I'll describe a number of cyclical processes that I watched take place in real time. The oscillations might seem extreme, and in fact they may be, since they're chosen from the experience of a half-century to prove a point. And they may give the impression that the events under discussion were compressed in time, whereas in truth they took months and years to develop. But these examples are real, and I hope they'll make my message clear.

II

THE NATURE OF CYCLES

Most people think of cycles in terms of a series of events. And most people understand that these events regularly follow each other in a usual sequence: upswings are followed by downswings, and then eventually by new upswings. But to have a full understanding of cycles, that's not enough. The events in the life of a cycle shouldn't be viewed merely as each being followed by the next, but—much more importantly—as each *causing* the next.

When I meet with Oaktree clients, they almost always ask me to help them make sense of what's going on in the world or in the market. They usually want to know about one particular cycle or another and where we stand in it. I invariably pull out a sheet of paper and make a drawing to aid the discussion.

There's usually a line that stretches from lower left to upper right. Another line fluctuates up and down around it. Together they look like this.

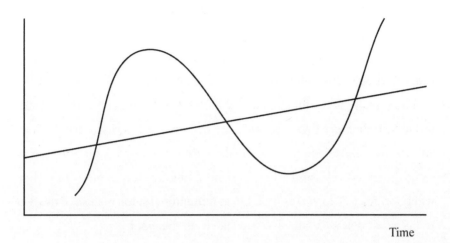

Time

When I started to organize for the task of writing this book, I went through my Oaktree bag and found a large number of such drawings. I had drawn them in the course of describing several different phenomena, and they were annotated differently. But each one related to a cycle worthy of discussion. The chapters in this book will generally be devoted to those cyclical phenomena.

Before moving ahead with my discussion of cycles, I want to return to something I mentioned in *The Most Important Thing*. I confess that I alternate between discussing the ups and downs of cycles and the side-to-side oscillations of pendulums, applying the cycle label to some phenomena and (as seen in chapter VII) the pendulum label to others (usually those connected to psychology). Sometimes I'll talk about a given phenomenon as a cycle, and sometimes as a pendulum. But when pressed, I find it hard to distinguish between the two or to say why one gets one label and not the other.

I tend to think about things visually, so perhaps I can use an image to describe the connection between cycles and pendulums. As I will describe at length later, cycles oscillate around a midpoint (or a secular trend). Similarly, pendulums hang over a midpoint (or norm) and swing back and forth from there. But if you take the hang-point of the pendulum, turn it on its side and drag it from left to right as it oscillates, what do you get? A cycle.

There really is no fundamental difference. I'll even admit that a pendulum is little more than a special case of a cycle, or perhaps just a different way to make reference to particular cycles. My reasons for referring to some things as cycles and others as pendulums are clear to me. I hope they will become clear to you as well. Or, at minimum, I hope my use of the two terms won't detract from what you take from this book.

The bottom line is that, in the world investors inhabit, cycles rise and fall, and pendulums swing back and forth. Cycles and pendulum swings come in many forms and relate to a wide variety of phenomena, but the underlying reasons for them — and the patterns they produce — have a lot in common, and they tend to be somewhat consistent over time. Or as Mark Twain is reputed to have said (although there's no evidence he actually said it), "History doesn't repeat itself, but it does rhyme."

Whether Twain said it or not, that sentence sums up a lot of what this book is about. Cycles vary in terms of reasons and details, and timing and extent, but the ups and downs (and the reasons for them) will occur forever, producing changes in the investment environment — and thus in the behavior that's called for.

The central line in my drawings constitutes a midpoint around which the cycle oscillates. It sometimes has an underlying direction or secular trend ("secular" as in "of or relating to a long term of indefinite duration" per *Webster's New Collegiate Dictionary*), and that's usually upward. So, over time and in the long run, economies tend to grow, companies' profits tend to increase and (largely because of those things) markets tend to rise. And if these developments were scientific or wholly natural, physical processes, economies, companies and markets might progress in a straight line and at a constant rate (at least for a while). But of course, they're not, so they don't.

The fact is that the performance of these things is heavily influenced in the short run by, among other things, the involvement of people, and people are far from steady. Rather they fluctuate from time to time, often because of things we can lump under the broad heading of "psychology." Thus people's behavior varies . . . certainly as the environment varies, but sometimes in the absence of changes in the environment, too.

It's the oscillation of things around the midpoint or secular trend that this book is largely about. The oscillation bedevils people who don't understand it, are surprised by it or, even worse, partake in and contribute to it. But as I've said before, it often presents profit opportunities for those who understand, recognize and take advantage of cyclical phenomena.

∾

It's clear from looking at my drawings for a few seconds that the movements of cyclical phenomena can be understood as taking place in a number of identifiable phases:

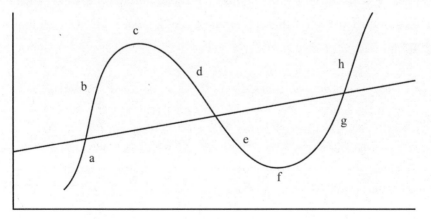

Time

a) recovery from an excessively depressed lower extreme or "low" toward the midpoint,

b) the continued swing past the midpoint toward an upper extreme or "high,"

c) the attainment of a high,

d) the downward correction from the high back toward the midpoint or mean,

e) the continuation of the downward movement past the midpoint, toward a new low,

f) the reaching of a low,

g) once again, recovery from the low back toward the midpoint,

h) and then, again, the continuation of the upward swing past the midpoint, toward another high.

It's important to note from the above that there cannot be said to be a single "starting point" or "ending point" for a cycle. Any of the phases listed above can be described as representing the beginning of a cycle . . . or the end . . . or any stage in between.

The simplistic narrator may find it easy to talk about the beginning of a cycle, but someone a bit more sophisticated can find that extremely hard. Here's what I wrote on this subject in "Now It's All Bad?" (September 2007):

> Henry Kissinger was a member of TCW's board when I worked there, and a few times each year I was privileged to hear him hold forth on world affairs. Someone would ask, "Henry, can you explain yesterday's events in Bosnia?" and he'd say, "Well, in 1722 . . ." The point is that chain reaction-type events can only be understood in the context of that which went before.

If someone asks, "How did we get to this point?" or "What caused us to reach that high (or low)?" invariably the explanation has to be based on the events that went before. But that being said, it may not be easy to figure out just how far back to reach for the starting point for your narrative.

People often ask me "what caused the cycle to begin?" or "are we close to the end of the cycle?" I consider these improper questions, since cycles neither begin nor end. Better questions might be: "what caused the current up-leg to begin?" or "how far have we gone since the beginning of the up-cycle?" or "are we close to the end of the down-leg?" You might even ask whether we're close to the end of a cycle, as long as you define it as running from one peak to the next, or from trough to trough. But — in the absence of such a definition — cycles do not have a defined beginning, and I believe they will never end.

≈

The cycle oscillates, as I mentioned, around the midpoint. The midpoint of a cycle is generally thought of as the secular trend, norm, mean, average or "happy medium," and generally as being in some sense as "right and proper." The extremes of the cycle, on the other hand, are thought of as aberrations or excesses to be returned from, and generally they are. While the thing that's cycling tends to spend much of the time above or below it, eventual movement back in the direction of the mean is usually the rule. The movement from either a high or a low extreme back toward the midpoint is often described as "regression toward the mean," a powerful and very reasonable tendency in most walks of life. But, thinking back to the cycle stages listed above, it can also be seen that the cyclical pattern generally consists as much of movement from the reasonable midpoint toward a potentially imprudent extreme (phases

b, e and h in the preceding graphic) as it does going from an extreme
back toward the midpoint (a, d and g).

The rational midpoint generally exerts a kind of magnetic pull, bringing
the thing that's cycling back from an extreme in the direction of "normal."
But it usually doesn't stay at normal for long, as the influences responsible
for the swing toward the midpoint invariably continue in force and thus
cause the swing back from an extreme to proceed through the midpoint
and then carry further, toward the opposite extreme.

It's important to recognize and accept the dependability of this pattern. The details vary — the timing, duration, speed and power of the
swings and, very importantly, the reasons for them — and that's likely
what's behind Twain's remark regarding history not repeating. But the
underlying dynamics are usually similar. In particular, that means the
swing back from a high or low almost never halts at the midpoint . . .
regardless of how "right" or "appropriate" the midpoint may be. The
continuation of the movement past the midpoint and toward the opposite extreme is highly dependable. For example, markets rarely go from
"underpriced" to "fairly priced" and stop there. Usually the fundamental
improvement and rising optimism that cause markets to recover from
depressed levels remain in force, causing them to continue right through
"fairly priced" and on to "overpriced." It doesn't have to happen, but
usually it does.

∾

Cycles have more potential to wreak havoc the further they progress from
the midpoint — i.e., the greater the aberrations or excesses. If the swing toward one extreme goes further, the swing back is likely to be more violent,
and more damage is likely to be done, as actions encouraged by the cycle's
operation at an extreme prove unsuitable for life elsewhere in the cycle.

In other words, the potential for havoc increases as the movement away from the midpoint increases: as economies and companies do "too well" and stock prices go "too high." Advances are followed by mere corrections, and bull markets by bear markets. But booms and bubbles are followed by much more harmful busts, crashes and panics.

∿

What is this midpoint around which things cycle? As I said, it's often a point astride a secular trend. For example, an economy's gross domestic product may exhibit a secular annual growth rate of, say, 2% for a few decades. But growth will be faster in some years and slower — even negative — in others. The performance in individual years is usually part of a cycle around the underlying secular trend.

Importantly, the secular growth rate may be subject to a cycle as well, but a longer-term, more gradual one. You have to step back further to see it. For example, societies tend to follow long-term patterns of rise and fall — think of the Roman Empire, for example — and the short term we talk about consists of ups and downs around the long-term trend (see pages 48–51).

The same can be true for industries. But since long-term cycles occur over decades and centuries, rather than quarters and years — and thus they can entail time frames that exceed any observer's lifetime — they can be hard to detect in real time and hard to factor into a decision process.

Here's what I wrote on the subject in my memo "The Long View" (January 2009):

> There's an old story about a group of blind men walking down the
> road in India who come upon an elephant. Each one touches a dif-
> ferent part of the elephant — the trunk, the leg, the tail or the ear —
> and comes up with a different explanation of what he'd encountered

based on the small part to which he was exposed. We are those blind
men. Even if we have a good understanding of the events we witness,
we don't easily gain the overall view needed to put them together. Up
to the time we see the whole in action, our knowledge is limited to the
parts we've touched. . . .

    . . . some of the most important lessons concern the need to (a)
study and remember the events of the past and (b) be conscious of
the cyclical nature of things. Up close, the blind man may mistake the
elephant's leg for a tree — and the shortsighted investor may think an
uptrend (or a downtrend) will go on forever. But if we step back and
view the long sweep of history, we should be able to bear in mind that
the long-term cycle also repeats and understand where we stand in it.

                                  ∾

This is a good time for me to make one of the most important points about
the nature of cycles. Most people think of cycles in terms of the phases
listed above and recognize them as a series of events. And most people understand that these events regularly follow each other in a usual sequence:
upswings are followed by downswings, and then eventually by new upswings.

    But to have a full understanding of cycles, that's not enough. The events
in the life of a cycle shouldn't be viewed merely as each being followed
by the next, but — much more importantly — as each *causing* the next. For
example:

- As the phenomenon swings toward an extreme, this movement
  gives it energy, which it stores. Eventually its increased weight
  makes it harder for the swing to continue further from the midpoint, and it reaches a maximum beyond which it can no longer
  proceed.

- Eventually it stops moving in that direction. And once it does, gravity then pulls it back in the direction of the central tendency or midpoint, with the energy it has amassed powering the swing back.

- And as the phenomenon in question moves from the extreme back toward the midpoint, the swing imparts momentum to it that causes it to overshoot the midpoint and keep moving toward the opposite extreme.

In this way, a cycle in the economic or investment world consists of a series of events that give rise to their successors. The process described in the three bullet points above sounds like a physical one, governed by forces such as gravity and momentum. But as I mentioned above and we'll see later on, the most important deviations from the general trend — and the variation in those deviations' timing, speed and extent — are largely produced by fluctuations in psychology.

If you consider the human psyche — rather than physical attributes — to be the source of much of the energy or momentum, these three points do a pretty good job of also explaining the swings and oscillations that investors are challenged to deal with. In the chapters that follow, some of the most important content will consist of descriptions of ways in which the events in each type of cycle generate their successors.

Owing to this view of cycles as progressions of causative events, this book contains several step-by-step accounts of progressions that took place in the past. The goal with each progression will be to illustrate what caused each event in the progression, what it meant in the progression, and how it contributed to the events that followed. The recounting of progressions may feel repetitive, and some of the ones covered actually will be touched on more than once (although with reference to different aspects). But hopefully these real-world examples will help readers achieve the goal of understanding cycles and how to position for them.

∾

It's extremely important to note this causal relationship: that the cycles I'm talking about consist of series of events that cause the ones that follow. But it's equally significant to note that while cycles occur in a variety of areas due to these serial events, cyclical developments in one area also influence cycles in others. Thus the economic cycle influences the profit cycle. Corporate announcements determined by the profit cycle influence investor attitudes. Investor attitudes influence markets. And developments in markets influence the cycle in the availability of credit . . . which influences economies, companies and markets.

Cyclical events are influenced by both endogenous developments (including the cyclical events that precede them) as well exogenous developments (events occurring in other areas). Many of the latter — but far from all — are parts of other cycles. Understanding these causative interactions isn't easy, but it holds much of the key to understanding and coping with the investment environment.

It must be understood that while I will describe cycles as separate and discrete, this is not entirely realistic. I will provide a smooth narrative that describes the operation of each type of cycle in isolation. I will give the impression that each cycle has an independent life of its own. I may also give the impression that the swing in a given direction of one type of cycle ends before the start of a corresponding or resultant swing in a cycle of another type — i.e., that they operate sequentially and independently. In other words, I will attempt to discuss each type of cycle in isolation . . . although in truth they don't operate in isolation.

My description might suggest that the different cycles are independent of each other and self-contained. It may seem that something happens in cycle A, which affects cycle B, which affects cycle C, which might feed all the way back to influence cycle A. This may give the impression that cycle A is on hold after it has influenced cycle B, and while cycle B's influence on cycle C takes place. But that's not the way it is.

The interrelationships among the various cycles are nowhere near as neat as my descriptions will be. The various cycles operate on their own, but they also continuously affect each other. I try to tease out the various threads in my mind and treat them separately, and that is the way this book will be organized. But the well-behaved, isolated cycles I'll describe are only an analytical concept. In life they're really a jumble of interrelated phenomena that can't be separated entirely. A affects B (and C), and B affects A (and C), and they all influence D, which influences all of them. They're all entangled with each other, but we must think about them in an orderly fashion if we are to understand cycles and their effects.

∿

Finally, perhaps under the heading of "miscellany," I want to point out a few more things about the nature of cycles that are essential for a thorough understanding (starting here with a few observations from my November 2001 memo, "You Can't Predict. You Can Prepare."):

- *Cycles are inevitable.* Every once in a while, an up- or down-leg goes on for a long time and/or to a great extreme, and people start to say "this time it's different." They cite the changes in geopolitics, institutions, technology or behavior that have rendered the "old rules" obsolete. They make investment decisions that extrapolate the recent trend. But then it usually turns out that the old rules do still apply, and the cycle resumes. In the end, trees don't grow to the sky, and few things go to zero. Rather, most phenomena turn out to be cyclical.

- *Cycles' clout is heightened by the inability of investors to remember the past.* As John Kenneth Galbraith says, "extreme brevity of the financial memory" keeps market participants from recognizing the recurring nature of these patterns, and thus their inevitability:

> When the same or closely similar circumstances occur again, sometimes in only a few years, they are hailed by a new, often youthful, and always supremely self-confident generation as a brilliantly innovative discovery in the financial and larger economic world. There can be few fields of human endeavor in which history counts for so little as in the world of finance. Past experience, to the extent that it is part of memory at all, is dismissed as the primitive refuge of those who do not have the insight to appreciate the incredible wonders of the present. (*A Short History of Financial Euphoria*, 1990)

- *Cycles are self-correcting,* and their reversal is not necessarily dependent on exogenous events. The reason they reverse (rather than going on forever) is that trends create the reasons for their own reversal. Thus I like to say success carries within itself the seeds of failure, and failure the seeds of success.
- Seen through the lens of human perception, *cycles are often viewed as less symmetrical than they are.* Negative price fluctuations are called "volatility," while positive price fluctuations are called "profit." Collapsing markets are called "selling panics," while surges receive more benign descriptions (but I think they may best be seen as "buying panics"; see tech stocks in 1999, for example). Commentators talk about "investor capitulation" at the bottom of market cycles, while I also see capitulation at the top, when previously prudent investors throw in the towel and buy.

Although this may be underestimated and overlooked, in my experience financial cycles generally are largely symmetrical. Every cycle movement has an "other side," meaning every upswing is invariably followed by — or, perhaps better said, leads to — a downswing, and vice versa.

"Boom/bust" — that's a phenomenon that's widely talked about and generally understood, and it's a good illustration of cycle symmetry. Most people understand that busts follow booms. Somewhat fewer grasp the fact that the busts are caused by the booms. From the latter, it makes sense that (a) booms usually won't be followed by modest, gradual and painless adjustments and (b) on the other hand, we're unlikely to have a bust if we haven't had a boom.

It must be noted, however, that this symmetry only applies dependably to direction, not necessarily to the extent, timing or pace of movement. (This is the point that Nick Train makes — you'll meet him in the next chapter.) Thus an upward movement may be followed by a downward movement of either greater or lesser magnitude. The downward turn may commence just after the apex is reached, or things may stay at a high for a long time before beginning to correct. And, perhaps most importantly, it can take years for a boom to grow to its full extent. But the bust that follows may seem like a fast-moving freight train; as my long-time partner Sheldon Stone says, "The air goes out of the balloon much faster than it went in."

Let's return to what Mark Twain is supposed to have said: "History doesn't repeat itself, but it does rhyme." Grasping this concept is absolutely critical to an understanding of cycles. What Twain must have meant by this statement — if he indeed was responsible for it — is that whereas the details vary from one event to another in a given category of history (say, the ascent of demagogues), the underlying themes and mechanisms are consistent.

This is true of cycles in finance, and absolutely true of financial crises. As you'll see later, the Global Financial Crisis of 2007–08 occurred
largely because of the issuance of a huge number of unsound sub-prime
mortgages, and that took place in turn because of an excess of optimism,
a shortage of risk aversion, and an overly generous capital market, which
led to unsafe behavior surrounding sub-prime mortgages. Thus the nar-
row-minded literalist would say, "I'll definitely turn cautious the next time
mortgage financing is made readily available to unqualified home buyers."
But that aspect of the Crisis need never recur for the lessons of the Global
Financial Crisis to be valuable. Rather, the themes that provide warning
signals in every boom/bust are the general ones: that excessive optimism
is a dangerous thing; that risk aversion is an essential ingredient for the
market to be safe; and that overly generous capital markets ultimately lead
to unwise financing, and thus to danger for participants.

In short, the details are unimportant and can be irrelevant. But the
themes are essential, and they absolutely do tend to recur. Understanding
that tendency — and being able to spot the recurrences — is one of the most
important elements in dealing with cycles.

Finally, I want to bring in the definition of insanity that Albert Einstein is
credited with: "doing the same thing over and over and expecting different
results." When people invest in things after they've been carried aloft because "everyone knows" they're both flawless and underpriced — thinking
they offer high returns without risk of loss — that's insanity. Such beliefs
have been defrocked in the aftermath of every bubble. But many people
— either unaware that bubbles tend to be followed by crashes, or blinded
to that risk by their eagerness to get rich quickly — buy into the next one
nevertheless.

Securities and markets that have benefitted from fabulous appreciation
are much more likely to succumb to a cyclical correction than they are to

appreciate *ad infinitum*. Try telling that to the eager investor who believes "it's different this time."

∾

The length of this chapter and the large variety of topics covered are indicative of the multi-faceted and challenging nature of cycles. For this reason, cycles have to be understood both analytically and intuitively. As with many other aspects of investing, those who possess the latter ability in addition to the former will go the furthest. Can an intuitive approach be taught? Yes, to some degree, but most fully to those who start off with the gift of insight. In short, some people just tend to "get it" (whatever "it" may be) and some don't.

Courses in accounting, finance and security analysis will equip the investor with the technical knowledge that is necessary for success but, in my opinion those courses are far from sufficient. The main element missing from them is an understanding of cyclical phenomena and how they develop as set forth in this book. Some cues will be found in the newly established fields of behavioral economics and behavioral finance, and I commend them to your attention. Psychology is an essential component in understanding the cycles that matter so much to investors.

The greatest lessons regarding cycles are learned through experience . . . as in the adage "experience is what you got when you didn't get what you wanted." I know so much more about this today than I did when I began as a young security analyst at First National City Bank 48 years ago.

However, since we usually see only one major cycle per decade, anyone who's going to rely solely on the amassing of experience for his progress had better have a lot of patience. I hope what you read here will add to your understanding and speed your education.

The ancient Greek historian Thucydides stated in *History of the Pelo-*

ponnesian War that he would be satisfied "if these words of mine are judged useful by those who want to understand clearly the events which happened in the past and which (human nature being what it is) will, at some time or other and in much the same ways, be repeated in the future." That's a good description of my goal here as well.

III

THE REGULARITY OF CYCLES

This effort to explain life through the recognition of patterns — and thus to come up with winning formulas — is complicated, in large part, because we live in a world that is beset by randomness and in which people don't behave the same from one instance to the next, even when they intend to. The realization that past events were largely affected by these things — and thus that future events aren't fully predictable — is unpleasant, as it makes life less subject to anticipation, rule-making and rendering safe.

In the fall of 2013, in response to something I'd written in *The Most Important Thing*, I received an email from Nick Train of Lindsell Train, a London-based money management firm. Nick took issue with my use of the word "cycle" to describe phenomena like those I'm discussing here. Nick and I had a healthy email colloquy regarding the issue and met for an enjoyable, spirited lunch.

By the time the main course arrived, it had become clear that what motivated Nick to write was his conviction that for something to be described as cyclical, its timing and extent have to be regular and thus predictable. A radio cycle or sine wave, for example, rises and falls in a regular, predictable pattern, with the same amplitude, frequency and ending point every time.

Dictionary.com defines a cycle in physics as "a complete alteration in which a phenomenon attains a maximum and minimum value, returning to a final value equal to the original one," and a cycle in mathematics as "a permutation of a set of elements that leaves the original cyclic order of the elements unchanged." In other words, these scientific and mathematical cycles follow patterns so regular that they end up back where they started, and that happens because the timing and path of the fluctuations is always the same. Score one for Nick.

But economies, companies and markets — and certainly investors' psyches and behavior — are not regular in this way. I asserted at our lunch, and I think Nick eventually agreed, that things can be cyclical without exhibiting this degree of consistency. It's all a matter of your definition of the word "cycle."

Here's part of what I wrote to Nick to follow up:

> What I claim is that, usually, things rise and fall. Most natural things have a birth/death cycle, and investor psychology has a very pronounced cycle of rising optimism (and price appreciation) followed by rising pessimism (and price declines). You may think that's simplistic and unhelpful. But one of the main points is that when something rises, investors have a tendency to think it'll never fall (and vice versa). Betting against those tendencies can be very profitable. . . .
>
> Little in the world — and certainly not in the investment world — is regular enough in time to profit from applying a mechanistic process. But that doesn't mean you can't take advantage of up-and-down cycles. . . .
>
> I don't think fluctuations have to end up back where they started to be called a cycle. Many cycles end up higher than they started —

that is, they are cycles around an underlying secular uptrend — but that doesn't mean they're not cyclical, or that it's not desirable to ride the up-cycle and avoid the down-cycle, as opposed to staying on throughout.

The *Cambridge Dictionary's* definition of a cycle — for use in the general, non-technical world — is "a group of events that happen in a particular order, one following the other, and are often repeated." I'm happy with that one; it reflects the sense in which I think about cycles and oscillations in my world.

∾

While I don't agree with Nick Train's objection that the irregularity of the phenomena I'm discussing disqualifies them from being described as cyclical, there is a great deal to be understood about their irregularity and what can be learned from it.

The most important thing to note here is that, as I said in the last chapter, the things I call cycles do not stem completely — or sometimes at all — from the operation of mechanical, scientific or physical processes. They would be much more dependable and predictable if they did — but much less potentially profitable. (This is because the greatest profits come from seeing things better than others do, and if cycles were totally dependable and predictable, there would be no such thing as superiority in seeing them.) Sometimes there is an underlying principle (and sometimes not), but much variation is attributable to the role of humans in creating cycles. The involvement of humans in this process enables their emotion- and psychology-induced tendencies to influence cyclical phenomena. Chance or randomness also plays a big part in some cycles, and human behavior contributes to their existence, too. Humans are a big part of the reason these cycles exist, but also — along with randomness — for their inconsistency and thus their undependability.

∾

We humans have to live in the real world. As described earlier, we look for patterns and rules that will permit us to live more easily and profitably. Perhaps it started with early man's experience with daily and annual cycles. He may have learned the hard way that it was unsafe to visit the watering hole at the time of day when mother lions went there with their cubs. And maybe he learned through experimentation that certain crops did better when planted in the spring than in the fall. The more absolute the rules, the easier life would be. It now seems to be ingrained in the human brain to look for explanatory patterns.

But this effort to explain life through the recognition of patterns — and thus to come up with winning formulas — is complicated, in large part, because we live in a world that is beset by randomness and in which people don't behave the same from one instance to the next, even when they intend to. The realization that past events were largely affected by these things — and thus that future events aren't fully predictable — is unpleasant, as it makes life less subject to anticipation, rule-making and rendering safe. Thus people search for explanations that would make events understandable . . . often to an extent beyond that which is appropriate. This is as true in investing as it is in other aspects of life.

I found some interesting statements on this subject in *The Drunkard's Walk,* a 2008 book about randomness by Leonard Mlodinow, a faculty member at Caltech. Here's the first, from his book's prologue:

> To swim against the current of human intuition is a difficult task. . . .
> The human mind is built to identify for each event a definite cause

and can therefore have a hard time accepting the influence of unrelated or random factors. And so the first step is to realize that success or failure sometimes arises neither from great skill nor from great incompetence but from, as the economist Armen Alchian wrote, "fortuitous circumstances." Random processes are fundamental in nature and are ubiquitous in our everyday lives, yet most people do not understand them or think much about them.

In a chapter about the unpredictability and capriciousness of success in the movie industry, Mlodinow describes producer William Goldman's view on the subject:

> Goldman didn't deny that there are reasons for a film's box office performance. But he did say that those reasons are so complex and the path from green light to opening weekend so vulnerable to unforeseeable and uncontrollable influences that educated guesses about an unmade film's potential aren't much better than the flips of a coin.

Mlodinow goes on to discuss how random elements apply to a batter in baseball:

> The result of any particular at bat (that is, an opportunity for success) depends primarily on the player's ability, of course. But it also depends on the interplay of many other factors: his health; the wind, the sun, or the stadium lights; the quality of the pitches he receives; the game situation; whether he correctly guesses how the pitcher will throw; whether his hand-eye coordination works just perfectly as he takes his swing; whether that brunette he met at the bar kept him up too late or the chili-cheese dog with garlic fries he had for breakfast soured his stomach. If not for all the unpredictable factors, a player would either hit a home run on every at bat or fail to do so [on every at bat].

We know that a variety of factors influence outcomes in all fields, and that many of them are random or unpredictable. That certainly includes a lot of the developments in economics and investing. Even if one's income is stable, an individual's propensity to consume may be affected by the weather, war or which country wins the World Cup (and that, in turn, by how a ball bounces off a defender's shin). A company may issue a favorable earnings report, but whether its stock rises or falls as a result will be influenced by how its competitors do, whether the central bank chooses that week for an interest rate increase, and whether the earnings announcement comes in a good or bad week in the market. Given this degree of variability, the cycles I'm concerned with certainly aren't regular and can't be reduced to reliable decision-making rules.

I can give you an example from the world of high yield bonds: something I've found quite annoying. At one point in my experience, a view arose that bonds tend to default around the second anniversary of their issuance. If true, that would be a very helpful bit of knowledge: to avoid defaults, all one would have to do is sell all bonds as they approach that anniversary and buy back the ones that have survived it. (Of course, this rule ignores the question of what price sellers would receive for bonds that are nearing that treacherous date — since everyone knows it poses risk — and how much they'd have to pay to buy back the ones that have cleared it.)

Perhaps a cluster of second anniversary defaults occurred around the time that notion became popular. But coincidence is very different from causality. Is that phenomenon dependable? What were the reasons for it? Would they repeat? Should you bet on it? In particular, the history of high yield bonds probably covered only twenty years or so at that time, making me wonder whether the experience and sample size were sufficient to justify reliance on that observation. Rather than intellectual rigor, I prefer to think the two-year rule was based more on people's thirst for simple, helpful rules, and thus their excessive tendency to extrapolate without any real foundation.

I think it would be better to recognize that bonds default in response to a wide variety of influences — like those that contribute to the success or failure of a hitter in baseball — and that most defaults have absolutely nothing to do with the number of years that have elapsed since the bonds were issued. To invert Mark Twain's purported remark, history may rhyme, but it rarely repeats exactly.

∾

I'm firmly convinced that markets will continue to rise and fall, and I think I know (a) why and (b) what makes these movements more or less imminent. But I'm sure I'll never know when they're going to turn up or down, how far they'll go after they do, how fast they'll move, when they'll turn back toward the midpoint, or how far they'll continue on the opposite side. So there's a great deal to admit uncertainty about.

I have found, however, that the little I do know about cycle timing gives me a great advantage relative to the majority of investors, who understand even less about cycles and pay less heed to them and their implications for appropriate action. The advantage I'm talking about is probably all anyone can achieve, but it's enough for me. It's been the source of a significant edge that my Oaktree colleagues and I have enjoyed over the last 22 years. And it's a lot of what I want to pass on in this book.

IV

THE ECONOMIC CYCLE

The output of an economy is the product of hours worked and output per hour; thus the long-term growth of an economy is determined primarily by fundamental factors like birth rate and the rate of gain in productivity (but also by other changes in society and environment). These factors usually change relatively little from year to year, and only gradually from decade to decade. Thus the average rate of growth is rather steady over long periods of time.

Given the relative stability of underlying secular growth, one might be tempted to expect that the performance of economies would be consistent from year to year. However, a number of factors are subject to variability, causing economic growth — even as it follows the underlying trendline on average — to also exhibit annual variability.

The economic cycle (also known — mostly in the past — as "the business cycle") provides much of the foundation for cyclical events in the business world and the markets. The more the economy rises, the more likely it is that companies will expand their profits and stock markets will rise. I'll touch briefly here on the factors that influence economic cycles. But before I do so, I want to make the confession I volunteer whenever I discuss economics (or is it a proud proclamation?): I'm no economist.

I took courses in economics as both an undergraduate and a graduate student. I think about economics. I deal with economics as a professional investor. And I consider myself to be largely an "economic man" who makes most decisions for logical reasons based on the relationship between cost and value, risk and potential return. But my thinking about economics is based largely on common sense and experience, and I'm sure I'll write things here with which many economists will disagree. (Of course, they also disagree with each other. The workings of economics are quite unclear and imprecise, and thus it's for good reason that it's called "the dismal science.")

The main measure of an economy's output is GDP, or gross domestic product, the total value of all goods and services produced for final sale in an economy. It can roughly be viewed as the result of multiplying the number of hours people spend working by the value of the output produced in each hour. (Earlier in my career it was called gross national product, but that term has gone out of style. The distinction between the two lies in the treatment of foreign manufacturers operating in a given country: GDP includes them in that country's output, while GNP does not.)

The main questions most people (and certainly most investors) care about with regard to the economy are whether we'll have growth or recession in a given year, and what the rate of change will be. Both of these are components of what I call the short-term economic cycle. (I'll introduce other considerations shortly.)

When we think about U.S. GDP growth in a given year, we usually start with an assumption in the range of 2% to 3% or so and then add or subtract for the specific circumstances. But the starting point for each year's GDP growth is invariably positive. For example, as last year began there was a lot of discussion about the rate at which GDP would grow. The optimists thought it'd be nearly 3%, and the pessimists thought it might not reach 2%. But just about everyone thought it would be positive. The official definition of a recession is two consecutive quarters of negative growth, and very few people thought GDP growth would fall into negative territory — last year or soon thereafter.

Long-Term Economic Trends

Many investors are concerned about year-to-year economic growth: high or low, positive or negative. The developments they're asking about are short-term considerations. They're important, but they're not everything. In the long run their importance fades and long-term considerations become more relevant.

As I mentioned early on, most of the cycles that attract investors' attention consist of oscillations around a secular trend or central tendency. While those oscillations matter a great deal to companies and markets in the short run, changes in regard to the underlying trendline itself will prove to be of much greater overall significance. The *oscillations around the trend* will cancel out in the long run (admittedly after causing much elation or distress in individual years), but *changes in the underlying trend* will make the biggest difference in our long-term experience.

In January 2009, I wrote a memo entitled "The Long View" that focused on this subject. I'm going to quote extensively from it here.

First, I described a number of "salutary secular trends" that the securities markets had been riding over the preceding decades. I'll list them below but omit the descriptions that accompanied them in the memo:

- macro environment
- corporate growth
- the borrowing mentality
- popularization of investing
- investor psychology

The developments enumerated above constituted a strong tailwind behind the economy and the markets over the last several decades, and they produced a long-term secular uptrend.

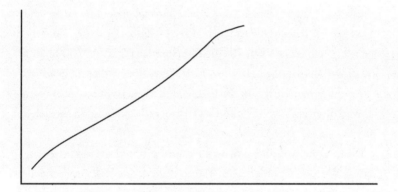

Yet, despite the underlying uptrend, there's been no straight line. The economy and markets were punctuated every few years by cyclical bouts of short-term fluctuation. Cycles around the trendline made for frequent ups and downs. Most were relatively small and brief, but in the 1970s, economic stagnation set in, inflation reached 16%, the average stock lost almost half its value in two years, and *Business Week* magazine ran a cover story trumpeting "The Death of Equities" (August 13, 1979). No, my forty years in the market haven't been all wine and roses.

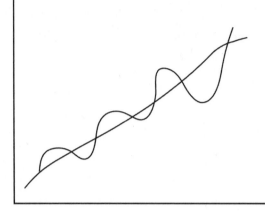

From time to time we saw better economies and worse — slowdown and prosperity, recession and recovery. Markets, too, rose and fell. These fluctuations were attributable to normal economic cycles and to exogenous developments (such as the oil embargo in 1973 and the emerging market crisis in 1998). The Standard & Poor's 500 had a few down years in the period from 1975 to 1999, but none in which it lost more than 7.5%. On the upside, however, 16 of those 25 years showed returns above 15%, and seven times the annual gain exceeded 30%.

Despite the ups and downs, investors profited overall, investing became a national pursuit, and Warren Buffett, one of America's richest men, got that way by buying common stocks and whole companies. A serious general uptrend was underway, reaching its zenith in 2007. . . .

Until mid-2007, my 39 years of experience as a money manager had been limited to part of the long-term story. Perhaps what looked like an underlying long-term uptrend should have been viewed instead as the positive part of a long-term cycle incorporating downs as well as ups. Only when you step back . . . can you gauge its full proportions.

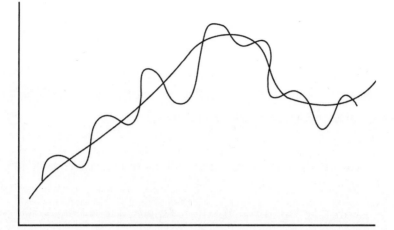

The main thing I want to discuss here is my realization that there are cycles in the long-term trend, not just short-term cycles around it, and we've been living through the positive phase of a big one.

Before I progress to a discussion of the short-term economic cycles that most investors concern themselves with, I'm going to spend some more time on the long term: the factors that shape it and the current outlook for it. After that I'll turn to the matter of the short-term economic cycle.

I have mentioned that one of the main determinants of each year's economic output is the number of hours worked. In turn, the most fundamental factor underlying increases in hours worked is population growth. Growth in the population means there are more people working each year to make and sell products (and also more people to buy and consume them, encouraging production). More production equals more GDP. If the population is growing, hours worked tend to grow, and so does GDP. Thus births are one of the main reasons for the usual presumption that economic growth will be positive. On the other hand, if the population is shrinking, positive GDP growth faces a significant headwind.

Population growth doesn't vary much from year to year. The number of people of child-bearing age doesn't change much in the short run, and neither does their tendency to have children. These things do change over decades or longer, however, so they cause changes in long-term population.

What are the kinds of the things that can alter a nation's birth rate (the average number of children each couple has)?

- rules like China's longstanding but recently revised one-child policy,
- wars (like World War II, which depressed the birth rate but gave rise to the Baby Boom when it ended),
- economic conditions, which, among other things, alter people's feelings about whether they can afford to have children, and
- social mores, like the recent tendency of young Americans to delay family formation

Changes in birth rates generally take place over long periods of time, and when they do, they require years to affect GDP growth. Take China's one-child policy, for example. You might say the shift was sudden: one day in 2015 the policy was in full force, and the next day its phase-out was announced. True as far as it goes. But while people who already had a child certainly might have gotten busy producing another on that new day, it would take roughly twenty years for that second child to become a worker and be able to contribute to China's economic output. Thus the bottom line is that year-to-year changes in GDP are unlikely to be attributed significantly to changes in the birth rate.

The other principal element in the GDP equation — the value of the output produced in each hour of labor — is determined by "productivity." Changes in productivity are fundamental determinants of changes in the long-term growth of GDP. Whatever the rate of population growth might

MASTERING THE MARKET CYCLE 53

be, GDP will grow faster if productivity is rising or slower if it's falling. And looking at second derivatives, the rate of growth in GDP will accelerate if the rate of gain in productivity is rising and decelerate if it's falling. It's all just math.

Changes in productivity, like changes in birth rate, take place in modest degrees and gradually, and they require long periods to take effect. They stem primarily from advances in the productive process. The first big gains occurred during the Industrial Revolution of roughly 1760 to 1830, when human labor was replaced by machines driven by steam and water power, and when large factories replaced the work that was done less efficiently in small shops and at home. The second major gains occurred in the late 19th and early 20th centuries, when electricity and automobiles replaced older and less-efficient forms of power and transportation. The third major change occurred in the latter half of the 20th century, when computers and other forms of automated control began to take the place of humans in guiding production machinery. And, of course, the fourth wave is underway now, during the Information Age, as massive advances in information acquisition, storage and application — and such activities as metadata and artificial intelligence — are permitting tasks to be accomplished that weren't dreamed of in the past.

Remember, each of these changes took place gradually, over decades. Each made a massive difference in GDP, but even with these, there weren't major accelerations and decelerations from year to year. The rate of gain in productivity tends to remain relatively steady for years, and certainly the short-term cycles of economic recession and recovery generally aren't attributed to changes in it.

It's clear that trends in hours worked and in output per hour combine to determine long-term trends in national output. But what factors produce changes in those two? Here's a partial, indicative list:

- **Demographic movements** — The migration of millions of Chinese from farms to cities is an example of what I'm talking about here. By increasing the availability of workers, this migration fueled China's rise as a site of low-cost manufacturing, and it is contributing to a related expansion of China's consumer class. Another example is immigration from Latin America to the United States. America, like other developed nations, is experiencing a declining birth rate. But ongoing immigration from south of the border — some of it illegal — takes the place of births in expanding the U.S.'s supply of productive labor and rate of consumption.

- **Determinants of inputs** — The number of hours worked can diverge from the number of people working, and certainly from the number interested in working.

  - "Workforce participation" reflects the percentage of people of working age who are either employed or looking for work.
  - The unemployment rate (the percentage of people participating in the workforce who don't have a job) rises and falls in response to changes in consumer and business spending (and thus to changes in demand for goods, and in the need for workers to produce goods).
  - The number of hours worked by each person with a job likewise varies with economic conditions — businesses shorten work weeks when demand for goods is low, and they authorize overtime when demand is high (until demand is strong enough to call for more hiring or another shift).

- **Aspiration** — The profit motive and the desire to live better are among the forces that drive workers (and thus societies) to work harder and to produce more. It might be tempting to think of these things as universal, but they aren't. For example, the profit motive was pretty much excluded from the economic system under the Soviets, and the willingness to work more is constrained in other economies (to wit, I've watched workers clock out at European banks — not to prove that they had worked until 5:00 as in the U.S., but rather that they had left by 5:00 and thus hadn't exceeded the 35-hour work week).

- **Education** — The deterioration of public education in the U.S. is likely to have a negative effect on workers' ability to contribute to the economy in the future, as well as their ability to generate substantial incomes with which to consume. These negative trends are likely to work counter to the positive effects from the influx of immigrants.

- **Technology** — Innovation causes new businesses to come into existence but brings about the demise of old ones. It both creates jobs and eliminates them. In short, it provides a hyper-example of the Darwinian nature of economic evolution: it creates winners *and* losers. New technologies overtake human effort as well as old technologies. But they are not in any way "safe," as they, too, can be displaced or — to use today's terminology — disrupted. Technology epitomizes the pattern of rise and fall, life and death ... and rebirth.

- **Automation** — The ability to replace human labor with machines is a particularly interesting factor. On the one hand, automation can be viewed as additive to the economic cycle, since it increases productivity, or the amount of output that is generated per hour of labor. The mechanization of agriculture, for instance, allowed many fewer farmers to produce much more food at much lower cost than ever before. But on the other hand, automation decreases the hours of labor applied to production. Today we see factories run by just a few workers that thirty years ago might have had a hundred. Thus the net effect of automation on GDP might be neutral or positive but, since it has the ability to eliminate jobs, automation might have the effect of reducing employment, and thus incomes, and thus consumption.

- **Globalization** — The integration of nations into a world economy may add to total world economic output, in part because of benefits from specialization, or it may not, leaving it a zero-sum (or negative-sum) exercise. But clearly, globalization can have differential effects on individual nations' economies (and create winners and losers within each nation). The massive increase in the number of factory workers described above certainly accelerated China's economic growth over the last thirty years by permitting it to become a leading exporter to the rest of the world. However, that same trend caused developed nations to buy a lot of goods from China that they otherwise might have produced themselves, thus curtailing their own GDP. The few million manufacturing jobs estimated to have been lost to China since 2000 certainly made U.S. economic growth lower than it otherwise would have been, although one would need to take into account the benefit of importing low-priced goods from China to estimate the total impact on the U.S. economy.

∾

The U.S. was blessed with an intact infrastructure coming out of World War II, and it benefitted greatly from the Baby Boom in post-war births, which created a massive upsurge in economic growth. American products were often the best in the world, and American corporations were wildly successful. In the yet-to-globalize world, American workers could remain the best-paid, safe from competition from goods produced more cheaply elsewhere. Improving management techniques and rapid increases in productivity were further contributors. Thus secular economic growth in the U.S. was rapid, contributing to demand for consumption and thus creating a virtuous circle from which many benefitted . . . but it was not one that could be counted on to continue unchanged.

More recently, economic growth appears to have slowed in the U.S. (as well as elsewhere). Is this a short-term cyclical change relative to the underlying long-term trend, or a change in the long-term trend itself? It will take many years before we know definitively. But there has arisen a school of thought blaming it on "secular stagnation"—that is, a fundamental slowing of the long-term trend.

Gains in population and productivity have declined in the U.S., as they have in other developed nations. Taken together, these two things suggest GDP will grow more slowly in the U.S. in the coming years than it did in the years following World War II. It is postulated that the major advances in productivity of the recent past will not be replicated in the future. In addition, the availability of much-cheaper labor elsewhere makes it unlikely that the U.S. will be able to compete on price to produce the manufactured goods it requires; this has obviously negative implications in the U.S. for employment among less-skilled and less-educated Americans, income inequality, and standards of living relative to people in other countries. These issues, of course, played an obvious part in the 2016 presidential election.

Changes in population growth and productivity growth can require decades to take effect, but clearly they can affect countries' economic growth rates. In the 20th century, the U.S. surpassed Europe as an economic power. Then Japan seemed to sprint forward in the 1970s and 1980s, threatening to take over the world, until the late '80s, when it fell back into negligible growth. The emerging markets—and especially China—were the site of rapid growth over the last few decades, and while their growth is slower at the moment, they may well outgrow the developed world in the next few decades. India has human resources that can make it a rapid-growth economy if it can increase its efficiency and reduce corruption. And frontier nations like Nigeria and Bangladesh stand behind the emerging nations, waiting for their turn as rapid growers.

Societies rise and fall, and they speed up and slow down in terms of economic growth relative to each other. This underlying trend in growth clearly follows a long-term cycle, although the short-run ups and downs around it are more discernible and thus more readily discussed.

Short-Term Economic Cycles

As I mentioned earlier, economic forecasters and the consumers of their work product are usually preoccupied by the rate of GDP growth in the coming year or two. In other words, they're concerned about the growth rate exhibited in the upward swing of the short-term economic cycle and its duration, as well as whether it'll go negative for two quarters in the downward swing and thus be termed a recession. These things represent short-term fluctuations around the long-term growth trend as illustrated a few pages back. Since the factors that produce the long-term trend change little from quarter to quarter and year to year, why should short-term changes be of great concern? In fact, why should they even occur? Why isn't there just growth at the average rate—say 2%—every year?

These questions provide a good opportunity to introduce some of this book's protagonists: psychology, emotion and decision-making processes.

Births and productivity often tend to be viewed as independent and al-most-mechanical variables. Births result from procreation, and the reasons for it and the rate at which it takes place are usually quite steady over time. Likewise, the rate of change in the level of productivity — in output per unit of labor — is viewed as being dictated largely by technological gains and their dissemination. In other words, although economies are made up of people, the level of economic growth isn't thought to be highly reflective of those people's ups and downs.

But, in fact, it is. While the long-term trend sets the potential economic growth rate, the actual level of each year's GDP will vary relative to that which the trend dictates . . . largely because of the involvement of people.

Birth rate may determine the long-term trends in the number of hours worked, but other factors can introduce variation in the short run. The willingness to work is not constant. There may be times when conditions discourage people from seeking a place in the workforce, as previously mentioned, and also times when world events alter the level of consumption.

The most obvious example is the ability of world events to create fear that discourages economic activity. The sub-prime mortgage crisis and fi-nancial institution meltdown that reached its apex with the bankruptcy of Lehman Brothers in September 2008 discouraged consumers from buy-ing, investors from providing capital, and companies from building fac-tories and expanding workforces. These cutbacks occurred even among people who hadn't lost jobs, suffered home foreclosure or seen declines in the value of their portfolios. These developments quickly affected the over-all economy, and the result was a serious recession lasting from December 2007 to June 2009.

If the number of workers working and the amount they earn were rela-tively constant, we might expect the amount they spend on consumption to be similarly constant. But it isn't. Spending fluctuates more than employment and earnings because of variation in something called "the marginal propensity to consume": of every additional dollar earned, it determines the percentage that will go to consumption. Because this propensity is variable in the short run, consumption can vary independently of income.

Earners may choose to spend a higher percentage of their earnings on consumption because:

- the daily headlines are favorable;
- they believe election results presage a stronger economy, higher incomes or lower taxes;
- consumer credit has become more readily available;
- asset appreciation has made them feel richer; or
- their team won the World Series.

The fourth of these factors — the so-called "wealth effect" — is particularly noteworthy. Asset owners (a) are probably unlikely to fund consumption by selling their stocks or homes and (b) should recognize that asset price gains can prove ephemeral and thus aren't a good reason to alter spending patterns. Yet asset appreciation does tend to lead them to spend more. This phenomenon demonstrates the contribution of psychology to behavior, and behavior to short-term economic variation.

It's particularly important in this vein to note the extent to which economic expectations can be self-fulfilling. If people (and companies) believe the future will be good, they'll spend more and invest more . . . and the future will be good, and vice versa. It's my belief that most companies concluded that the Crisis of 2008 wouldn't be followed by a V-shaped recovery, as had been the rule in the last few recessions. Thus they declined to expand factories or workforces, and the resulting recovery was modest and gradual in the U.S. (and even more anemic elsewhere).

Another reason for short-term variation concerns inventories. Businesses may overestimate the demand for their products in a given period and thus increase production such that it exceeds the amount they can sell. Or they may hold production constant but encounter surprisingly soft demand. In either case, more goods will be produced than sold. The excess will be added to inventories. That, in turn, is likely to cause production in subsequent periods to be adjusted downward until inventories are restored to desired levels. In this way, additions to and reductions in inventories often lead to short-term ups and downs in economic output.

These are only a few examples of the factors that can cause the output of an economy to vary in a given quarter or year from the growth in potential output that birth rate and productivity gains might suggest. They are the result of factors that are not "mechanical" or reliable in nature. Many of them stem from human behavior, and thus they are uncertain and unpredictable.

∾

This leads me to add a few words about economic forecasts. Many investors predicate their actions on forecasts that they make themselves or obtain from economists, banks or the media. And yet I doubt many such forecasts contain information that's likely to add value and lead to investment success. (For a more extensive discussion of "what we don't know," see chapter 14 of *The Most Important Thing*.)

Here's how I view the foundation for considering this issue:

- In investing, it's easy to achieve performance that is equal to that of the average investor or a market benchmark.

- Since it's easy to be average, real investment success must consist of outperforming other investors and the averages. Investment success is largely a relative concept, measured on the basis of relative performance.

- Simply being right about a coming event isn't enough to ensure superior relative performance if everyone holds the same view and as a result everyone is equally right. Thus success doesn't lie in being right, but rather in being more right than others.

- Similarly, one doesn't have to be right in order to be successful: just less wrong than others.

- Success doesn't come from having a *correct* forecast, but from having a *superior* forecast. Can such forecasts be obtained?

Most economic forecasts consist of extrapolations of current levels and long-term trends. And since the economy usually doesn't depart much from those levels and trends, most extrapolation forecasts turn out to be correct. But those extrapolation forecasts are likely to be commonly shared, already reflected in the market prices for assets, and thus not generators of superior performance — even when they come true. Here's how Nobel Prize–winning economist Milton Friedman put it:

> All these people see the same data, read the same material, and spend their time trying to guess what each other is going to say. [Their forecasts] will always be moderately right — and almost never of much use.

The forecasts that are potentially valuable are those that correctly foresee deviation from long-term trends and recent levels. If a forecaster makes a non-conforming, non-extrapolation prediction that turns out to be correct, the outcome is likely to come as a surprise to the other market participants.

When they scramble to adjust their holdings to reflect it, the result is likely to be gains for the few who correctly foresaw it. There's only one catch: since major deviations from trend (a) occur infrequently and (b) are hard to correctly predict, most unconventional, non-extrapolation forecasts turn out to be incorrect, and anyone who invests on their basis is usually likely to do below average.

So these are the possibilities I see with regard to economic forecasts:

- Most economic forecasts are just extrapolations. Extrapolations are usually correct but not valuable.
- Unconventional forecasts of significant deviation from trend would be very valuable if they were correct, but usually they aren't. Thus most forecasts of deviation from trend are incorrect and also not valuable.
- A few forecasts of significant deviation turn out to be correct and valuable — leading their authors to be lionized for their acumen — but it's hard to know in advance which will be the few right ones. Since the overall batting average with regard to them is low, unconventional forecasts can't be valuable on balance. There are forecasters who became famous for a single dramatic correct call, but the majority of their forecasts weren't worth following.

Taken together, these three conclusions on economic forecasting aren't very encouraging. Thus it's not for nothing that John Kenneth Galbraith said, "We have two classes of forecasters: those who don't know — and those who don't know they don't know."

Secular changes in long-term economic cycles are hard to predict, and the correctness of forecasts of such changes is hard to assess. The ups and downs of short-term economic cycles, too, are hard for any one person to consistently predict better than others. It's tempting to act on economic predictions, especially since the payoff for correct ones theoretically could be high. But the difficulty of being able to do so correctly and consistently mustn't be underestimated.

∾

Here is what I believe to be the bottom line on economic cycles:

- The output of an economy is the product of hours worked and output per hour; thus the long-term growth of an economy is determined primarily by fundamental factors like birth rate and the rate of gain in productivity (but also by other changes in society and environment). These factors usually change relatively little from year to year, and only gradually from decade to decade. Thus the average rate of growth is rather steady over long periods of time. Only in the longest of time frames does the secular growth rate of an economy significantly speed up or slow down. But it does.

- Given the relative stability of underlying secular growth, one might be tempted to expect that the performance of economies would be consistent from year to year. However, a number of factors are subject to variability, causing economic growth — even as it follows the underlying trendline on average — to also exhibit annual variability. These factors can perhaps be viewed as follows:

  o **Endogenous** — Annual economic performance can be influenced by variation in decisions made by economic units: for consumers to spend or save, for example, or for businesses to expand or contract, to add to inventories (calling for increased production) or sell from inventories (reducing production relative to what it might otherwise have been). Often these decisions are influenced by the state of mind of economic actors, such as consumers or the managers of businesses.

- **Exogenous** — Annual performance can also be influenced by (a) man-made events that are not strictly economic, such as the occurrence of war; government decisions to change tax rates or adjust trade barriers; or changes caused by cartels in the price of commodities, or (b) natural events that occur without the involvement of people, such as droughts, hurricanes and earthquakes.

- Long-term economic growth is steady for long periods of time but subject to change pursuant to long-term cycles.
- Short-term economic growth follows the long-term trend on average, but it oscillates around that trendline from year to year.
- People try hard to predict annual variation as a source of potential investing profit. And on average they're close to the truth most of the time. But few people do it right consistently; few do it that much better than everyone else; and few correctly predict the major deviations from trend.

∾

I often find — miraculously — that just as I'm just about to conclude something I'm writing, the perfect example pops up in real life or in something I read. Thus, as I was completing the first draft of this chapter on June 23, 2016, it was reported that a majority of voters in the United Kingdom had chosen to leave the European Union.

This decision was generally unexpected: the British pound and London stock market had strengthened in the days leading up to the vote, and the London bookmakers were giving odds that Brexit would be voted down. So much for forecasting.

This decision may have significant ramifications — economic, social and political — for the U.K. and Europe, but also for the rest of the world. The negative impact on the psyches of consumers, investors or businesspeople may cause near-term economic growth to slow. So may increases in trade barriers and reduced global efficiency.

Further, there's a chance that this event (and follow-ons such as the possible departure of Scotland and Northern Ireland from the United Kingdom) will alter long-term growth for the nations directly involved, and possibly for others. This event may be cited fifty years from now as having changed the growth trajectory of major parts of the world economy, and thus the whole, and as having contributed to a redirection of the long-term cycle.

Certainly there's a good chance the economic environment will be different in the years ahead from what it would have been if the Brexit vote had gone the other way — that is, that Brexit will cause a turn in Britain's long-term economic cycle. We just can't be sure how, to what extent, or what the knock-on effects on other economies will be.

V

GOVERNMENT INVOLVEMENT WITH
THE ECONOMIC CYCLE

Extreme economic cyclicality is considered undesirable. Too
much strength can kindle inflation and take the economy so
high that a recession becomes inevitable. Too much weakness,
on the other hand, can cause companies' profits to fall and can
cost people their jobs. Thus it is part of the job of central bankers and Treasury officials to manage cycles.

Since cycles produce ups and downs that can be excessive,
the tools for dealing with them are counter-cyclical and applied
with a cycle of their own — ideally inverse to the economic cycle
itself. However, like everything else involving cycles, managing
them is far from easy. If it weren't, we wouldn't see the extremes
we do.

In most of the world, capitalism and free markets are accepted today
as constituting the best system for allocating economic resources and
encouraging economic output. Nations have tried other systems, such as

socialism and communism, but in many cases they have either switched wholesale to or adopted aspects of free markets.

Despite the widespread acceptance of the free-market system, markets are rarely left entirely free. Government involvement takes many forms, ranging from the enactment and enforcement of laws and regulations to direct participation in the economy through entities like the U.S.'s mortgage agencies. Perhaps the most important form of government involvement, however, comes in the attempts of central banks and national treasuries to control and affect the ups and downs of economic cycles.

Central Banks

Over the centuries, significant power and responsibility has been vested in central banks such as the U.S. Federal Reserve Bank. Whereas in the past their primary roles may have been to issue currency and exchange it on request for gold or silver, today central banks are concerned primarily with managing economic cycles.

Early on, many central banks issued currency. As time passed and central banks took responsibility for cycles, their primary concern usually has been with inflation. In particular, the world went through periods of hyperinflation, with inflation running in the hundreds of percent per year, as was seen in Germany during the post–World War I Weimar Republic. Thus central banks turned to managing inflation. The goal wasn't to eliminate inflation — since it is accepted as (a) having a variety of salutary aspects and (b) being largely unavoidable — but to control it.

The reasons for inflation are somewhat mysterious and, like many other processes described here, unreliable and sporadic. Sometimes a given set of circumstances will give rise to inflation, and at other times the same circumstances will lead to more or less inflation, or to none at all. But in general, inflation is viewed as a result of a strong upward movement of the economic cycle.

- When the demand for goods increases relative to the supply, there can be "demand-pull" inflation.
- When inputs to production such as labor and raw materials increase in price, there can be "cost-push" inflation.
- Finally, when the value of an importing country's currency declines relative to that of an exporting country, the cost of the exporter's goods can rise in the importing country.

The cost of goods can escalate for any of these reasons. That's inflation. But, as I just said, sometimes these events can occur without an accompanying acceleration of inflation. And sometimes inflation can increase without these things being present. There is a large psychological component that influences all of this.

Since inflation results from economic strength, the efforts of central bankers to control it amount to trying to take some of the steam out of the economy. They can include reducing the money supply, raising interest rates and selling securities. When the private sector purchases securities from the central bank, money is taken out of circulation; this tends to reduce the demand for goods and thus discourages inflation. Central bankers who are strongly dedicated to keeping inflation under control are called "hawks." They tend to do the things listed above sooner and to a greater extent.

The problem, of course, is that actions of this kind are anti-stimulative. They can accomplish the goal of keeping inflation under control, but they also restrain the growth of the economy, with effects that can be less than beneficial.

The issue is complicated by the fact that in the last few decades, many central banks have been given a second responsibility. In addition to controlling inflation, they are expected to support employment, and, of course, employment does better when the economy is stronger. So central banks encourage this through stimulative actions such as increasing the money supply, decreasing interest rates, and injecting liquidity into the economy by buying securities — as in the recent program of "quantitative easing." Central bankers who focus strongly on encouraging employment and lean toward these actions are called "doves."

The bottom line is that most central bankers have two jobs: to limit inflation, which requires restraining the growth of the economy, and to support employment, which calls for stimulating economic growth. In other words, their dual responsibilities are in opposition to each other, and thus their job requires a delicate balancing act.

We have discussed the fact that the economy is cyclical, growing strongly at some times and weakly (or contracting) at others. An economic upswing tends to encourage employment but can cause inflation to accelerate. Stagnation or contraction, on the other hand, discourages inflation but can cut into employment. So the job of the central banker is to behave appropriately counter-cyclically: that is, to limit the extent of cycles, slowing the economy in times of prosperity in order to keep inflation under control, and stimulating the economy during slowdowns to support employment.

But just as the investor's insight into cycles is limited and uncertain, so is the central banker's. His two tasks — stimulating the economy and restraining it — obviously can't both be done at once. Is it time for stimulus or restraint? Whichever one is chosen, how much of it? If interest rates are low (as they have been since the Global Financial Crisis, in order to provide stimulus) but economic growth is weak (also as it has been), can rates be raised to forestall an increase in inflation without choking off the economy's tepid growth? If cycles are challenging for investors to understand and predict, they are no easier for central bankers to manage.

Governments

Governments have a greater variety of responsibilities than central bankers, only a small portion of which are related to the economic matters. Like central banks, they also are charged with stimulating the economy when appropriate, albeit not directly with controlling inflation. In their work with the economy, treasuries, too, are concerned with regulating the cycle: not too fast and not too slow.

Governments' main tools for managing the economic cycle are fiscal, defined as being concerned primarily with taxing and spending. Thus when governments want to stimulate their countries' economies, they can cut taxes, increase government spending and even distribute stimulus checks, making more money available for spending and investment. On the other hand, when they think economies are growing so fast as to be at risk of overheating — setting the scene for a resulting slowdown — governments can increase taxes or cut spending, reducing demand in their economies and thereby slowing economic activity.

The ultimate topic under this heading concerns national deficits. In the distant past, most governments ran balanced budgets. In short, they weren't able to spend more money than they brought in through taxes (or conquests). But then the concept of national debt arose, and the ability to incur debt introduced the potential for deficits: that is, for governments to spend more than they take in.

I seem to remember from my youth that there was active debate regarding the propriety of countries having national debt, but we no longer hear much resistance on that subject. It is generally accepted that countries can owe money, although questions do arise from time to time about how much debt is prudent. The answer generally seems to be "not too much more than we have now."

The economic theory propounded by John Maynard Keynes in the 1930s dwelled heavily on the role of governments vis-à-vis cycles. Keynesian economics focuses on the role of aggregate demand in determining the level of GDP, in contrast with earlier approaches that emphasized the role of the supply of goods. Keynes said governments should manage the economic cycle by influencing demand. This, in turn, could be accomplished through the use of fiscal tools, including deficits.

Keynes urged governments to aid a weak economy by stimulating demand by running deficits. When a government's outgo — its spending — exceeds its income — primarily from taxes — on balance it puts funds into the economy. This encourages buying and investing. Deficits are stimulative, and thus Keynes considered them helpful in dealing with a weak economy.

On the other hand, when economies are strong, Keynes said governments should run surpluses, spending less than they take in. This removes funds from the economy, discouraging spending and investment. Surpluses are contractionary and thus an appropriate response to booms. However, the use of surpluses to cool a thriving economy is little seen these days. No one wants to be a wet blanket when the party is going strong. And spending less than you bring in attracts fewer votes than do generous spending programs. Thus surpluses have become as rare as buggy whips.

∾

Extreme economic cyclicality is considered undesirable. Too much strength can kindle inflation and take the economy so high that a recession becomes inevitable. Too much weakness, on the other hand, can cause companies' profits to fall and cost people their jobs.

Thus it is part of the job of central bankers and Treasury officials to manage cycles through the techniques described above. Since cycles produce ups and downs that can be excessive, the tools for dealing with them are counter-cyclical and applied with a cycle of their own — ideally inverse to the economic cycle itself.

However, like everything else involving cycles — such as knowing where we are and what to do about them — managing them is far from easy. If it weren't, we wouldn't see the extremes we do.

VI

THE CYCLE IN PROFITS

The process that determines a company's profits is complex and multivariate. The economic cycle has a profound effect on some companies' sales but less on others. Largely because of differences in operating and financial leverage, a given percentage change in sales has a much greater impact on profits for some companies than for others.

These days, as I said earlier, the normal growth rate for U.S. GDP seems to be about 2–3% per year. Growth might come in at 1% or so in a sluggish year or hit 4% or 5% in boom times (or during a recovery from a slowdown). The annualized growth rate might even turn negative by a couple of percent in tough times, and if it stays negative for two successive quarters, be termed a recession. So there are fluctuations, but they are moderate: annual growth in U.S. GDP almost always falls between 5% and minus 2%, and even those extremes are seen only once every decade at most.

Does that mean companies' profits also are stable from year to year? Far from it. Profits can gain much more than 5% in good times and decline much more than 2% in bad. They, too, follow a cycle — one that is influenced by the economic cycle, but that rises and falls much more than the economy as a whole. So profits are more volatile than GDP. The question is why? What factors cause the profit cycle to perform differently from the economic cycle?

First, the ups and downs of the economy absolutely are very important in determining the rise and fall of corporate profits. More GDP means — more than anything else — more consumption, and thus stronger demand for goods. That, in turn, means greater volumes sold and higher selling prices, more work and higher wages, and thus still more consumption. All those things together mean increased revenues for businesses.

By definition, the collective sales of all businesses are one and the same as GDP, and they reflect the same rate of change. But that doesn't mean all companies follow the same pattern.

Sales are responsive to the economic cycle in some industries, and in some they aren't. And some respond a lot, while others respond just a little.

- Sales of industrial raw materials and components are directly responsive to the economic cycle. When business collectively increases its output — that is, when GDP expands — it takes more chemicals, metals, plastic, energy, wire and semiconductors to do so, and vice versa.

- On the other hand, everyday necessities like food, beverages and medicine aren't highly responsive to the economic cycle. People generally consume them regardless of what's going on in the economy. (But demand isn't absolutely constant: people trade down in recessions — buying cheaper food and eating at home rather than in restaurants — and they trade up in times of prosperity. And, sadly, people who are struggling financially may cut down even on their consumption of "necessities" when forced to choose between food, medications and rent payments.)

- Demand for low-cost consumer items (like everyday clothing, newspapers and digital downloads) isn't very volatile, while demand for luxury goods and vacation trips may be.

- Purchases of big-ticket "durable goods"—things like cars and homes for individuals and trucks and factory equipment for businesses—are highly responsive to the economic cycle. First, the fact that they're durable means they last a long time, so replacement can be deferred in times of economic weakness. Second, because they cost a lot, they're hard to afford in bad times and easier to afford good times. And third, businesses generally need more of them when business is good and less when it isn't. These things make the demand for durables highly responsive to the economic cycle.

- Demand for everyday services generally isn't volatile. If they're necessary (like transportation to work) and low-priced (like haircuts), demand won't be highly sensitive to changes in the economy. Further, services like these have a limited shelf life and can't be stored. Thus they have to be purchased continually. But demand still can vary based on economic conditions: for example, a haircut can be made to last five weeks rather than three.

In addition, sales of some products respond to cycles other than economic. Because durables are expensive and can be paid for over their long lives, the demand for them can go up and down (everything else being equal) as fluctuations in the credit cycle make financing more and less readily available. And some things are influenced by non-cyclical developments: for example, the demand for new cell phones and laptops responds to price reductions, new product introductions and improvements in technology.

For the most part, however, economic growth dominates the process through which sales are determined. Sales generally rise strongly when GDP growth is strong and less so (or they decline) when it isn't.

∾

But the linkage between economic growth and profit growth is highly imperfect. This is because the movements of the economic cycle aren't the only thing that influences sales (as just shown), and also because a change in sales doesn't necessarily result in an equivalent change in profits. One of the main reasons for this latter phenomenon is the fact that most businesses are characterized by leverage of two types. These are elements that magnify the response of profits to a change in sales. The meaning of "leverage" may be more immediately obvious from the British word for it: gearing.

First, businesses are subject to operating leverage. Profits equal revenues minus costs (or expenses). Revenues are the result of sales, and we know that sales fluctuate for a large number of reasons. So do costs, and different kinds of costs fluctuate in different ways, particularly in response to changes in sales.

Most businesses have some costs that are fixed, some that are semi-fixed, and some that are variable. For example, take a taxicab company:

- It has its headquarters in an office building, but when ridership increases a bit, it doesn't need to add more office space. This is an example of a fixed cost.
- It has a fleet of taxis. The current fleet can accommodate a moder-

ate increase in ridership, but if trips increase enough, it may have to buy additional cabs. Thus the expense for cabs is semi-fixed.

- Its cabs are powered by gasoline. If an increase in business causes its cabs to go x% more miles, their consumption of gasoline is likely to increase by that same x%. For the taxi company, then, the cost of gasoline is variable.

The sum of the above means that if the company's ridership (and thus its revenues) increases by 20%, its spending on office facilities won't increase; its spending on cabs probably won't increase initially, but may later; and its spending on gasoline will increase immediately and proportionately. Thus the taxicab company's total costs will increase with an increase in ridership, but usually less than its revenues. This will cause its profit margin to rise, meaning the increase in operating profits will be considerably greater than the increase in sales: that's operating leverage. In general, it's higher for companies for whom a larger percentage of costs are fixed and lower for the ones whose costs are more variable.

Operating leverage is great for companies when the economy does well and sales rise. But when the opposite happens, it's less good: profits can fall more than sales, and if conditions are bad enough, profits can turn into losses. Companies can, however, take actions to limit the effect on profits of a sales decline. These can include laying off employees and closing stores. But (a) economy measures usually need time to take effect; (b) they sometimes entail increased expense in the short run, as in the case of severance pay; (c) they generally can limit the negative effect but not eliminate it; and (d) they rarely work as well as projected.

The second form of leverage affecting most companies is financial leverage. Let's say a given company's operating profits decline by $1,000 (or 33%), from $3,000 to $2,000. If the company's $30,000 capital requirement has been sourced entirely through equity, meaning it hasn't borrowed any of its capital and doesn't have to make any interest payments, that decline would flow through to the company's net income — the "bottom line" — and it, too, would fall by 33%.

But most companies are financed with a combination of equity and debt. Debtholders occupy a senior position relative to the equity investors, who are said to be in the "first-loss" position; this means the equity holders suffer all declines in profits, and then all losses, until the equity is wiped out, at which time any further losses fall to the debtholders. As long as there's equity in the company, the outcome for the debtholders remains unchanged — they merely receive the interest payments they were promised. (That's why bonds and notes are called "fixed income securities": the outcome is fixed.)

Let's assume the capital structure of this company consists of $15,000 of debt (requiring annual interest payments of $1,500) and $15,000 of equity. That means the $1,000 decline in operating profits reduces the net income from $1,500 ($3,000 of operating profit before interest payments, minus $1,500 of interest) to $500 ($2,000 minus $1,500). In other words, a 33% decline in operating profit (from $3,000 to $2,000) causes this company's net income to decline by 67% (from $1,500 to $500). The magnified impact of a decline in operating profit on the net income illustrates financial leverage at work.

∾

The process that determines a company's profits is complex and multivariate. The economic cycle has a profound effect on some companies' sales but less on others. Largely because of differences in operating and financial leverage, a given percentage change in sales has a much greater impact on profits for some companies than for others.

And, of course, idiosyncratic developments can have a very significant impact on profits. These can include things like management's decisions regarding inventories, production levels, and capital investment; technological advancements (on the part of a company, its industry competitors, and even companies in competing industries — see below); changes in regulation and taxation; and even developments exogenous to the industry, or even to the business world, such as weather, war and fads. The economic cycle provides the backdrop for changes in companies' sales and profits, but the potential for deviation from the cycle-based expectation is vast. Idiosyncratic developments are the main reason.

I'll take a moment here to deal with the subject of technology (rather than devote a separate chapter to it). "Disrupt" is the word of the day, and the ability of new technologies to disrupt traditional industries can create new competition and dismantle the incumbents' profit margins. Take, for example, the newspaper industry. As recently as the 1990s:

- Newspapers were considered an indispensable source of information.
- Most people bought a newspaper daily — or maybe one on the way to work and another on the way home — and the cost was small.
- Even if you bought the newspaper on Monday, you still had to buy another on Tuesday; there was no "shelf life" or protracted usefulness.
- Newspapers were one of the very few ways local businesses like movie theaters and used-car dealers could reach their customers, and a newspaper from one city generally couldn't compete for local advertising from another.
- Competition came primarily from other newspapers, television and radio. Once a newspaper was strongly established in a city,

however, it would be hard to displace — thus newspapers were viewed as businesses with strong "moats."

Because this combination of factors was seen as making newspapers' position largely impregnable, newspaper company stocks were thought of as "defensive," benefiting from highly stable revenues and profits.

Who would have thought that the Internet and other forms of online communication would significantly impact the fortunes of newspapers in less than twenty years? Today many companies compete to bring information directly to consumers. Newspapers are struggling to maintain their market share and profitability, as "free" has come to characterize many aspects of the digital world, knocking newspapers' business models off stride.

Newspapers provide an excellent example of the ability of an idiosyncratic factor to influence a company's sales and profits, completely apart from of the economic and traditional profit cycle. But isn't technology cyclical itself? Technologies are born, they prosper, and then they are replaced by still newer ones. The innovation of a few years ago can be supplanted more rapidly than ever these days, and the list of industries that are perceived as being immune to disruption seems to shrink every day.

Thirty or forty years ago, it seemed as if the world was a stable place that provided a relatively unchanging backdrop for life, and economic developments — including cycles — played out against that unchanging backdrop. Today, largely because of technological developments (but also social and cultural), nothing seems unchanging. In fact, much appears to be changing too fast for most of us to keep up with it.

VII

THE PENDULUM OF INVESTOR PSYCHOLOGY

In business, financial and market cycles, most excesses on the upside—and the inevitable reactions to the downside, which also tend to overshoot—are the result of exaggerated swings of the pendulum of psychology. Thus understanding and being alert to excessive swings is an entry-level requirement for avoiding harm from cyclical extremes, and hopefully for profiting from them.

So far we have discussed the economic cycle, governments' efforts to influence the economic cycle, and the profit cycle. To a great extent these things provide the backdrop or environment for investing. And they can seem to be exogenous to investing—independent processes that operate on their own. But anyone who thinks these things are "mechanical" in their operation and in full control of investment results underestimates the role of psychology or, I tend to say interchangeably, emotion. (Psychology and emotion are certainly different elements, but I see no meaningful way to distinguish between the two in terms of their effect on the investment environment.)

First, swings in emotion/psychology strongly influence the economic and corporate profit cycles, as indicated. And second, they play a very prominent part in causing ups and downs in the investment world — especially in the short run.

As I noted in chapter I, there is no fundamental distinction between cycles and pendulum swings. In fact, I could have made life easier for all of us by titling this chapter "The Cycle in Psychology" and fitting this phenomenon within a consistent nomenclature. But, for some unspecified reason, I first introduced the notion of the "pendulum" in emotion/psychology in just my second memo to clients, "First Quarter Performance" (April 1991). And since I haven't found a reason to distance myself from it in the 26 years since, I'm going to continue to refer to it here.

To introduce the pendulum, I'm going to borrow from what I wrote in 1991:

> The mood swings of the securities markets resemble the movement of a pendulum. Although the midpoint of its arc best describes the location of the pendulum "on average," it actually spends very little of its time there. Instead, it is almost always swinging toward or away from the extremes of its arc. But whenever the pendulum is near either extreme, it is inevitable that it will move back toward the midpoint sooner or later. In fact, it is the movement toward an extreme itself that supplies the energy for the swing back.
>
> Investment markets make the same pendulum-like swing:
>
> - between euphoria and depression,
> - between celebrating positive developments and obsessing over negatives, and thus
> - between being overpriced and underpriced.

This oscillation is one of the most dependable features of the investment world, and investor psychology seems to spend much more
time at the extremes than it does at a "happy medium."

I returned to the topic in "It's All Good" (July 2007). Before going on to
make a new observation, I listed a half-dozen additional elements in which
pendulum swings are seen:

- between greed and fear,
- between optimism and pessimism,
- between risk tolerance and risk aversion,
- between credence and skepticism,
- between faith in value in the future and insistence of concrete
  value in the present, and
- between urgency to buy and panic to sell.

I find particularly interesting the degree to which the polarities listed
above are interrelated. When a market has been rising strongly for a
while, we invariably see all nine of the elements listed first. And when
the market's been declining, we see all of the elements listed second.
Rarely do we see a blend of the two sets, given that the components in
each are causally related, with one giving rise to the next.

A lot of what I wrote then about the pendulum corresponds directly with
what I wrote about cycles back in chapter I. There's a swing toward one
extreme or the other; then the attainment of an extreme that can't be exceeded; and then a swing back toward the midpoint, fueled by the reversal of
momentum. It might be said that the pendulum also tends to regress toward
the mean or midpoint, but—like most cycles—it usually overshoots and
continues toward the extreme opposite from whence it came.

~

Why is the pendulum important? In essence, the too-strong upward and downward swings of the cycles I'm covering in this book largely result from — and represent — psychological excesses in action.

- The trendline rate of growth in economic output and corporate profits is moderate, and when participants' pro-cyclical decisions cause growth to be abnormally rapid (other than in times of recovery from recession), this usually represents a too-optimistic expansion from which there will be a retreat.
- Likewise, it seems rational that, in the long run, stocks overall should provide returns in line with the sum of their dividends plus the trendline growth in corporate profits, or something in the mid-to-high single digits. When they return much more than that for a while, that return is likely to prove to have been excessive — borrowing from the future and thus rendering stocks risky — meaning a downward correction is now in order.

In business, financial and market cycles, most excesses on the upside — and the inevitable reactions to the downside, which also tend to overshoot — are the result of exaggerated swings of the pendulum of psychology. Thus understanding and being alert to excessive swings is an entry-level requirement for avoiding harm from cyclical extremes, and hopefully for profiting from them.

The norms in terms of growth and appreciation are in some sense "right" and "healthy." And if the participants built their behavior around those norms — instead of occasionally building up hopes for more and thus setting the stage for eventual moves toward less — the world would be a steadier, less-tempestuous, and less-error-prone place. But that's not the nature of things.

I touched on the inapplicability of norms in "The Happy Medium" (from July 2004, but now with data brought up to date through 2016):

> Putting it all together, fluctuations in attitudes and behavior combine to make the stock market the ultimate pendulum. In my 47 full calendar years in the investment business, starting with 1970, the annual returns on the S&P 500 have swung from plus 37% to minus 37%. Averaging out good years and bad years, the long-run return is usually stated as 10% or so. Everyone's been happy with that typical performance and would love more of the same.
>
> But remember, a swinging pendulum may be at its midpoint "on average," but it actually spends very little time there. The same is true of financial market performance. Here's a fun question (and a good illustration): for how many of the 47 years from 1970 through 2016 was the annual return on the S&P 500 within 2% of "normal"—that is, between 8% and 12%?
>
> I expected the answer to be "not that often," but I was surprised to learn that it had happened *only three times!* It also surprised me to learn that the return had been more than 20 percentage points away from "normal"—either up more than 30% or down more than 10% —more than one-quarter of the time: 13 out of the last 47 years. So one thing that can be said with total conviction about stock market performance is that the average certainly isn't the norm. Market fluctuations of this magnitude aren't nearly fully explained by the changing fortunes of companies, industries or economies. They're largely attributable to the mood swings of investors.
>
> Lastly, the times when return is at the extremes aren't randomly distributed over the years. Rather they're clustered, due to the fact that investors' psychological swings tend to persist for a while—to paraphrase Herb Stein, they tend to continue until they stop. Most

of those 13 extreme up or down years were within a year or two of another year of similarly extreme performance in the same direction.

How about an example of the pendulum in action?

One of the most time-honored market adages says that "markets fluctuate between greed and fear." There's a fundamental reason for this: it's because *people* fluctuate between greed and fear. In other words, sometimes people feel positive and expect good things, and when that's the case, they turn greedy and fixate on making money. Their greed causes them to compete to make investments, and their bidding causes markets to rise and assets to appreciate.

But at other times, they feel less good and their expectations turn negative. In that case, fear takes over. Rather than enthuse about making money, they worry about losing it. This causes them to shrink from buying — eliminating the upward impetus beneath asset prices — and perhaps to sell, pushing prices down. When they're in "fear mode," people's emotions bring negative forces to bear on the markets.

Here's part of the discussion of the swing between greed and fear, from "The Happy Medium" (July 2004):

> When I was a rookie analyst, we heard all the time that "the stock market is driven by greed and fear." When the market environment is in healthy balance, a tug-of-war takes place between optimists intent on making money and pessimists seeking to avoid losses. The former want to buy stocks, even if they have to pay a price a bit above yesterday's close, and the latter want to sell them, even if it's on a downtick.
>
> When the market doesn't go anyplace, it's because the sentiment behind this tug-of-war is evenly divided, and the people — or feelings — on the two ends of the rope carry roughly equal weight. The optimists may prevail for a while, but as securities are bid up they become

more highly priced, and then the pessimists gain sway and sell them down. . . .

It didn't take long in my early days, however, for me to realize that often the market is driven by greed *or* fear. At the times that really count, large numbers of people leave one end of the rope for the other. Either the greedy or the fearful predominate, and they move the market dramatically. When there's only greed and no fear, for example, everyone wants to buy, no one wants to sell, and few people can think of reasons why prices shouldn't rise. And so they do — often in leaps and bounds and with no apparent governor.

Clearly that's what happened to tech stocks in 1999. Greed was the dominant characteristic of that market. Those who weren't participating were forced to watch everyone else get rich. "Prudent investors" were rewarded with a feeling of stupidity. The buyers moving that market felt no fear. "There's a new paradigm," was the battle cry, "get on board before you miss the boat. And by the way, the price I'm buying at can't be excessive, because the market's always efficient." Everyone perceived a virtuous cycle in favor of tech stocks to which there could be no end.

But eventually something changes. Either a stumbling block materializes, or a prominent company reports a problem, or an exogenous factor intrudes. Prices can also fall under their own weight or based on a downturn in psychology with no obvious cause. Certainly no one I know can say exactly what it was that burst the tech-stock bubble in 2000. But somehow the greed evaporated and fear took over. "Buy before you miss out" was replaced by "Sell before it goes to zero."

And thus fear comes into the ascendancy. People don't worry about missing opportunities; they worry about losing money. Irrational exuberance is replaced by excessive caution. Whereas in 1999 pie-in-the-sky forecasts for a decade out were embraced warmly, in 2002 investors chastened by the corporate scandals said, "I'll never

trust management again" and "How can I be sure any financial statements are accurate?" Thus almost no one wanted to buy the bonds of
the scandal-plagued companies, for example, and they sunk to giveaway prices. It's from the extremes of the cycle of fear and greed that
arise the greatest investment profits, as distressed debt demonstrated
in 2003.

"Greed/fear" is the most obvious psychological or emotional continuum along which investors swing, and in many ways the most illustrative.
What are some of the other key emotional or psychological swings? Most
operate in a manner similar to the greed/fear pendulum, and usually this
isn't a coincidence. The various parameters are interrelated. Here are a few
examples.

Underlying the swing between greed and fear is the swing between euphoria and depression. As previously described, for example, it may not
be simply that positive events give rise to greed. Rather, positive events
encourage euphoria, which abets greed (and vice versa for negative events,
depression and fear). Euphoria and depression are the foundation emotions that give rise to the swings that follow.

Euphoric investors may be excited about current developments and
those that may arise in the future, and this may accentuate their fixation
with—and expectation of—profit. On the other hand, depressed investors are unlikely to feel positive enough to be greedy. If you think about
it, euphoria is inconsistent with fear, and depression is inconsistent with
greed.

In a similar vein, investors also swing between optimism and pessimism. Positive events generally give rise to expectations of further positive events and positive outcomes ... a state better known as optimism.
Optimism has to underlie greed; it makes no sense to think people can be

greedy and driven forward to invest when their expectations are negative. Clearly, optimism and pessimism encourage other emotions and influence behavior.

∾

The next phenomenon I want to touch on is the tendency of investors to swing between credulousness and skepticism, and to fluctuate between being entranced by the possibility of profit in the future and insistent on tangible value in the here and now.

Sometimes — usually when things are going well in the world and asset prices are rising — investors become willing to swallow favorable stories regarding future developments, buy into appreciated assets, and shoulder elevated risk. But when things take a turn for the worse, they become more likely to reject even reasonable projections and decline to buy, largely because prices are down (even though that increases the likelihood that assets are cheap).

> Some investors spend their time working hard to quantify this year's earnings and the growth thereafter. Others strive to value real assets, intellectual property and business advantages (and predict what others will pay for them). Still others try to deduce the value implications of mergers and acquisitions, balance sheet restructurings and private-to-public transactions. In all of these ways and many more, it's the job of those in the investment business to predict the future and put a value on it.
>
> Let me give you an example. In 2000–01, our distressed debt funds invested a few hundred million dollars in bankrupt telecom companies. In each case, the purchase price implied a value for the company that was a small fraction of the amounts that had been invested in hard assets such as switching gear or fiber-optic cable. If we

could resell the equipment for a higher percentage of its cost than we had paid, the investment would be profitable.

The first sale went well, and we made a quick 50%. But soon thereafter, people stopped showing up to bid on these assets. Whereas the party to whom we had sold the first company thought he had a bargain, in later instances the possible buyers shied away from assets that were turning out to be in heavy oversupply. And that brings me to my point. In 1999, investors accepted at face value their telecom companies' rosy predictions of the future, and they were willing to pay handily for that potential. But in 2001, they saw the potential as largely empty and wouldn't pay a dime for it, given that the industry's capacity vastly exceeded its current needs and no one could imagine the excess being absorbed in their lifetime. This cycle in investors' willingness to value the future is one of the most powerful cycles that exists.

A simple metaphor relating to real estate helped me to understand this phenomenon: What's an empty building worth? An empty building (a) has a replacement value, of course, but it (b) throws off no revenues and (c) costs money to own, in the form of taxes, insurance, minimum maintenance, interest payments and opportunity costs. In other words, it's a cash drain. When investors are in a pessimistic mood and can't see more than a few years out, they can only think about the negative cash flows and are unable to imagine a time when the building will be rented and profitable. But when the mood turns upward and interest in future potential runs high, investors envision it full of tenants, throwing off vast amounts of cash, and thus salable at a fancy price.

Fluctuation in investors' willingness to ascribe value to possible future developments represents a variation on the full-or-empty cycle. Its swings are enormously powerful and mustn't be underestimated. ("The Happy Medium," July 2004)

∾

The superior investor is mature, rational, analytical, objective and unemotional. Thus he performs a thorough analysis of investment fundamentals and the investment environment. He calculates the intrinsic value of each potential investment asset. And he buys when any discount of the price from the current intrinsic value, plus any potential increases in intrinsic value in the future, together suggest that buying at the current price is a good idea.

In order to be able to do all the above, the superior investor strikes an appropriate balance between fear (which is shorthand for risk aversion, dislike for loss, and respect for uncertainty and randomness) and greed (a.k.a. aspiration, aggressiveness and acquisitiveness). All people feel emotions, but the superior investor keeps these conflicting elements in balance. The presence of the two offsetting forces leads to responsible, wise and even-keeled behavior.

But the important points are these:

- Few people are always even-keeled and unemotional.
- For this reason, few investors are capable of staking out a midpoint position that balances greed and fear — and staying there — as more- and less-positive developments arise.
- To the contrary, most investors swing between being greedy when they're optimistic and fearful when they're pessimistic.
- Most swing to those positions at the wrong time — becoming greedier after the emergence of positive developments has caused prices to become elevated, and becoming more fearful after negative events have caused prices to become depressed.

Here's some of what I wrote about the swing of psychology in "On the Couch" (January 2016):

There are many more ways in which non-objective, non-rational quirks commonly affect behavior. As Carol Tavris pointed out in her May 15, 2015 *Wall Street Journal* review of Prof. Richard Thaler's book *Misbehaving: The Making of Behavioral Economics* (2015):

> As a social psychologist, I have long been amused by economists and their curiously delusional notion of the "rational man." Rational? Where do these folks live? Even 50 years ago, experimental studies were demonstrating that people stay with clearly wrong decisions rather than change them, throw good money after bad, justify failed predictions rather than admit they were wrong, and resist, distort or actively reject information that disputes their beliefs.

The difficulty of understanding events, their significance and their potential ramifications comes in good part from the kinks in investors' psyches, and it contributes to — and feeds back to exacerbate — investors' responses. Thus investors tend to emphasize just the positives or the negatives much more often than they take a balanced, objective approach. And they tend to become optimistic and eager to buy when good news, positively interpreted, has forced prices up . . . and vice versa. All of this is obvious (especially in retrospect). Thus, equally obviously, understanding and dealing with it presents a potential way to improve results.

The basic point is that psychology does swing, and most people's behavior swings with it. The fluctuation between greed and fear is typical of the swing of the psychological pendulum. In fact, it explains not only the behavior of most investors, but also — taking investors collectively — the behavior of entire markets. Markets move upward when events are positive and psychology turns up, and they fall when events are negative and psychology turns down.

The pendulum spends only a little of the time at the midpoint of its arc.

Rather, the pendulum is usually swinging toward one extreme or the other, first recovering from one psychological extreme — either too high or too low — and then continuing toward the other.

The superior investor resists psychological excesses and thus refuses to participate in these swings. The vast majority of the highly superior investors I know are unemotional by nature. In fact, I believe their unemotional nature is one of the great contributors to their success.

This is one of my most persistent observations and — in a related way — one of the questions I'm most often asked is whether people can learn to be unemotional. My answer is "yes and no." I think it's possible for people to be on the lookout for potential emotional influences and to try to restrain their effect. But I also think people who are inherently unemotional will have it much easier. A lack of emotionality is a gift (in investing, that is, but perhaps not in other areas, like marriage). It's not my point that emotional people can't be good investors, but it will require a great deal of self-aware-ness and self-restraint.

∾

In addition to the interrelatedness of the various emotional swings de-scribed on the last few pages, it's also important to note the causal nature of these phenomena. Just as positive events give rise to euphoria, and eupho-ria gives rise to optimism, and optimism abets an increase in greed, swings in the sum of all these elements cause the way investors perceive things to fluctuate between rosy and dark. Investors' perception of events is colored by their swings along the various emotional or psychological arcs. And this colored perception feeds back, creating more euphoria, optimism and greed.

Here's how I put it in "On the Couch" (January 2016):

One of the most significant factors keeping investors from reaching appropriate conclusions is their tendency to assess the world with emotionalism rather than objectivity. Their failings take two primary forms: selective perception and skewed interpretation. In other words, sometimes they take note of only positive events and ignore the negative ones, and sometimes the opposite is true. And sometimes they view events in a positive light, and sometimes it's negative. But rarely are their perceptions and interpretations balanced and neutral.

Ever since the events of August 2015 in China, I've repeatedly found myself harking back to one of the oldest cartoons in my file, and still one of the very best:

"Everything that was good for the market yesterday is no good for it today."

The bottom line is that investor psychology rarely gives equal weight to both favorable and unfavorable developments. Likewise, investors' interpretation of events is usually biased by their emotional reaction to whatever is going on at the moment. Most developments have both helpful and harmful aspects. But investors generally obsess about one or the other rather than consider both. And that recalls another classic cartoon:

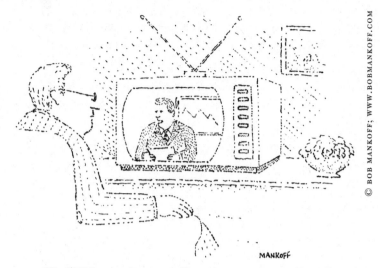

"On Wall Street today, news of lower interest rates sent the stock market up, but then the expectation that these rates would be inflationary sent the market down, until the realization that lower rates might stimulate the sluggish economy pushed the market up, before it ultimately went down on fears that an overheated economy would lead to a reimposition of higher interest rates."

BobMankoff.com

It all seems so obvious: investors rarely maintain objective, rational, neutral and stable positions. First they exhibit high levels of optimism, greed, risk tolerance and credulousness, and their resulting behavior causes asset prices to rise, potential returns to fall, and risk to increase. But then, for some reason—perhaps the arrival of a tipping point—they switch to pessimism, fear, risk aversion and skepticism, and this causes asset prices to fall, prospective returns to rise, and risk to decrease. Notably, each group of phenomena tends to happen in unison, and the swing from one to the other often goes far beyond what reason might call for.

That's one of the crazy things: in the real world, things generally fluctuate between "pretty good" and "not so hot." But in the world of investing, perception often swings from "flawless" to "hopeless." The pendulum careens from one extreme to the other, spending almost no time at "the happy medium" and rather little in the range of reasonableness. First there's denial, and then there's capitulation.

The world is full of positive and negative events, and on most days we see some of each. And some of the events that occur are ambiguous, having elements of both good and bad, making them subject to either positive or negative interpretation.

Take the example of the second cartoon. Low interest rates are good, because they stimulate business activity and increase the discounted present value of future cash flows. But they're also bad, since the stronger business activity they abet can give rise to inflation and thus signal the central banks that rates should be raised, withdrawing stimulus from the economy. Interpretation may not fluctuate between the extremes several times a day, as the cartoon suggests. But it does fluctuate excessively, and in fact it can turn on a dime.

A few years ago my friend Jon Brooks supplied this great illustration of skewed interpretation at work. Here's how investors react to events when they're feeling good about life (which usually means the market has been rising):

- Strong data: economy strengthening — stocks rally
- Weak data: Fed likely to ease — stocks rally
- Data as expected: low volatility — stocks rally

- Banks make $4 billion: business conditions favorable — stocks rally
- Banks lose $4 billion: bad news out of the way — stocks rally

- Oil spikes: growing global economy contributing to demand — stocks rally
- Oil drops: more purchasing power for the consumer — stocks rally

- Dollar plunges: great for exporters — stocks rally
- Dollar strengthens: great for companies that buy from abroad — stocks rally

- Inflation spikes: will cause assets to appreciate — stocks rally
- Inflation drops: improves quality of earnings — stocks rally

Of course, the same behavior also applies in the opposite direction. When psychology is negative and markets have been falling for a while, everything is capable of being interpreted negatively. Strong economic data is seen as likely to make the Fed withdraw stimulus by raising interest rates, and weak data is taken to mean companies will have trouble meeting earnings forecasts. In other words, it's not the data or events; it's the interpretation. And that fluctuates with swings in psychology.

At the greatest extremes of the pendulum's swing, a process can take on the appearance of a virtuous circle or a vicious circle. When events are predominantly positive and psychology is rosy, negative developments tend to be overlooked, everything is interpreted favorably, and things are often thought to be incapable of taking a turn for the worse. The logic supporting an expectation of further advances appears irresistible; past constraints and norms are ignored or rationalized away; and anyone imagining limitations on the positive future is dismissed as an old fogey lacking imagination. The potential for gains comes to be viewed as infinite. Asset prices rise, encouraging further optimism.

But on the other hand, when things have been going badly for months or years and psychology is highly negative, it's the potential for improvement that can be forgotten. Unpleasant events are emphasized and positive ones are ignored. The case for further deterioration seems rock-solid, its error can't be imagined, and now it's the downside that seems to be unlimited. Prices fall, resulting in further pessimism.

The virtuous circle and the vicious circle are both unrealistic exaggerations. While they've been dreamed up many times in the past, they've never proved out. But that fact doesn't enable most people to resist them while they're rampant.

Again, the superior investor — who resists external influences, remains emotionally balanced and acts rationally — perceives both positive and negative events, weighs events objectively and analyzes them dispassionately. But the truth is that sometimes euphoria and optimism cause most investors to view things more positively than is warranted, and sometimes depression and pessimism make them see only bad and interpret events with a negative cast. Refusing to do so is one of the keys to successful investing.

∿

> For a bullish phase to hold sway, the environment has to be characterized by greed, optimism, exuberance, confidence, credulity, daring, risk tolerance and aggressiveness. But these traits will not govern a market forever. Eventually they will give way to fear, pessimism, prudence, uncertainty, skepticism, caution, risk aversion and reticence. . . . Busts are the product of booms, and I'm convinced it's usually more correct to attribute a bust to the excesses of the preceding boom than to the specific event that sets off the correction. ("Now What?," January 2008)
>
> Usually, when either set of polar extremes is in the ascendancy, that fact is readily observable, and thus the implications for investors should be obvious to objective observers. But of course, the swing of the market pendulum to one extreme or the other occurs for the simple reason that the psyches of most market participants are moving in the same direction in a herd-like fashion.
>
> Few of the people involved actually are objective. To continue a

thread from my memo "Everyone Knows" (April 2007), expecting widespread clinical observation during a market mania makes about as much sense as saying "everyone knows the market has gone too far." If many people recognized that it had gone too far, it wouldn't be there. ("It's All Good," July 2007)

VIII

THE CYCLE IN ATTITUDES
TOWARD RISK

The rational investor is diligent, skeptical and appropriately
risk-averse at all times, but also on the lookout for opportunities
for potential return that more than compensates for risk. That's
the ideal. But in good times, we hear most people say, "Risk?
What risk? I don't see much that could go wrong: look how
well things have been going. And anyway, risk is my friend — the
more risk I take, the more money I'm likely to make."

Then, in bad times, they switch to something simpler: "I
don't care if I ever make another penny in the market; I just
don't want to lose any more. Get me out!"

Now that we've moved on from considering cycles in the abstract to
discussing their operation in the investment world, I'm going to provide a brief aside regarding the fundamental nature of investing, in order
to establish a foundation for the discussion that will follow. Some of this
admittedly will be familiar from earlier chapters.

What is investing? One way to think of it is as bearing risk in pursuit of
profit. Investors try to position portfolios so as to profit from future devel-

opments rather than be penalized by them. The superior investor is simply someone who does this better than others.

Do we know what will happen in the future? Some investors think they do — or think they have to act as if they do, because if they don't they'll lose their jobs and their clients — or they have been pursuing profit through forecasts for so long that they've brainwashed themselves into believing it's possible to be right about the future (and have become conditioned to ignore their low past success rates). Other investors — the smarter, more self-aware ones, I think — understand that the future isn't knowable with certainty. They may form opinions regarding future events, but they don't bet heavily that those opinions will prove correct.

Since (a) investing consists of dealing with the future but (b) the future isn't knowable, that's where the risk in investing comes from. If future events were predictable, investing would be easy and profit would be sure. (The general level of returns might be low in that case because so little risk is involved; that's a topic for another day.) But the fact that events aren't predictable introduces risk. Because the events that actually occur may be different than those that were predicted, or the market's reaction to events may differ from what was expected, a portfolio may be positioned incorrectly for the future that unfolds.

Since risk (that is, uncertainty with regard to future developments, and the possibility of bad outcomes) is the primary source of the challenge in investing, the ability to understand, assess and deal with risk is the mark of the superior investor and an essential — I'm tempted to say *the* essential — requirement for investment success.

Finally as to foundation, it's important to recognize that while the investment environment varies over time, at any particular point in time it is a given. What I mean is that we can accept the environment as it is and invest, or we can reject it and stay on the sidelines, but we don't have a third option of saying, "I don't like the environment as it is today; I demand a different one." Or rather we can demand another, but of course that won't make it materialize.

My view that risk is the main moving piece in investing makes me conclude that at any given point in time, the way investors collectively are viewing risk and behaving with regard to it is of overwhelming importance in shaping the investment environment in which we find ourselves. And the state of the environment is key in determining how we should behave with regard to risk at that point. Assessing where attitudes toward risk stand in their cycle is what this chapter is about — perhaps the most important one in this book.

∾

One of the luckiest breaks I received in my lifetime came in the form of the opportunity to attend the University of Chicago's Graduate School of Business (since renamed the Booth School) in 1967–69. I, like many people in those days, went straight from college to graduate school, perhaps as the most efficient route to success, but with the added incentive provided by the Vietnam War and accompanying draft.

Over the four prior years, I had received a nuts-and-bolts education in finance at Wharton: practical, non-theoretical and qualitative. My choice of graduate school was most fortuitous, as Chicago had just begun to teach a new theory of finance and investment that had been developed, largely there, in the early 1960s. Thus my Wharton training was paired with — or rather juxtaposed against — further study in finance that was almost entirely academic, theoretical and quantitative.

Soon after arriving at Chicago, I was exposed to a graphic that provided

much of the foundation for the new theory of investment, and that has
served as the starting point for much of my thinking and writing ever since.

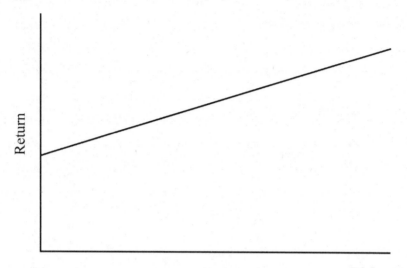

Risk

This graphic has become ubiquitous in the investment world in the time
since my first exposure to it fifty years ago. Its essence lies in the fact that
the line slopes up and to the right, indicating a positive relationship between risk and return. This is usually misinterpreted, in my view, as meaning "riskier assets produce higher returns," and thus "if you want to make
more money, the answer is to take more risk." This formulation cannot
be correct, since if riskier assets could be counted on to produce higher
returns, they by definition wouldn't be riskier.

The linearity with which the relationship between risk and return
is presented in the graphic above ignores the fact that at every level of
risk there is a range of potential outcomes regarding return, and thus
it overstates the reliability of the relationship. That's what makes people say riskier investments produce higher returns. Instead, I think the

graphic should be interpreted as saying, "Investments that seem risk-ier have to appear to promise higher returns, or else no one will make them." Words like "seem" and "appear" are the right ones, since they indicate that risk and potential return can only be estimated, and that the investment world doesn't work like a machine. That makes those words highly appropriate — actually, compelling — for use when discuss-ing investing. (For a more thorough discussion, see chapter 5 of *The Most Important Thing.*)

People who immediately "get" concepts like risk and risk/return usually have an intuitive sense that prepares them to be good investors. I hope the reasons behind my interpretation of the graphic will become immediately clear once I have prompted you to think about it.

Let's suppose a logical investor is offered two investments with the same expected return, but in one case the return is virtually assured and in the other it is highly uncertain. We would expect him to choose the former, since most people prefer certainty over uncertainty. If a Treasury bond and a high-tech startup both seemed likely to return 7%, for example, the vast majority of people would go with the Treasury. Why take the extra risk associated with the startup if no potential increase in return is offered to compensate for the incremental risk?

Well, that's the point: most people would prefer a sure 7% over a pos-sible 7%. In other words, most people are risk-averse. That's the essential assumption that underlies the "Chicago school" of finance.

To describe risk aversion, I say most people prefer safety and disprefer risk — even though I've never seen the word "disprefer" in a dictionary. (There's a big difference of opinion regarding the propriety of that word, with the linguistic establishment railing against it, but I think it's a great word. If it doesn't exist, it should.)

The widespread dislike for risk and the resultant insistence on incremental potential return if incremental risk is to be borne are the reasons why long-term Treasurys carry higher yields than short-term Treasurys; why high yield bonds promise higher returns than investment grade bonds; why stocks are generally expected to return more than bonds; and why venture capital investing is expected to provide higher returns than public stocks. Note that I'm only talking here about "expectations" and "promises"—or what "may happen" or "should happen"—rather than things that "will happen" or "are sure to happen." But that expectation of incremental return generally has to be present in order for most people to voluntarily take on added risk.

Because of the natural dispreference for risk, it's entirely reasonable to expect that if they're going to bear it, investors have to be induced through the possibility of an incremental reward. Non-daredevils will do risky things only if they expect a generous reward for doing so. Nothing else makes sense.

Risk aversion is an essential element in investing. People's aversion to loss causes them to police the markets. Because most people are averse to risk:

- they approach investing with caution,
- they perform careful analysis when considering investments, and especially risky ones,
- they incorporate conservative assumptions and appropriate skepticism into their analysis,
- they demand greater margins of safety on risky investments to protect against analytical errors and unpleasant surprises,
- they insist on healthy risk premiums—the expectation of incre-

mental returns—if they're going to undertake risky investments, and

- they refuse to invest in deals that make no sense.

These are all essential parts of the investment process. Because risk-averse investors perform them, investing is a rational field in which reasonable propositions are offered. In short, risk aversion is the main element that keeps markets safe and sane.

Please note, however, that the above is a normative description, or a description of how things *should* be. These are things the superior investor does, and that all investors *should* do. But the bottom line is that not everyone does them, and certainly not all investors do them equally at all times.

It's one of the absolute truths that attitudes toward risk change, and in so doing they alter the investment environment. That's what the rest of this chapter will be about.

∾

Here's another aside: How is the investment environment formed? In short, it is the result of discussions that take place in the marketplace—either within each investor's consciousness or among investors, spoken or signaled through their actions. Here's how I described the creation of the investment environment in "Risk and Return Today" in October 2004:

> I'll use a "typical" market of a few years back to illustrate how this works in real life: The interest rate on the 30-day T-bill might have been 4%. So an investor says, "If I'm going to go out five years, I want 5%. And to buy the 10-year note I have to get 6%." He demands a

higher rate to extend maturity because he's concerned about the risk
to purchasing power, a risk that is assumed to increase with time to
maturity. That's why the yield curve, which in reality is a portion of
the capital market line, normally slopes upward with the increase in
asset life.

Now let's factor in credit risk. "If the 10-year Treasury pays 6%,
I'm not going to buy a 10-year single-A corporate unless I'm promised 7%." This introduces the concept of credit spreads. Our hypothetical investor wants 100 basis points to go from a "guvvie" to a
"corporate." If the consensus of investors feels the same, that's what
the spread will be.

What if we depart from investment grade bonds? "I'm not going
to touch a high yield bond unless I get 600 over a Treasury note of
comparable maturity." So high yield bonds are required to yield 12%,
for a spread of 6% over the Treasury note, if they're going to attract
buyers.

Now let's leave fixed income altogether. Things get tougher, because you can't look anywhere to find the prospective return on investments like stocks (that's because, simply put, their returns are
conjectural, not "fixed"). But investors have a sense for these things.
"Historically S&P stocks have returned 10%, and I'll only buy them
if I think they're going to keep doing so." So in theory, the common
stock investor determines earnings per share, earnings growth rate
and dividend payout ratio and inputs them into a valuation model to
arrive at the price from which S&P stocks will return 10% (although
I'm not sure the process is nearly that methodical in actuality). "And
riskier stocks should return more; I won't buy on the NASDAQ unless I think I'm going to get 13%."

From there it's onward and upward. "If I can get 10% from stocks,
I need 15% to accept the illiquidity and uncertainty associated with
real estate. And 25% if I'm going to invest in buyouts . . . and 30% to
induce me to go for venture capital, with its low success ratio."

That's the way it's supposed to work, and in fact I think it generally
does (although the requirements aren't the same at all times). The

result is a capital market line of the sort that has become familiar to many of us, as shown below.

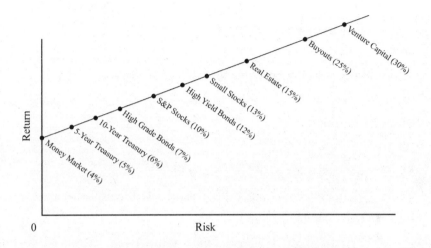

The process described above results in the formation of the risk/return continuum or "capital market line." The process establishes the general level of return relative to risk, as well as the quantum of incremental promised return — or the "risk premium" — that will be expected for the bearing of incremental risk. In a rational world, the result will be as follows:

- Investments that seem riskier will be priced so that they appear to offer higher returns.
- The increase in return per unit of incremental risk will be reasonable and appropriate.
- The increase in expected return generally will appear to be consistently proportional to the incremental risk (that is, bearing a unit of incremental risk at one point on the continuum will appear likely to bring the same amount of incremental return as bearing a similar unit of incremental risk elsewhere on the continuum).

- Thus there won't be particular points on the continuum where risk-bearing is rewarded much more or much less than at others (that is, investments whose promised risk-adjusted return is obviously superior to the rest).

In a rational world, any violations of these provisions would cause capital to move such that the prices of mispriced assets are bid up or pushed down. As a result:

- the violations would be corrected,
- all investments would offer risk-adjusted returns that are fair relative to each other, and
- investors could increase their returns only by increasing the amount of risk they bear.

If investors always behaved that way, their actions would cause the world to be marked by "efficient markets" where no investment offers a better risk-adjusted return than any other. Of course markets don't always operate as they're supposed to — things certainly aren't always priced right — but the general suggestion of efficiency is too logical to be disregarded. (Market efficiency is another essential topic, but I won't go into it further — see chapter 2 of *The Most Important Thing*, as well as the latter half of "Getting Lucky" from January 2014.)

∾

The key thing to note is that fluctuations in attitudes toward risk can cause exceptions to the principles described here. Sometimes investors become too risk-averse, and sometimes they relax their risk aversion and become too risk-tolerant.

When positive events occur as described in the last chapter and euphoria, optimism and greed rise, investors tend to become less risk-averse than usual and less risk-averse than they should be. What are the effects (following on from the list of the functions investors perform on page 106–107)?

- Since they feel better about the environment and are more optimistic about likely outcomes, they reduce the amount of caution they bring to the investing process.
- Since they no longer consider investing to be risky, they don't see the need for painstaking analysis.
- They tend to make assumptions that are more generous, and they replace skepticism with credulousness.
- They're willing to make do with a reduced margin of safety.
- Viewing risk as less worrisome, they no longer demand risk premiums as cushy as in the past.
- They behave less as sticklers, since they're more attracted to the returns on risky investments and less leery of the risk they involve.

It is for these reasons that, as you'll see in the next chapter, the shakiest financings are completed in the most buoyant economies and financial markets. Good times cause people to become more optimistic, jettison their caution, and settle for skimpy risk premiums on risky investments. Further, since they are less pessimistic and less alarmed, they tend to lose interest in the safer end of the risk/return continuum. This combination of elements makes the prices of risky assets rise relative to safer assets. Thus it shouldn't come as a surprise that more unwise investments are made in good times than in bad. This happens even though the higher prices on risky investments may mean the prospective risk premiums offered for making those riskier investments are skimpier than they were in more risk-conscious times.

The reduced insistence on adequate risk premiums causes the slope of the capital market line to flatten. Going back to high school geometry, we recall that the slope of a line on a graph is the distance traveled on the vertical axis per unit change along the horizontal axis. The slope of the capital market line reflects the amount of incremental potential return that is offered per unit of incremental risk borne. Thus it is a direct indication of the degree of risk aversion present in the market.

In times of obliviousness toward risk — or high risk tolerance — the reduced demand in terms of risk premiums causes the slope of the line to flatten and the amount of risk compensation to shrink.

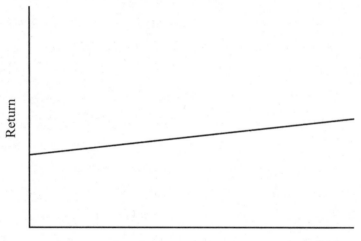

The lower slope of the capital market line means, by definition, that the there's less of a return increment per unit increase in risk. In simpler terms, the payoff for risk-bearing is sub-par.

In my opinion, all of the above follows logically from direct observation. The process is as follows:

- positive events lead to increased optimism,

- increased optimism makes people more risk-tolerant,

- an increase in risk tolerance causes lower risk premiums to be demanded,

- a reduction in demanded risk premiums equates to lower demanded returns on risky assets,

- a reduction of demanded returns on risky assets causes their prices to rise, and

- higher prices make assets even riskier (but also attract buying on the part of "momentum investors" who chase rising stocks).

It follows from the above that risk is high when investors feel risk is low. And risk compensation is at a minimum just when risk is at a maximum (meaning risk compensation is most needed). So much for the rational investor!

For me, the bottom line of all of this is that the greatest source of investment risk is the belief that there is no risk. Widespread risk tolerance — or a high degree of investor comfort with risk — is the greatest harbinger of subsequent market declines. But because most investors are following the progression described just above, this is rarely perceived at the time when perceiving it — and turning cautious — is most important.

∾

Since the other side of the coin should be obvious, I won't belabor it. But I will take a minute to talk about what happens when the downward swing of the cycle in attitudes toward risk makes investors more risk-averse.

One of the most important characteristics of psychological cycles is their extremeness. Cycles swing not only in directions and degrees

that make sense, but also in wacky ways and to excess. For example, investors gang up from time to time and say, "Let's disregard risk. We'll
all get rich." Their ardor and excitement cause them to bid prices to
levels that are so high — and to accept tales that clearly are so unrealistic — that after the fact it would be laughable if the damage done weren't
so great.

And after they have committed these sins of excess — and lost a lot of
money in the resultant downswing toward greater prudence — they casti-
gate themselves for their excesses of greed and credulousness. They wonder how they could have behaved so foolishly. They confess that they never
really understood the exotic and exciting investment activities in which
they had engaged. And they vow never to do it again.

Just as the inadequacy of their risk aversion allowed them to push
prices up and buy at the top — egged on by the vision of easy money in
a world in which they couldn't discern any risk — now they push prices
down and sell at the bottom. Their unpleasant recent experience convinces them — contrary to what they had thought when everything was
going well — that investing is a risky field in which they shouldn't engage.
And, as a consequence, their risk aversion goes all the way from inadequate to excessive.

- Given their recent painful experience and the negativity they've
developed about what lies ahead, they amp up their caution.
- Since they now associate investing with loss rather than profit,
their process comes to emphasize the avoidance of further loss
over prospecting for opportunity.
- They ensure that their assumptions are conservative enough to
rule out all potential for disappointment, and they apply extreme
skepticism.

- They find it impossible to identify — even to imagine — investments that offer an adequate margin of safety.
- Since they see risk everywhere, they consider even the current swollen risk premiums insufficient.
- They become worrywarts. Just as risk tolerance had positioned them to become buyers of overpriced assets at the highs, now their screaming risk aversion makes them sellers — certainly not buyers — at the bottom.

That's the point. Under these circumstances, the perception of risk is exaggerated and the slope of the capital market line becomes excessive.

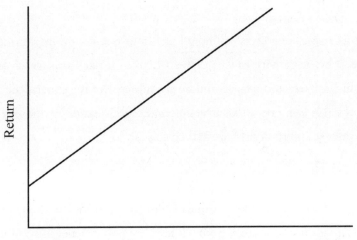

In precisely the reverse of my description of the flat capital market line, the higher slope of this one means the expected return increment per unit increase in risk is unusually generous. This is a risk-averse market, and it offers an exaggerated payoff for risk-bearing. Thus the reward for bearing incremental risk is greatest at just the moment when — no, rather, just because — people absolutely refuse to bear it.

As risk attitudes swing from high to low, so do opportunities for profit or loss. When everything's going well and asset prices are soaring, investors tend to view the future as rosy, risk as their friend, and profit as easily achieved. Everyone feels the same, meaning little risk aversion is incorporated in prices, and thus they're precarious. Investors become risk-tolerant just when they should increase their risk aversion.

And when events are down, so are investors. They think of the markets as a place to lose money, risk as something to be avoided at all cost, and losses as depressingly likely. As I described at the end of the last chapter, under the excess of caution that prevails, (a) no one will accept possibilities that incorporate any optimism at all and (b) they likewise cannot countenance the possibility that an assumption could be "too *bad* to be true."

Just as risk tolerance is unlimited at the top, it is non-existent at the bottom. This negativity causes prices to fall to levels from which losses are highly unlikely and gains could be enormous. But the sting of the prior declines tends to increase risk aversion and send investors to the sidelines just as prices (and thus risk) are at their lowest.

∾

I'd like to provide a real-life example of changing attitudes, with the benefit of some quantification, taken from "The Happy Medium" (July 2004):

> The prevalence of risk-tolerance (or risk-obliviousness) in the late 1990s was clear. I personally heard a prominent brokerage house strategist say, "Stocks are overpriced, but not enough to keep them from being a buy." And we all heard the man on the street say, "I'm up so much in my 401(k), it wouldn't bother me if it fell by a third." (Where was that guy two or three years later?)
>
> No, those risk-tolerant attitudes will not persist forever. Eventually,

something will intrude, exposing securities' imperfections and too-high prices. Prices will decline. Investors will like them less at $60 than they did at $100. Fear of losing the remaining $60 will overtake the urge to make back the lost $40. Risk aversion eventually will reassert itself (and usually go to excess).

How about some quantification of this cycle? In mid-1998, just before the collapse of Long-Term Capital Management brought investors other than techies to their senses, only $12.5 billion of non-defaulted bonds yielded more than 20% (one possible threshold for the label "distressed debt"). Because investors weren't very worried about risk, they demanded ultra-high returns from relatively few non-defaulted bonds; the word "blithe" might best describe their attitude.

But Long-Term's demise awakened investors to the existence of risk, and a year later, the amount of bonds yielding more than 20% had more than tripled to $38.7 billion. By mid-2002, when the corporate scandals held the debt market in a grip of terror, the 20% yielders had grown to $105.6 billion, eight and a half times the level just four years earlier. Risk aversion had come a long way from inadequate and, as later events showed, had become excessive. By March 31, 2004, this figure had fallen 85%, back to just $16.2 billion; risk aversion had subsided (and possibly had become inadequate again). I'm sure that fundamentals didn't fluctuate anywhere near the degree reflected in prices, yields and thus the distressed debt tally. As usual, reality was greatly exaggerated by swings in psychology.

When investors in general are too risk-tolerant, security prices can embody more risk than they do return. When investors are too risk-averse, prices can offer more return than risk.

The title of the memo cited above — "The Happy Medium" — was inspired by my mother's wisdom and her constant reminders that we should avoid extremes in behavior. Rather we should tend toward the middle on most things — toward a reasonable balance between too much and too little.

But my experience as an investor convinces me that the happy medium is rarely seen. If you reflect on what I said about the graph of a typical cycle back on page 25, you may be impressed to find that in stages "a," "d" and "g," cyclical phenomena tend to return from extremes and move toward the more reasonable mean. What a rational thing that is!

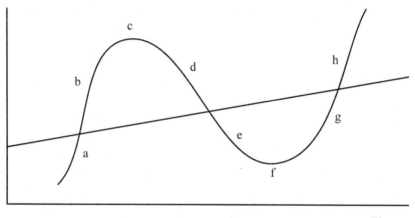

Time

But then, as I pointed out, it's usually the case that those "corrections from extremes" continue past the fair midpoint in stages "b," "e" and "h," toward the opposite extreme.

A statistician who looks at the above graphic will tell you that *on average* the phenomenon charted is at the central value or astride the secular trend. But the rest of us see it as almost always in motion: swinging away from or back toward those midpoints. In fact, it spends about as much time at extreme highs and lows as it does at the happy medium. Most investors' attitude toward risk do the very same.

What's the greatest source of investment risk? Does it come from negative economic developments? Corporate events that fall short of forecasts? Companies whose products become uncompetitive? Earnings declines? Low creditworthiness? No, it comes when asset prices attain excessively high levels as a result of some new, intoxicating investment rationale that can't be justified on the basis of fundamentals, and that causes unreasonably high valuations to be assigned. And when are these prices reached? When risk aversion and caution evaporate and risk tolerance and optimism take over. This condition is the investor's greatest enemy.

What Happens When Risk Aversion Is Insufficient?

The Global Financial Crisis of 2007–08 represented the greatest financial downswing of my lifetime, and consequently it presents the best opportunity to observe, reflect and learn. The scene was set for its occurrence by a number of developments. Here's a partial list:

- Government policies supported an expansion of home ownership —which by definition meant the inclusion of people who historically couldn't afford to buy homes—at a time when home prices were soaring;
- The Fed pushed interest rates down, causing the demand for higher-yielding instruments such as structured/levered mortgage securities to increase;
- There was a rising trend among banks to make mortgage loans, package them and sell them onward (as opposed to retaining them);
- Decisions to lend, structure, assign credit ratings and invest were made on the basis of unquestioning extrapolation of low historic mortgage default rates;
- The above four points resulted in an increased eagerness to ex-

tend mortgage loans, with an accompanying decline in lending standards;

- Novel and untested mortgage backed securities were developed that promised high returns with low risk, something that has great appeal in non-skeptical times;
- Protective laws and regulations were relaxed, such as the Glass-Steagall Act (which prohibited the creation of financial conglomerates), the uptick rule (which prevented traders who had bet against stocks from forcing them down through non-stop short selling), and the rules that limited banks' leverage, permitting it to nearly triple;
- Finally, the media ran articles stating that risk had been eliminated by the combination of:

  - the adroit Fed, which could be counted on to inject stimulus whenever economic sluggishness developed,
  - confidence that the excess liquidity flowing to China for its exports and to oil producers would never fail to be recycled back into our markets, buoying asset prices, and
  - the new Wall Street innovations, which "sliced and diced" risk so finely, spread it so widely and placed it with those best suited to bear it.

The existence of all the above elements indicated the presence of risk tolerance. In fact, they couldn't have arisen if risk tolerance hadn't dominated the psyches of investors, lenders, borrowers and regulators. The existence of risk tolerance like that seen in the years immediately preceding the Crisis should be very worrisome, as it implies an absence of worry, caution and skepticism.

It is inescapable that these developments—and the risk tolerance or risk obliviousness that was behind them — ultimately would lead to unsafe financial behavior, particularly via the issuance of financial instruments that were unsound and likely to fail. The ability to borrow large amounts of capital at low interest rates caused asset buyers to consider the period a "golden age." But it wasn't marked by the availability of sound, bargain-priced investments. Rather, the ready availability of leverage made it easy to invest heavily in assets whose prices had risen a great deal, and in innovative, untested, synthetic, levered investment products, many of which would go on to fail.

Perhaps most importantly among the contributing factors, the period was marked by risky behavior on the part of financial institutions. When the world is characterized by benign macro events, hyper-financial activity and financial innovation, there is a tendency for providers of capital to compete for market share in a process I call "the race to the bottom" (I'll make reference later on to a memo of that name). The mood in the years 2005–07 was summed up by Citigroup CEO Charles Prince in June 2007, virtually on the eve of the Global Financial Crisis, in a statement that became emblematic of the era: "When the music stops, in terms of liquidity, things will be complicated. But as long as the music's playing, you've got to get up and dance. We're still dancing."

In other words, banks had to do — and were doing — things that depended for their success on the continuation of abnormally favorable conditions, and that would turn into problems if those conditions normalized. But no banker could decline to participate for fear of losing market share. The instruments were untested and potentially defective, but no one was willing to pass up his share. That's the kind of crowd behavior that typifies . . . creates . . . and exacerbates cycles.

In theory a bank CEO could have declined to join in this folly. But under the realities of the times, anyone who sat out the dance, lost market share and failed to rake in the "easy money" that his competitors were reaping could be forced out of his job by activist investors. Thus banks bid aggressively for the opportunity to provide capital as if the music would never stop. But cognizance of cycles makes it clear that eventually it will. This kind of risk tolerance and risk obliviousness plays an essential part in the up-phase that precedes — and sets the scene for — every dramatic down-phase.

As the period 2005–07 was rolling along, it presented a great opportunity to observe events that made manifest market participants' attitudes toward risk, and to reach helpful conclusions. I believe the following excerpt from "The Race to the Bottom," a memo I wrote on the subject in February 2007 — just a few months before the first indication that bad times were coming — provides an excellent example. It demonstrates the potential value of inferences drawn from isolated and perhaps anecdotal experiences:

> While the last few years have given me many opportunities to marvel at excesses in the capital markets, in this case the one that elicited my battle cry — "that calls for a memo" — hit the newspapers in England during my last stay. As the *Financial Times* reported on November 1, 2006:
>
> > Abbey, the UK's second-largest home loans provider, has raised the standard amount it will lend homebuyers to five times either their single or joint salaries, eclipsing the traditional borrowing levels of around three and a half times salary. It followed last week's decision by Bank of Ireland Mortgages and Bristol and West to increase standard salary multiples from four to 4.5 times.
>
> In other words, there had been a traditional rule of thumb saying that borrowers can safely handle mortgages with a face amount equal to

three-plus times their salaries. But now they can have five times —
roughly 50% more. What inference should be drawn? There are at
least four possibilities:

- the old standard was too conservative, and the new one's
  right;
- conditions have changed, such that the new standard is
  as conservative for today as the old one was for its times;
- it's reasonable for mortgage lenders to accept higher default experience, and thus lower net returns, because their
  cost of capital has declined; or
- the rush to place money has caused a supplier of capital to
  loosen its standards.

Now, I am no expert on the U.K. mortgage market, and it's my inten-
tion in this memo to comment on general capital market trends, not
any one sector. Further, it's certainly true that today's lower interest
rates mean a given salary can support a bigger mortgage (and that's
likely to hold true so long as (1) borrowers keep their jobs and (2)
their mortgages carry fixed rates). But if you think Abbey's reason for
taking this step might be a logical one like that, the question to ask is
"why now?"

Logical reasons and sober decision making might be involved here.
But so might competition to put out money and the usual late-stage
belief that "it's different this time." Lenders and investors invariably
depart from time-honored disciplines when cycles move to extremes,
out of a belief that current conditions are different from those that pre-
vailed in the past, when those disciplines were appropriate. And just as
invariably, they're shown that cycles repeat and nothing really changes.

What did we see in the U.S. mortgage market as home prices rose
and interest rates declined? First, low teaser rates. Then higher loan-
to-value ratios. Then 100% financing. Then low-amortization loans.
Then no-amortization loans. Then loans requiring no documentation

of employment or credit history. All these things made it possible for more buyers to stretch for more expensive homes, but at the same time they made mortgages riskier for lenders. And these developments took place when home prices were sky-high and interest rates were at multi-generation lows. In the end, buyers took out the biggest mortgage possible given their incomes and prevailing interest rates. Such mortgages would land them in the houses of their dreams . . . and leave them there for as long as conditions didn't deteriorate, which they invariably do.

Do you remember the game Bid-a-Note from the TV show *Name That Tune*? Contestant x said, "I can name that tune in six notes." Then contestant y said, "I can name that tune in five notes." Then contestant x said, "I can name that tune in four notes." The contestant who eventually got the chance to guess the name of the tune was the one who was willing to accept the riskiest proposition — to try on the basis of the least information.

So the Bank of Ireland entered the competition to lend money for home purchases and said, "I'll lend four and a half times the borrower's salary." And Abbey said, "I'll lend five times." The so-called winner in this auction is the one who'll put out the most money with the least safety. Whether that's really winning or losing will become clear when the cycle turns, as it did in the U.S. last year. But certainly there's a race to the bottom going on . . . a contest to become the institution that'll make loans with the slightest margin for error. . . .

Any way you slice it, standards for mortgage loans have dropped in recent years, and risk has increased. Logic-based? Perhaps. Cycle-induced (and exacerbated)? I'd say so. The *FT* quoted John-Paul Crutchley, a banking analyst at Merrill Lynch, as saying "When Abbey are [*sic*] lending a multiple of five times salary, that could be perfectly sensible — or it could be tremendously risky." Certainly mortgage lending was made riskier. We'll see in a few years whether that was intelligent risk taking or excessive competitive ardor. . . .

Today's financial market conditions are easily summed up: There's a global glut of liquidity, minimal interest in traditional investments, little apparent concern about risk, and skimpy prospective returns everywhere. Thus, as the price for accessing returns that are potentially adequate (but lower than those promised in the past), investors are readily accepting significant risk in the form of heightened leverage, untested derivatives and weak deal structures. The current cycle isn't unusual in its form, only its extent. There's little mystery about the ultimate outcome, in my opinion, but at this point in the cycle it's the optimists who look best.

As is often the case, I could have made this a shorter memo by simply invoking my two favorite quotations, both of which have a place here.

The first is from John Kenneth Galbraith, who passed away last year. I was fortunate to be able to spend a few hours with Mr. Galbraith a year and a half earlier and to have the benefit of his wisdom firsthand. This quote, once again, is from his invaluable book, *A Short History of Financial Euphoria*. It seems particularly apt under the current circumstances:

> Contributing to . . . euphoria are two further factors little noted in our time or in past times. The first is the extreme brevity of the financial memory. In consequence, financial disaster is quickly forgotten. In further consequence, when the same or closely similar circumstances occur again, sometimes in only a few years, they are hailed by a new, often youthful, and always supremely self-confident generation as a brilliantly innovative discovery in the financial and larger economic world. There can be few fields of human endeavor in which history counts for so little as in the world of finance. Past experience, to the extent that it is part of memory at all, is dismissed as the primitive refuge of those who do not have the insight to appreciate the incredible wonders of the present.

The second is Warren Buffett's bedrock reminder of the need to adjust our financial actions based on the investor behavior playing out around us. Fewer words, but probably even more useful:

> The less prudence with which others conduct their affairs, the greater the prudence with which we should conduct our own affairs.

> This memo can be summed up simply: there's a race to the bottom going on, reflecting a widespread reduction in the level of prudence on the part of investors and capital providers. No one can prove at this point that those who participate will be punished, or that their long-run performance won't exceed that of the naysayers. But that is the usual pattern.
>
> If you refuse to fall into line in carefree markets like today's, it's likely that, for a while, you'll (a) lag in terms of return and (b) look like an old fogey. But neither of those is much of a price to pay if it means keeping your head (and capital) when others eventually lose theirs. In my experience, times of laxness have always been followed eventually by corrections in which penalties are imposed. It may not happen this time, but I'll take that risk. In the meantime, Oaktree and its people will continue to apply the standards that have served us so well over the last twenty years.

Warren Buffett puts it well in the above quote; it's one I use all the time. I think it aptly sums up this phenomenon, as well as the contrarian response that is required as a result. When others fail to worry about risk and fail to apply caution, as Buffett says, we must turn more cautious. But it must also be said that when other investors are panicked and depressed and can't imagine conditions under which risk would be worth taking, we should turn aggressive.

What Happens When Risk Aversion Is Excessive?

The symmetry of financial cycles, described at length in chapter II, essentially guaranteed that the risk-tolerant environment of 2005–07 — and the boom in financial instrument issuance that it abetted — would be followed by a serious correction. And, of course, such a correction materialized.

As I said earlier, the Global Financial Crisis of 2007–08 provided what I hope will turn out to be a once-in-a-lifetime opportunity to witness an irrational swing of the pendulum of emotion to total negativity, and a turn of the cycle in attitudes toward risk in the direction of excessive risk aversion.

The actions that had been abetted by excessive risk tolerance in 2005–07 — as just described — were exposed as having been foolhardy, and as a result they brought great pain and loss:

- It became clear that the effort to expand home ownership had led to purchases of homes by many people who couldn't afford them. Thousands lost the money they had put into home equity, along with moving costs and any improvements they made.

- Sub-prime mortgages that had been issued without proof of income or employment were shown to have been unwise.

- Weak mortgage lending practices — along with extensive mortgage fraud that those practices failed to catch — turned out, not surprisingly, to have led to the issuance of many mortgages on which borrowers were unable to make the required payments.

- The extrapolation of low historic default rates on mortgages turned out to have ignored the possibility that weakened mortgage lending practices would result in defaults at unprecedented rates.

- Since actual defaults exceeded the historic rates that had been the basis for security structuring decisions, debt ratings and loss projections, structured and levered securities that had been built from sub-prime mortgages also defaulted in stunning numbers, proving their high ratings to have been erroneous.

- Levered mortgage backed securities (and financial derivatives, most of which contain high levels of built-in leverage) generally switched from being return-enhancing tools to weapons of financial mass destruction, as levered funds and securities breached loan covenants, and issuers ultimately proved unable to service their debt.

- Of course, the new financial products demonstrated — as usual — that financial innovations promising high returns with low risk rarely keep that promise.

- As for the relaxed regulations, the financial conglomerates permitted by revocation of the Glass-Steagall Act had extensive problems; the repeal of the uptick rule allowed the stocks of financial institutions to be driven down relentlessly; and several banks proved unable to survive under the high levels of leverage that had been allowed.

Because of everything that had gone before, the consequences included massive mortgage defaults and home repossessions; downgradings and failures on the part of mortgage backed securities; collapsing home prices and the inability to sell existing homes; collapsing stock and corporate bond markets and the disappearance of liquidity; a total drying up of credit availability; and failures, bailouts and bankruptcies at a number of banks.

> Of course, it's improbable events that brought on the credit crisis. Lots of bad things happened that had been considered unlikely (if not impossible), and they happened at the same time, to investors who'd taken on significant leverage. ("The Limits to Negativism," October 2008)

What was the cumulative psychological effect of all of the above on investors and other financial-system participants? In short, it scared them to death. When total fear replaces a high degree of confidence, excessive risk aversion takes the place of unrealistic risk tolerance. And that's what happened in late 2008 following the bankruptcy of Lehman Brothers. Sellers came forward in droves, exhibiting a high degree of urgency. Buyers took to the sidelines. Asset prices collapsed. And market liquidity went to zero.

All these things resulted from the replacement of high risk tolerance with high risk aversion. And they all contributed to still more fear, still more risk aversion, further negative events, and widespread fear of more of the same. The same people who had bought untried instruments on the basis of positive assumptions and promises that were too good to be true now were convinced that the entire financial system might melt down.

To provide an example of the swing toward excessive risk aversion and its impact, I'll share the story of something that happened a few weeks after the Lehman bankruptcy. It's the event that inspired me to write my low-point memo quoted above, "The Limits to Negativism."

Participating to a minor degree in the general trends that were afoot, Oaktree formed its first levered funds in the years just preceding the Crisis. We used less leverage than others — for example, four times equity in our European senior loan fund versus the more conventional seven or eight — and we tried to be conservative about what assets we bought, but events nevertheless brought us to the brink of a meltdown. Prior to the Crisis, senior or "leveraged" loans — even those with credit problems — had rarely traded at prices below 96 cents on the dollar. Thus we felt we were well insulated from the possibility of margin calls (demands from lenders for additional equity capital) that, under our borrowing agreement, could come only if the average market price of the loans in the portfolio got down to 88.

But in the aftermath of the Lehman bankruptcy, loan prices fell to unprecedented levels, pressured by, among other things, banks' fire sales of portfolios abandoned by levered holders who received margin calls of their own and failed to meet them. Thus 88 — and a margin call and meltdown — became a real possibility for us. We were able to get time to respond from our lender, and we set about raising additional equity from the fund's investors with which to reduce the fund's leverage from 4-to-1 to 2-to-1. When we asked the investors to put up more additional equity, they understood that this represented an opportunity to retain loans at discounted prices rather than give up on them; to enjoy the loans' high implied yields; and to benefit from the fund's low-cost leverage. Thus most of them came forward with the increased equity we requested. At the newly reduced level of leverage, the fund was protected from a margin call unless the average price of our loans fell to an unimaginable 65.

But with the total absence of buyers and the continuation of margin-call- and hedge-fund-withdrawal-related selling, the loan market continued to spiral downward, as the notion of "the right price" gave way to widespread concern that no price could be counted on to hold. Thus the average price on our loan portfolio neared 70. It fell to me to get the leverage down from 2-to-1 to 1-to-1, in which case we could completely eliminate the contractual covenant that introduced the risk of a margin call.

Now I was offering the fund's investors a chance to pay to retain the fund's loans at yields to maturity that were well into double digits, and levered returns on the overall fund in the 20s (before fees and potential losses due to defaults). Of course, if a pre-existing investor failed to put up his pro rata share of the additional equity and allowed someone else to do so instead, that would be tantamount to selling off part of his interest in the fund's portfolio at those yields.

And yet, the combination of non-stop price declines, portfolio liquidations and a total absence of buyers made it challenging for some fund investors to take the step of again adding capital. Some were fatigued from having to deal with the issues popping up everywhere in their portfolios. Some viewed this chance not as rescuing their investments, but as possibly "throwing good money after bad." Some didn't have liquid funds on hand. And some just didn't have the willingness to defend additional investment to their bosses. At bottoms, it can be extremely hard to take actions that require conviction and staunchness. And that led to the event I'm going to describe.

I went to a pension fund that was an investor in the fund, to make the case for an additional equity investment. The yields I laid out were attractive, they admitted, but they were worried about the possibility of loan defaults. The conversation went like this:

Pension fund: What about the potential that defaults will render the investment unsuccessful?

HM: Well, our average default rate over the last 26 years in high yield bonds—which are junior in the capital structure to loans like the fund holds—has been about 1% a year (and bear in mind that there are recoveries in the case of default, meaning our credit losses have been less than a percent per year). Thus defaults at our historic rate would do little to diminish the fund's promised return in the 20s.

Pension fund: But what if it's worse than that?

HM: The worst five-year period we've ever had showed defaults averaging 3% per year; obviously not a problem relative to the yields we're talking about.

Pension fund: But what if it's worse than that?

HM: The average default rate in the high yield bond universe—without assuming any ability to avoid defaults through skillful credit selection—has been 4.2% per year. Resulting credit losses of 2–3% clearly wouldn't do much to jeopardize the results on this investment.

Pension fund: But what if it's worse than that?

HM: The worst five years in history for the universe averaged 7.3% — still not a problem.

Pension fund: But what if it's worse than that?

HM: The worst one-year default rate in high yield bond history was 12.8%. That still leaves plenty of return here.

Pension fund: But what if it's worse than that?

HM: One and a half times the worst year in history would be 19%, and we would still make a little money given the portfolio yield in the 20s. And for such a minimal return to be the result, defaults of that order of magnitude would have to happen every year — not just once.

Pension fund: But what if it's worse than that?

At this point I asked, "Do you have any equities?" and I told them if they did — and really believed the doomsday scenarios toward which they had been pushing me — they'd better leave the room immediately and sell them all.

My point is that, in a negative environment, excessive risk aversion can cause people to subject investments to unreasonable scrutiny and endlessly negative assumptions (just as they may have performed little or no scrutiny and applied rosy assumptions when they made investments in the preceding heady times). During panics, people spend 100% of their time making sure there can be no losses . . . at just the time that they should be worrying instead about missing out on great opportunities.

In times of extreme negativism, exaggerated risk aversion is likely to cause prices to already be as low as they can go; further losses to be highly unlikely; and thus the risk of loss to be minimal. As I've indicated earlier, the riskiest thing in the world is the belief that there's no risk. By the same token, the safest (and most rewarding) time to buy usually comes when everyone is convinced there's no hope.

If I could ask only one question regarding each investment I had under consideration, it would be simple: How much optimism is factored into the price? A high level of optimism is likely to mean the favorable possible developments have been priced in; the price is high relative to intrinsic value; and there's little margin for error in case of disappointment. But if optimism is low or absent, it's likely that the price is low; expectations are modest; negative surprises are unlikely; and the slightest turn for the better would result in appreciation. The pension fund meeting described above was important for the simple reason that it indicated that all optimism had been wrung out of investors' thinking.

After that meeting, I practically ran to my office to write "The Limits to Negativism" at roughly the point in that cycle when one could have bought the most debt at the lowest prices. In it I shared the following realization:

> Lots of bad things happened that had been considered unlikely (if not impossible), and they happened at the same time, to investors who'd taken on significant leverage. So the easy explanation is that the people who were hurt in the credit crisis hadn't been skeptical — or pessimistic — enough.
>
> But that triggered an epiphany: *Skepticism and pessimism aren't synonymous. Skepticism calls for pessimism when optimism is excessive. But it also calls for optimism when pessimism is excessive.* I'll write some more on the subject, but it's really as simple as that.
>
> Contrarianism — doing the opposite of what others do, or "leaning against the wind" — is essential for investment success. But as the credit crisis reached a peak last week, people succumbed to the wind rather than resisting. I found very few who were optimistic; most were pessimistic to some degree. Some became genuinely depressed — even a few great investors I know. Increasingly negative tales of the coming meltdown were exchanged via email. *No one applied skepticism, or said "that horror story's unlikely to be true."* Pessimism fed on itself. People's only concern was bullet-proofing their portfolios

to get through the coming collapse, or raising enough cash to meet redemptions. The one thing they weren't doing last week was making aggressive bids for securities. So prices fell and fell several points at a time — the old expression is "gapped down."

Hopefully this contemporary account will give you a sense for what excessive, unreasonable risk aversion feels like, and also a sense for what you should be doing under circumstances like those.

Postscript: a few of the fund's investors (including the one I visited that day) declined to post the additional equity. Feeling I should do everything I could to keep the fund afloat, I put it up in their place. The chance to invest in a levered portfolio of depressed senior loans at a time of highly excessive risk aversion made that one of the best investments I've ever made . . . since the unwillingness of others to participate in that market had rendered the loans absurdly cheap.

∿

This chapter regarding the cycle in attitudes toward risk has grown to be one of the longest in this book. There's a good reason for that: I believe it covers one of the most important cycles. In *The Most Important Thing*, a key chapter talks about the importance of knowing where we stand in the various cycles. Understanding how investors are thinking about and dealing with risk is perhaps the most important thing to strive for. In short, excessive risk tolerance contributes to the creation of danger, and the swing to excessive risk aversion depresses markets, creating some of the greatest buying opportunities.

The rational investor is diligent, skeptical and appropriately risk-averse at all times, but also on the lookout for opportunities for potential return that more than compensates for risk. That's the ideal. But in good times, we hear most people say, "Risk? What risk? I don't see much that could go wrong: look how well things have been going. And anyway, risk is my friend — the more risk I take, the more money I'm likely to make." Then, in bad times, they switch to something simpler: "I don't care if I ever make another penny in the market; I just don't want to lose any more. Get me out!"

It's essential to note that since rational, unemotional investors are very much in the minority, the totality of investors rarely achieve equilibrium regarding their attitudes toward risk, or any of the other aspects of psychology or emotion as to which the cycle oscillates or the pendulum swings. They tend not to maintain a healthy balance between the risk aversion that compels them to be cautious and the risk tolerance that urges them on: usually one or the other is in the pronounced ascendency. The same is very much true with regard to greed and fear, skepticism and credulousness, the willingness to sometimes see only positives and sometimes only negatives, and many other things. The cycles in psychology amply demonstrate that investors spend very little of their time at the happy medium.

The fluctuation — or inconstancy — in attitudes toward risk is both the result of some cycles and the cause or exacerbator of others. And it will always go on, since it seems to be hard-wired into most people's psyches to become more optimistic and risk-tolerant when things are going well, and then more worried and risk-averse when things turn downward. That means they're most willing to buy when they should be most cautious, and most reluctant to buy when they should be most aggressive. Superior investors recognize this and strive to behave as contrarians.

IX

THE CREDIT CYCLE

Superior investing doesn't come from buying high-quality assets, but from buying when the deal is good, the price is low, the potential return is substantial, and the risk is limited. These conditions are much more the case when the credit markets are in the less-euphoric, more-stringent part of their cycle. The slammed-shut phase of the credit cycle probably does more to make bargains available than any other single factor.

Now our foundation is complete. We've covered the economic and profit cycles that provide the fundamental backdrop for investment activities, and also the psychological and attitudinal swings that occur in response to changes in fundamentals (and that tend to exaggerate them). Now we're going to take up some specific types of financial cycles. You will note that fluctuations in all the above strongly affect the cycles covered in the following chapters.

As we've already discussed, some activities—like home buying—are highly responsive to movements in the economic cycle, and others—like purchasing food—are not. Some cycles have a profound effect on other aspects of the economy and on other cycles, and some do not. The subject of this chapter, the credit cycle, is in each case the former: it is both highly responsive to economic developments and highly influential. Lastly, it is also extremely volatile. Thus its movements are powerful and extreme, and they greatly affect activity in many other areas. And all these things are exacerbated by the swings of psychology described in chapters VII and VIII.

Please note that the subject here is sometimes referred to as the capital market cycle rather than the credit cycle. I don't find the distinction important. Strictly speaking, "capital" refers to all the money used to finance a business, while "credit" refers to that portion of a company's capital that's made up of debt rather than equity. In practice, these two cycle names seem to be used interchangeably, although I do find many fewer references to the capital market cycle. I'm going to stick to "the credit cycle" when I'm only talking about debt markets, and I may lapse into "the capital market cycle" when I'm talking about the general availability of financing. But either way and most importantly, the considerations that apply to one apply equally to the other.

The following passage from my memo "Open and Shut" (December 2010) calls on some of what I wrote earlier and places the credit cycle in context within the range of cycles:

> Consider this: the ups and downs of economies are usually blamed for fluctuations in corporate profits, and fluctuations in profits for the rise and fall of securities markets. However, in recessions and recoveries, economic growth usually deviates from its trendline rate by only a few percentage points. Why, then, do corporate profits increase and decrease so much more? The answer lies in things like financial leverage and operating leverage, which magnify the impact on profits of rising and falling revenues.
>
> And if profits fluctuate this way — more than GDP, but still relatively moderately — why is it that the securities markets soar and col-

lapse so dramatically? I attribute this to fluctuations in psychology and, in particular, to the profound influence of psychology on the availability of capital.

In short, whereas economies fluctuate a little and profits a fair bit, the credit window opens wide and then slams shut . . . thus the title of this memo. I believe the credit cycle is the most volatile of the cycles and has the greatest impact. Thus it deserves a great deal of attention.

And here's how I put it, more succinctly, in "You Can't Predict. You Can Prepare." (November 2001):

> The longer I'm involved in investing, the more impressed I am by the power of the credit cycle. It takes only a small fluctuation in the econ-omy to produce a large fluctuation in the availability of credit, with great impact on asset prices and back on the economy itself.

Changes in the availability of capital or credit constitute one of the most fundamental influences on economies, companies and markets. Even though the credit cycle is less well-known to the man on the street than most of the other cycles discussed in this book, I consider it to be of para-mount importance and profound influence.

As suggested in the citation just above, the credit cycle can be easily un-derstood through the metaphor of a window. In short, sometimes it's open and sometimes it's closed. And, in fact, people in the financial world make frequent reference to just that: "the credit window," as in "the place you go to borrow money." When the window is open, financing is plentiful and easily obtained, and when it's closed, financing is scarce and hard to get. Finally, it's essential to always bear in mind that the window can go from wide open to slammed shut in just an instant. There's a lot more to fully understanding this cycle — including the reasons for these cyclical move-ments and their impact — but that's the bottom line.

∼

Why does this cycle have the importance I ascribe to it? First, capital or credit is an essential ingredient in the productive process. Thus the ability of companies (and economies) to grow usually depends on the availability of incremental capital. If the capital markets are closed, it can be hard to finance growth.

Second, capital must be available in order for maturing debt to be refinanced. Companies (as well as most other economic units, such as governments and consumers) generally don't pay off their debts. Most of the time they merely roll them over. But if a company is unable to issue new debt at the time that its existing debt comes due, it may default and be forced into bankruptcy. Where we stand in the credit cycle — whether credit is readily available or difficult to obtain — is the greatest determinant of whether debt can be refinanced at a given time.

Many corporate assets are long-term in nature (like buildings, machinery, vehicles and goodwill). Yet corporations often raise the money with which to buy those things by issuing short-term debt. They do this because the cost of borrowing is generally lowest on short maturities. This arrangement — "borrowing short to invest long" — works out well most of the time, when the credit market is open and fully functioning, meaning debt can be rolled over with ease when it comes due. But the mismatch between long-term assets that can't be easily liquidated and shorter-term liabilities can easily bring on a crisis if the credit cycle turns negative so that maturing debt can't be refinanced. This classic mismatch, when combined with stringency in the financing markets, is often the cause of the most spectacular financial meltdowns.

When the Global Financial Crisis began to build in 2007 and the credit markets froze up, the U.S. Department of the Treasury took the unprecedented step of guaranteeing all commercial paper. If it hadn't done so, these debt instruments — which have maturities of 270 days or less — might not have been capable of being rolled over, and thus could have caused defaults among even the strongest of companies. In fact, the defaults may well have been concentrated among top companies, since they issue commercial paper in billions precisely for the reason that their strong creditworthiness gives them easy access to the commercial paper market. (The importance of the market being open — and of the ability to roll over maturing paper — underlines the essential difference between positive net worth and liquidity. Even a wealthy company can get into trouble if it doesn't have cash on hand and can't obtain enough to meet its debt maturities, bills and other calls on cash as they arise.)

Third, financial institutions represent a special, exaggerated case of reliance on the credit markets. Financial institutions are in the business of trading in money, and they need access to financing to keep that business going. They also are often the site of the greatest short/long mismatches and potential meltdowns. Consider, for example, the bank that takes deposits that can be withdrawn any day and uses them to make mortgage loans that won't be repaid for thirty years. What happens if all the depositors demand their money back on the same bad day (a "run on the bank")? If there's no access to the credit market (and no government bailout), that bank may fail.

Fourth and finally, the credit market gives off signals that have great psychological impact. A closed credit market causes fear to spread, even out of proportion to businesses' negative realities. Difficult conditions can cause the capital market to close . . . and closed capital markets can have a negative impact on business conditions (as well as on market participants' opinions of businesses). This kind of "vicious circle" is part of most financial crises.

The Credit Cycle in Operation

By now you should have an understanding of the nature and importance of the credit cycle. The next topic to tackle is why credit cycles occur: what causes credit to be more available at some times and less available at others?

The credit window doesn't have a mind of its own, opening and closing of its own accord. Rather, it follows events elsewhere. In "You Can't Predict. You Can Prepare." (November 2001), I put the expand-and-contract process in context and explained it in some detail:

> The process is simple:
>
> - The economy moves into a period of prosperity.
> - Providers of capital thrive, increasing their capital base.
> - Because bad news is scarce, the risks entailed in lending and investing seem to have shrunk.
> - Risk averseness disappears.
> - Financial institutions move to expand their businesses — that is, to provide more capital.
> - They compete for market share by lowering demanded returns (e.g., cutting interest rates), lowering credit standards, providing more capital for a given transaction, and easing covenants.

At the extreme, providers of capital finance borrowers and projects that aren't worthy of being financed. As *The Economist* said earlier this year, "the worst loans are made at the best of times." This leads to capital destruction — that is, to the investment of capital in projects where the cost of capital exceeds the return *on* capital, and eventually to cases where there is no return *of* capital.

When this point is reached, the up-leg is reversed.

- Losses cause lenders to become discouraged and shy away.
- Risk averseness rises, and along with it, interest rates, credit restrictions and covenant requirements.
- Less capital is made available — and at the trough of the cycle, only to the most qualified of borrowers.
- Companies become starved for capital. Borrowers are unable to roll over their debts, leading to defaults and bankruptcies.
- This process contributes to and reinforces the economic contraction.

Of course, at the extreme the process is ready to be reversed again. Because the competition to make loans or investments is low, high returns can be demanded along with high creditworthiness. Contrarians who commit capital at this point have a shot at high returns, and those tempting potential returns begin to draw in capital. In this way, a recovery begins to be fueled.

Sometimes people are eager to put money to work, and that makes the credit window open wide. But when circumstances cause them to change their minds, financing can become unavailable. As with so many other things in this book, it's essential that the reader gain a clear understanding of the workings of the cycles, and especially of the way in which each element leads to the next. Thus the thorough, step-by-step explanation provided here is essential and must be absorbed.

But in "You Can't Predict. You Can Prepare." I went on to reduce the process to just a few words. They truly do constitute the bottom line on the credit cycle, and they make clear the never-ending chain-reaction nature of the cycle:

Prosperity brings expanded lending, which leads to unwise lending, which produces large losses, which makes lenders stop lending, which ends prosperity, and on and on.

A market is an auction house where the item being offered goes to the person who'll pay the most for it. The financial markets are no different. The opportunity to make an investment or provide a loan goes to the market participant who'll pay the most for that opportunity. The bidding takes the price to higher dollar levels and higher valuation parameters (such as higher price/earnings ratios). In the credit market, a high price or high valuation parameter translates directly into a low yield on the debt instrument in question, and the chance to provide capital goes to the lender who'll accept the lowest yield.

My memo "The Race to the Bottom," published in February 2007, was primarily about the eagerness of providers of capital to expand their "book of business" in good times, and its effect:

> It helps to think of money as a commodity. Everyone's money is pretty much the same. Yet institutions seeking to add to loan volume, and private equity funds and hedge funds seeking to increase their fees, all want to move more of it. So if you want to place more money — that is, get people to go to you instead of your competitors for their financing — you have to make your money cheaper. As with the other commodities, low price is the most dependable route to increased market share.
>
> One way to lower the price for your money is by reducing the interest rate you charge on loans. A slightly more subtle way is to agree to a higher price for the thing you're buying, such as by paying a higher p/e ratio for a common stock or a higher total transaction price when you're buying a company. Any way you slice it, you're settling for a lower prospective return. But there are other ways to cheapen your money, and they're the primary subject of this memo.

With debt, structure is important. Thus easier terms for the borrower can bring added risk for the lender. For example, lenders would like to have protective covenants that limit the extent to which a borrower can engage in certain actions that increase the risk that is present. They may restrict the total debt the borrower can assume, limit the cash it can pay out in dividends, or require that it maintain a certain minimum net worth. But, especially when the credit market is heated, the "best buyer" of debt — the most eager lender — might be willing to accept a structure with fewer covenants, and thus more risk.

So in an auction, the chance to make a loan or buy a debt security goes to the provider of capital who's willing to accept a combination of the least yield and the riskiest structure. When risk aversion is present and the demand for lending opportunities is reasonable relative to the supply of such opportunities, the bidding is usually prudent. But when risk tolerance takes over and lenders compete avidly for opportunities, the bidding is likely to become overheated. The resulting opportunity to lend is likely to be at too high a price: a yield that's too low and/or risk that's excessive. Thus an overheated auction in the credit market — as elsewhere — is likely to produce a "winner" who's really a loser. This is the process I call the race to the bottom.

On the other hand, there are times when buyers show up for auctions in small numbers, and the few who do attend are interested in buying only at giveaway prices. The bidding stalls, and the result is low prices, eye-popping yields, and loan structures that afford excellent protection. Unlike the overheated climate that spawns the race to the bottom, ice-cold markets in which no one's eager to lend can create real winners.

The degree of openness of the credit window depends almost entirely on whether providers of capital are eager or reticent, and it has a profound impact on economies, companies, investors, and the prospective return and riskiness of the investment opportunities that result.

> In the short term, the effect of generous capital market conditions is to make more money available to more companies for more reasons, at lower rates of interest and with fewer covenants. This leads to higher levels of acquisitions, buyouts and corporate expansion (not to mention rapid recapitalizations of buyout companies and thus high short-term rates of return). In the short run, this contributes to a high level of general financial activity.
>
> Another effect is to forestall financial stringency at weak companies. When lenders are strict and covenants are tight, operating problems can lead quickly to both technical defaults (violations of covenants) and "money defaults" (non-payment of interest or principal). But looser conditions can permit default to be forestalled: if covenants are lax or absent; if borrowers have the option to convert cash-pay bonds into payment-in-kind bonds (through a recent innovation, "toggle bonds"); or if they can raise new money and thus postpone the day of reckoning.
>
> Eventually, many of the forestalled defaults will demonstrate their inevitability, with the companies falling from more highly leveraged heights. And certainly the capital markets' willingness to finance less-than-deserving companies will lead ultimately to a higher level of corporate distress. Thus, everything else being equal, the bigger the boom—and the greater the excesses of the capital markets in the upward direction—the greater the bust. Timing and extent are never predictable, but the occurrence of cycles is the closest thing I know to inevitable. ("The Race to the Bottom," February 2007)

The Impact of the Credit Cycle

One of the main points in this book is the extent to which events within one cycle have influence in other fields and on other kinds of cycles. Nowhere is this clearer than in the credit cycle.

> In "Genius Isn't Enough" on the subject of Long-Term Capital Management (October 1998), I wrote "Look around the next time there's a crisis; you'll probably find a lender." Over-permissive providers of capital frequently aid and abet financial bubbles. There have been numerous recent examples where loose capital markets contributed to booms that were followed by famous collapses: real estate in 1989–92; emerging markets in 1994–98; Long-Term Capital in 1998; the movie exhibition industry in 1999–2000; venture capital funds and telecommunications companies in 2000–01. In each case, lenders and investors provided too much cheap money and the result was over-expansion and dramatic losses. In the movie *Fields of Dreams* Kevin Costner was told, "If you build it, they will come." In the financial world, if you offer cheap money, they will borrow, buy and build — often without discipline, and with very negative consequences.
>
> The capital cycle contributed tremendously to the tech bubble. Money from venture capital funds caused far too many companies to be created, often with little in terms of business justification or profit prospects. Wild demand for IPOs caused their hot stocks to rise meteorically, enabling venture funds to report triple-digit returns and attract still more capital requiring speedy deployment. The generosity of the capital markets let telecom companies sign on for huge capital projects that were only partially financed, secure in the knowledge that more financing would be available later, at higher p/e's and lower interest rates as the projects were further along. This ease caused far more optical fiber capacity to be built than was needed at the time, a lot of which is sitting idle. Much of the investment that went into it may never be recovered. Once again, easy money has led to capital destruction.

In making investments, it has become my habit to worry less about the economic future — which I'm sure I can't know much about — than I do about the supply/demand picture relating to capital. Being positioned to make investments in an uncrowded arena conveys vast advantages. Participating in a field that everyone's throwing money at is a formula for disaster. ("You Can't Predict. You Can Prepare.")

To restate, here's further proof from "The Happy Medium" (July 2004) that a lengthy and important description like that above with regard to the cyclical process can be summed up in fewer words:

> From time to time, providers of capital simply turn the spigot on or off — as in so many things, to excess. There are times when anyone can get any amount of capital for any purpose, and times when even the most deserving borrowers can't access reasonable amounts for worthwhile projects. The behavior of the capital markets is a great indicator of where we stand in terms of psychology and a great contributor to the supply of investment bargains.

I went on in that memo to discuss the way in which the credit cycle contributes to the creation of excess:

> Looking for the cause of a market extreme usually requires rewinding the videotape of the credit cycle a few months or years. Most raging bull markets are abetted by an upsurge in the willingness to provide capital, usually imprudently. Likewise, most collapses are preceded by a wholesale refusal to finance certain companies, industries, or the entire gamut of would-be borrowers.

My goal in what follows is to describe the effect of the credit cycle. And to do so I'll return again to the Global Financial Crisis (GFC), since it provides the best teaching moments.

In the late 1960s, in my early years as an equity analyst, I was highly aware of the economic cycle and the way corporate profits rise and fall in response to it. While I had a lot more to learn, I already knew a bit about fluctuations in psychology and risk attitudes (and about their importance). But I had almost no appreciation for the role or operation of the credit cycle. In short, it's hard to fully understand most phenomena in the investment world unless you've lived through them. Now I've come to the conclusion that the credit cycle is a really big deal. In fact, when asked about the causes of the Global Financial Crisis of 2007–08, I put it right at the top of the list.

The very choice of the name "Global Financial Crisis" for the painful 2007–08 experience reflects the fact that it was essentially a *financial* phenomenon—caused almost entirely by events within the financial markets—and not one with primarily economic or other origins. Here are the attitudinal and behavioral factors in the financial world that led to a wide-reaching crisis:

- The existential cause was the too-liberal attitudes toward financial risk described on pages 119–120.
- Those carefree attitudes were inflamed by strong demand for high-yielding investments that resulted from the Fed's lowering of general interest rates.
- Those two factors led to, among other things, an excessive willingness on the part of investors to accept innovative financial products, and to swallow whole the favorable extrapolation of history and the other optimistic assumptions on which those products were based.
- The predominance of mortgage backed securities among those in-

novations gave rise to a rapidly increasing need for mortgages from which to fashion the new securities.

- That demand facilitated the selling onward of mortgages, which in turn allowed mortgage lenders to be careless in choosing the prospective home buyers to whom they would lend. Since mortgage originators wouldn't be retaining the mortgages they created, they didn't have to worry about their soundness. In an extreme example of this trend, the category of "sub-prime" mortgages was created for borrowers who couldn't satisfy traditional lending standards in terms of employment or income, or who chose to pay higher interest rates rather than document these things. The fact that weak borrowers like these could borrow large sums was indicative of irrational credit market conditions.

- Relaxed credit diligence on the part of mortgage lenders, and the availability to home buyers of generous sub-prime financing, made home ownership possible for more Americans than ever, including many who wouldn't have been able to afford it under the tighter traditional mortgage standards.

- Seduced by potential profits from rating vast numbers of securities backed by sub-prime mortgages (and enabled by their own naiveté, or perhaps their greed), the credit-rating agencies competed for business by offering inflated ratings, in a race to the bottom of their own.

- Home affordability increased substantially, fueled by the fact that interest rates are low on short maturities, as originators hit upon low initial monthly payments as a way to maximize mortgage issuance. This contributed to the widespread use of floating-rate mortgages entailing low starting monthly payments based on low initial "teaser" rates of interest. Obviously, these non-fixed rates posed a potential risk to borrowers who could barely afford their payments before they increased. But borrowers were assured that, thanks to the generous capital market conditions, they would always be able to refinance into yet another mortgage, again with a sub-market teaser rate.

- Investment banks were eager to turn the raw material of plentiful sub-prime mortgages into tranched mortgage backed securities with the highest average credit rating, in order to maximize their salability. The ardor for this activity at just the time that "financial engineering" came into favor gave rise to ratings for tranches that turned out to have been totally divorced from how they actually would perform under stress.

- The investment banks that created and sold these securities often were willing to retain the equity layer at the bottom of the tranched structure in order to facilitate a high volume of issuance or simply out of a desire to hold high-yielding assets (i.e., even they were oblivious to the toxic nature of their product). And other banks took advantage of the high levels of permissible leverage to create assets at very favorable yield spreads by using low-cost borrowings to buy the risky, high-yielding equity and junior debt tranches of structured mortgage securities.

As you can see from the above, virtually all the conditions on which the GFC was built were endogenous to the financial system and the credit cycle. The developments that constituted the foundation for the Crisis weren't caused by a general economic boom or a widespread surge in corporate profits. The key events didn't take place in the general business environment or the greater world beyond that. Rather, the GFC was a largely financial phenomenon that resulted entirely from the behavior of financial players. The main forces that created this cycle were the easy availability of capital; a lack of experience and prudence sufficient to temper the unbridled enthusiasm that pervaded the process; imaginative financial engineering; the separation of lending decisions from loan retention; and irresponsibility and downright greed.

It must be noted, however, that this chain reaction was abetted by elected officials who were eager to expand the American dream of home ownership and naively thought it would be great if everyone was enabled to buy a home. In a speech in October 2002, President George W. Bush repeated what he'd been told by one of his friends: "You don't have to have a lousy home for the first-time home buyers. If you put your mind to it, the first-time home buyer, the low-income home buyer can have just as nice a house as anybody else." I wonder if the people who heard that statement at the time found it as illogical as it seems today.

After the GFC hit, Congressman Barney Frank, formerly one of the strongest proponents of broadened home ownership, said: "Home ownership is a good thing. But we have made a great mistake in this society. There are people in the society who should not be allowed to borrow money to buy a home. And we have pushed people into home ownership who shouldn't be there." (As you can see, political rhetoric is cyclical, too.)

In other words, the events that provided the basis for the GFC were almost all about money. The pursuit of money took a powerful upswing. The economic realities that reflect on and constrain the attainment of money were often ignored. And the caution and risk aversion that usually bear on the willingness of market participants to provide money were largely absent. Thus the capital cycle rose to an irrational extreme, the consequences of which are generally foreseeable.

When the cycle rises to an extreme, it invariably can't stay there forever.

Sometimes it corrects under its own weight, and sometimes this happens because of events outside the cycle. In this case it was more the former. Like the laying of the foundation for the Crisis, the unraveling of the markets was essentially all financial in nature, although the first step came from "the real world."

- Most influentially, in 2006, sub-prime mortgage borrowers began to default in large numbers. Some of the borrowers, who had received loans without proving their ability to make payments, turned out in fact to be unable. Some loans, secured through fraud, went bad when fictitious borrowers disappeared. Other loans, for the full home purchase price—which had allowed home buyers to gamble on continued home appreciation without risking any money of their own—were abandoned when the market stopped rising.
- Regardless of the reason, the historic basis that allowed sub-prime mortgage backed securities to achieve high leverage and high ratings—insistence that there wouldn't be a nationwide wave of mortgage defaults—failed to hold. As it turned out, lending decisions had been made unwisely, with undue reliance on that history. Importantly, lenders and investors had ignored the chance that such reliance would give rise to lending behavior so careless that it in itself would render the history irrelevant.
- Large numbers of mortgage defaults led to downgradings, covenant breaches and payment defaults on mortgage backed securities.
- The downgradings, breaches and defaults caused the prices of mortgage backed securities to collapse, and the resultant loss of

confidence caused the market liquidity for these instruments to dry up.

- With terrified buyers taking to the sidelines — and terrified holders increasingly eager to sell (or forced to sell by margin calls) — the result was a dramatic downward spiral in the prices of mortgage backed securities.

- These negative developments collided head-on with new regulations, designed to increase transparency, which required banks' assets to be "marked to market." But with prices in free-fall and liquidity non-existent, it was hard to have faith in any price chosen. When banks marked down their assets to be appropriately conservative, the implied losses shocked investors, contributing to further panic, which caused prices to decline further, and so on.

- In many cases the very viability of banks came into question. Many had to be absorbed by other banks (with support from the government) or bailed out by the government.

- Each bank failure, acquisition (at pennies on the dollar) or bailout brought losses to investors and further sapped confidence. In addition, the interlocking relationships among banks caused grave concern regarding the remaining ones' ability to rely on amounts due from the others. "Counterparty risk" became the newest source of worry.

- Banks reported massive losses. The rising prices quoted for credit default swaps — derivatives used to bet against banks' creditworthiness — implied increased odds of insolvency. Shareholders dumped bank stocks in response, forcing down their prices. Short sellers sold unremittingly, adding to the downward pressure, rendering their pessimistic predictions self-fulfilling, and further extending the vicious circle.

- Ultimately, Lehman Brothers was denied absorption or bailout, leading to its bankruptcy. That collapse, when added to the many other unsettling events taking place simultaneously, led to nothing short of panic.

- Whereas the markets had reacted adversely to the problems in mortgages in mid-2007 but overlooked the potential for contagion to other areas, in late 2008 everyone threw in the towel on everything. The prices of all assets other than Treasurys and gold collapsed.

- Funds that had invested using borrowed capital — "leverage" or "margin" — saw asset values marked down precipitously and received demands from lenders to post additional capital. When they appealed to the banks for more time, the banks generally couldn't or wouldn't grant it. The result was distressed selling of portfolios *en masse,* which further increased the downward pressure on prices.

- The capital markets slammed shut in this environment, meaning new financing became virtually impossible in all quarters of the financial markets, even those totally unrelated to homes and mortgages.

- Given the sum of the above, all economic units pulled back, refusing to buy, invest or expand. The result was an economic retrenchment that has been labeled "the Great Recession."

Taken to its extreme in the last fifteen weeks of 2008, the downswing of the credit cycle seemed universal and unstoppable. Few people were able to imagine any forces capable of arresting it or — as described in the last chapter — any hypothetical scenario that was too dire to come true. A total meltdown of the financial system was considered a real possibility.

> The bottom line is that the willingness of potential providers of capital to make it available on any given day fluctuates violently, with a profound impact on the economy and the markets. There's no doubt that the recent credit crisis was as bad as it was because the credit markets froze up and capital became unavailable other than from governments. ("Open and Shut")

I truly believe a system meltdown — with ramifications like those seen in the Great Depression — could have occurred. Former Treasury secretary Timothy Geithner's book *Stress Test* bears this out. Fortunately, however, the U.S. government took steps that turned the tide. These included the guaranteeing of commercial paper, mentioned earlier, as well as of money market funds. The bank bailouts showed that help was available, and the September 2008 bankruptcy of Lehman Brothers suggested that the government was differentiating between the banks that were worth saving and those that weren't. Whereas panicky market participants were convinced that Morgan Stanley was next in line for collapse after Lehman — and that Goldman Sachs would follow that — the downward spiral was arrested when Japan's Mitsubishi UFJ went through with a promised $9 billion investment in Morgan Stanley.

Importantly, events in the credit markets eventually demonstrated that cycles can't go in one direction forever, even given widespread cataclysmic events. Debt prices were generally in free-fall from the time of the Lehman bankruptcy on September 15 through the end of 2008. By the end of 2008, however, the ingredients for a solid market recovery were in place.

- The over-levered funds that had received margin calls either raised additional capital, sold assets to de-lever as required, or liquidated.
- Funds and investment managers that received notices from investors desiring to withdraw at year-end either put up "gates" postponing withdrawals or completed the asset sales needed to meet them.
- The prices of debt securities reached a point where they implied yields so high that selling was unpalatable and buying became attractive.
- And, ultimately, market participants demonstrated that when negative psychology is universal and "things can't get any worse," they won't. When all optimism has been driven out, and panicked risk aversion is everywhere, it becomes possible to reach a point where prices can't go any lower. And when prices eventually stop going down, people tend to feel relief, and so the potential for a price recovery begins to arise.

The quoted prices for debt continued downward in the first quarter of 2009, as composure, confidence and a "base" of buying power had yet to return in full. But the ability of investors to buy in large scale dried up as the year began, because of the factors listed just above. And when buying interest materialized in the second quarter — perhaps because distressed debt buyers came to the realization that they had shrunk unreasonably from the daunting task of "catching a falling knife" — the dearth of supply for sale contributed to a powerful move to the upside.

The Global Financial Crisis shows the credit cycle at the greatest extreme since the Great Depression. Debt markets historically had been marked by general conservatism, meaning excesses on the upside were limited and most bubbles took place in the equity market. Certainly it was the site of the Great Crash of 1929.

But the creation of the high yield bond market in the late 1970s kicked off a liberalization of debt investing, and the generally positive economic environment of the subsequent three decades provided those who ventured in with a favorable overall experience. This combination led to a strong trend toward acceptance of low-rated and non-traditional debt instruments.

There were periods of weakness in debt in 1990–91 (related to widespread bankruptcies among the highly levered buyouts of the 1980s) and in 2002 (stemming from excessive borrowing to fund overbuilding in the telecom industry, which led to prominent downgrades that coincided with several high-profile corporate accounting scandals). But the effects of these were limited because of the isolated nature of their causes. It wasn't until 2007–08 that the financial markets witnessed the first widespread, debt-induced panic, with ramifications for the entire economy. Thus the GFC provided the ultimate example of the credit cycle's full effect.

∽

As I described it in "Open and Shut," the capital market cycle is simple in its operation, and its message is easy to perceive. An uptight, cautious credit market usually stems from, leads to or connotes things like these:

- fear of losing money
- heightened risk aversion and skepticism
- unwillingness to lend and invest regardless of merit
- shortages of capital everywhere
- economic contraction and difficulty refinancing debt
- defaults, bankruptcies and restructurings

- low asset prices, high potential returns, low risk and excessive risk premiums

Taken together, these things are indicative of a great time to invest. Of course, however, because of the role played by fear and risk aversion in their creation, most people shy away from investing while they are in force. That makes it difficult for most people to invest when the capital cycle is negative, just as it is potentially lucrative.

On the other hand, a generous capital market is usually associated with the following:

- fear of missing out on profitable opportunities
- reduced risk aversion and skepticism (and, accordingly, reduced due diligence)
- too much money chasing too few deals
- willingness to buy securities in increased quantity
- willingness to buy securities of reduced quality
- high asset prices, low prospective returns, high risk and skimpy risk premiums

It's clear from this list of elements that excessive generosity in the capital markets stems from a shortage of prudence and thus should give investors one of the clearest red flags. The wide-open capital market arises when the news is good, asset prices are rising, optimism is riding high, and all things seem possible. But it invariably brings the issuance of unsound and overpriced securities, and the incurrence of debt levels that ultimately will result in ruin.

The point about the quality of new issue securities in a wide-open capital market deserves particular attention. A decrease in risk aversion and skepticism — and increased focus on making sure opportunities aren't missed rather than on avoiding losses — makes investors open to a greater quantity of issuance. The same factors make investors willing to buy issues of lower quality.

When the credit cycle is in its expansion phase, the statistics on new issuance make clear that investors are buying new issues in greater amounts. But the acceptance of securities of lower quality is a bit more subtle. While there are credit ratings and covenants to look at, it can take effort and inference to understand the significance of these things. In feeding frenzies caused by excess availability of funds, recognizing and resisting this trend seems to be beyond the ability of the majority of market participants. This is one of the many reasons why the aftermath of an overly generous capital market includes losses, economic contraction, and a subsequent unwillingness to lend.

The bottom line of all of the above is that generous credit markets usually are associated with elevated asset prices and subsequent losses, while credit crunches produce bargain-basement prices and great profit opportunities. ("Open and Shut")

∿

The ultimate purpose of this book isn't to help you understand cycles *after* they've taken place, like the Global Financial Crisis as described at such great length. Rather it is to enable you to sense where we stand in the various cycles in real time, and thus to take the appropriate action.

The key to dealing with the credit cycle lies in recognizing that it reaches its apex when things have been going well for a while, news has been good, risk aversion is low, and investors are eager. That makes it easy for borrowers to raise money and causes buyers and investors to compete for the opportunity to provide it. The result is cheap financing, low credit standards, weak deals, and the unwise extension of credit. Borrowers hold the cards when the credit window is wide open — not lenders or investors. The implications of all of this should be obvious: proceed with caution.

The exact opposite becomes true at the other extreme of the credit cycle. Its nadir is reached when developments are unpleasant, risk aversion is heightened, and investors are depressed. Under such circumstances, no one wants to provide capital, the credit market freezes up, and proposed offerings go begging. This puts the cards into the hands of providers of capital rather than the borrowers.

Because borrowing is difficult and capital is generally unavailable, those who possess it and are willing to part with it can apply rigorous standards, insist on strong loan structures and protective covenants, and demand high prospective returns. It's things like these that provide the margin of safety required for superior investing. When these boxes can be ticked, investors should swing into an aggressive mode.

Superior investing doesn't come from buying high-quality assets, but from buying when the deal is good, the price is low, the potential return is substantial, and the risk is limited. These conditions are much more the case when the credit markets are in the less-euphoric, more-stringent part of their cycle. The slammed-shut phase of the credit cycle probably does more to make bargains available than any other single factor.

X

THE DISTRESSED DEBT CYCLE

Few lenders and bond buyers are imprudent enough to advance money that won't be repaid if conditions remain as they are. And in sober times, they insist on a margin of safety sufficient to ensure that interest and principal will be paid even if conditions for the debtor deteriorate.

But when the credit market heats up — when the race to the bottom causes avid lenders to finance less-deserving borrowers and accept weaker debt structures — bonds are issued that lack that margin of safety and won't be able to be serviced if things get a little worse. This is the unwise extension of credit. This process, as we say at Oaktree, "stacks the logs in the fireplace" for the next bonfire.

I was fortunate to partner with Bruce Karsh three decades ago, and together in 1988 we formed our first fund for distressed debt investing, which we believe was one of the very first from a mainstream financial institution. That took us into a highly specialized investment niche.

Rather than companies that are doing well or have bright futures, our distressed debt investments are generally in companies that are doing so poorly that they've defaulted on their outstanding debt or are considered highly likely to do so: they're either in bankruptcy or viewed as heading for it. To be clear, our typical company isn't challenged operationally, just overloaded with debt; thus our mantra is "good company, bad balance sheet."

Normally investors buy debt securities or make loans because they expect to be paid interest periodically and have their principal repaid when the debt matures. With distressed debt, however, the consensus is that these things won't occur: instead it is expected that the debt won't "stay current" or "be serviced." So if interest and principal aren't expected to be paid, what is the distressed debt investor's motivation?

The answer is that debtholders who aren't paid as scheduled have a "creditor claim" against the debtor. In short — and to over-simplify — when a company goes through bankruptcy, the old owners are wiped out and the old creditors become the new owners. Each creditor receives his share of the value of the company — depending on the amount and seniority of the debt he holds — in some combination of cash, new debt and ownership of the company going forward.

A distressed debt investor tries to figure out (a) what the bankrupt company is worth (or will be worth at the time it emerges from bankruptcy), (b) how that value will be divided among the company's creditors and other claimants, and (c) how long this process will take. With correct answers to those questions, he can determine what the annual return will be on a piece of the company's debt if purchased at a given price.

Getting our start in distressed debt investing in 1988 was extremely advantageous, as there were few competitors and the field was little known and little understood — two conditions that can help make for superior returns possible in any field. As a result, our funds have been able to earn a high average return over the 29 years since. But, as with many things, the average is of only limited significance. The funds we formed at less-than-great times generally have yielded good returns, but the results on funds formed at the right times have been superlative.

In other words, the opportunities for top returns in distressed debt come and go. Given the subject matter of this book, what I'll review here is what it is that makes the opportunities rise and fall. Unsurprisingly, the answer lies in the fluctuations in the distressed debt cycle. What, in turn, causes those fluctuations?

∾

The opportunities to profit in distressed debt are highly cyclical and determined by developments in other cycles. Thus they are illustrative of the workings of cycles and ripe for discussion here.

In the beginning—in 1988, 1989 and early 1990—our funds benefitted from the often-ignored benefits of distressed debt investing, and our returns were good. But in the latter half of 1990, the market for sub-investment grade debt collapsed in the first of the three major crises Bruce and I have worked through together. In addition to creating the low purchase prices that made our 1990 funds above-average gainers, this episode was highly educational, as it gave us our first glimpse of the process through which superior opportunities arise in distressed debt.

The first of the two essential ingredients in their creation consists of "the unwise extension of credit." Given the discussion in the last chapter, you should have an understanding of what I have in mind and how this develops. I'll explain through the example of high yield bonds:

- At the start, appropriately risk-averse investors apply stringent credit standards to the issuance of high yield bonds.
- The same healthy economic environment that facilitates bond is-

suance makes it easy for companies to service their existing debt (meaning defaults are scarce).

- Thus high yield bonds — with their generous interest coupons and little damage from defaults — provide solid realized returns.

- Those returns convince investors that high yield bond investing is safe, attracting increased capital to the market.

- Increased capital for investment translates into increased demand for bonds. Since Wall Street never allows demand to go unmet, this results in increased bond issuance.

- The same condition that allows larger amounts of bonds to be issued — strong investor demand — invariably also allows bonds of lesser creditworthiness to be issued.

Few lenders and bond buyers are imprudent enough to advance money that won't be repaid if conditions remain as they are. And in sober times, they insist on a margin of safety sufficient to ensure, as I said earlier, that interest and principal will be paid even if conditions for the debtor deteriorate.

But when the credit market heats up — when the race to the bottom causes avid lenders to finance less-deserving borrowers and accept weaker debt structures — bonds are issued that lack that margin of safety and won't be able to be serviced if things get a little worse. This is the unwise extension of credit. This process, as noted earlier, "stacks the logs in the fireplace" for the next bonfire.

But that's only the first half the process. Even after the fuel for a bonfire has been assembled, there won't be a conflagration until the second ingredient arrives: an igniter. It usually comes in the form of a recession, which causes corporate profits to decline. This is often accompanied by a credit crunch — the slamming shut of the credit window — such that existing debt can't be refinanced and goes into default instead. And often conditions are exacerbated by exogenous events that sap confidence and damage the economy and the financial markets. In 1990 these consisted of:

- the Gulf War, which was set off by the Iraqi invasion of Kuwait;
- the bankruptcy of many of the prominent, highly levered buyouts of the 1980s; and
- the imprisonment of Michael Milken (the principal investment banker behind high yield bonds) and the collapse of Drexel Burnham (Milken's employer and the investment bank most closely associated with high yield bonds). With Drexel and Milken gone from the scene, the remedial exchanges that had helped weakened companies avoid default were hard to effect.

When the igniter arrives, bonds that shouldn't have been issued — and perhaps even some that should have — begin to fail.

- A slower economy makes it harder for companies to service their debt.
- With the credit market closed, refinancing can't be accomplished, meaning defaults rise.
- Rising defaults damage investor psychology.
- Investors who were risk-tolerant when things were going well now become risk-averse.
- Advancing capital to financially distressed companies — which seemed like a good idea just a short time earlier — now goes out of favor.
- Potential debt buyers back away, refusing to "catch a falling knife" and saying they'll wait until the uncertainty has been resolved.

- Capital that is mobile flees from the market. Buyers become scarce, and sellers predominate.
- Selling of bonds increases; bond prices cascade downward; funds that receive withdrawals become forced sellers; and eventually bonds are available for sale at any price.

These are the conditions that give rise to the ability to effect bargain purchases of distressed debt, and thus to opportunities for elevated returns.

Of course, the cycle doesn't go in just one direction. Eventually the economy begins to recover and the credit market reopens. These two developments cause the default rate on high yield bonds to recede. The combination of an improving economy and a declining default rate causes selling to abate. Thus the downward pressure on bond prices eases, and some buying begins. Prices rise rather than fall, and balance sheet restructurings restore companies to viability, remove stumbling blocks and unlock value. When gains on bond purchases made at the bottom begin to be noticed, additional capital is attracted to the market. The combination of better results and increased capital causes the demand for bonds to grow. And with that we've gone full cycle: we're back to the beginning.

A while back I put together a concise synopsis of the way the cycle in bond issuance underlays the rise and fall of the distressed debt cycle. Here it is:

- Risk-averse investors limit quantities issued and demand high quality.
- High-quality issuance leads to low default rates.
- Low default rates cause investors to become complacent and risk-tolerant.

- Risk tolerance opens investors to increased issuance and lower quality.
- Lower-quality issuance eventually is tested by economic difficulty and gives rise to increased defaults.
- Increased defaults have a chilling effect, making investors risk-averse once more.
- And so it resumes.

This is a cycle I've seen in action repeatedly. My 29 years of experience in distressed debt tells me its themes definitely do rhyme. And the preceding description of the cycle gives me an excellent opportunity to make my point that each event in a cycle causes the one that follows. In fact, I designed this description specifically to achieve that goal. Take a look at the progression just described: you'll see that the final words of each line are the same as the first words of the line that follows. This is a true chain reaction, and one I expect to continue in the future.

∾

As you can see, the rise and fall of opportunities in the market for distressed debt stems from the interaction of other cycles: in the economy, investor psychology, risk attitudes and the credit market.

- The economic cycle influences investor psychology, company profitability and the incidence of default.
- The cycle in psychology contributes to fluctuations in credit market conditions and the desire of investors to lend, buy and sell.
- The cycle in attitudes toward risk facilitates the issuance of weak bonds at the top and denies capital for refinancing at the bottom.

- The credit cycle has a profound effect on the availability of refinancing and the degree to which would-be debt issuers are subjected to stringent credit standards.

Hopefully it's clear that multiple underlying cycles have effects on the
distressed debt market that are far from discrete and isolated. As I wrote
earlier, each of these cycles rises and falls; each causes the others to rise and
fall; and each is affected by the rise and fall of others. But the result of all
of this is a dramatic cycle in distressed debt opportunities, and one that is
subject to explanation.

XI

THE REAL ESTATE CYCLE

Much of investing is subject to gross generalizations and sweeping statements—usually stressing the positives, because of humans' tendency toward greed and wishful thinking—and for some reason this seems particularly true in real estate. Over the course of my career I've heard investment in real estate rationalized by easily digested statements like "they're not making any more" (in connection with land), "you can always live in it" (in connection with houses), and "it's a hedge against inflation" (in connection with properties of all types). What people eventually learn is that regardless of the merit behind these statements, they won't protect an investment that was made at too high a price.

The cycle in real estate has a lot in common with other cycles, such as the one that controls the provision of capital or credit.

- Positive events and increased profitability lead to greater enthusiasm and optimism.
- Improved psychology encourages increased activity. That in-

cludes doing more of something; doing it on the basis of rosier assumptions; paying higher prices to do it; and/or lowering the standards that have to be met if one is to do it. All of these things tend to entail the assumption of greater risk.

- The combination of positive psychology and the increase in activity causes asset prices to rise, which encourages still more activity, further price increases, and greater risk-bearing.

- Inevitably this virtuous circle takes on the appearance of being unstoppable, and this appearance causes asset prices and the level of activity to go too far to be sustained.

But when the news eventually turns less positive and the environment becomes less hospitable, the levels of psychology, activity and risk-bearing prove to have been excessive, and the same goes for asset prices. The resulting price correction causes psychology to become less positive, which causes disinvestment, which puts further downward pressure on prices, and so forth.

These are all elements that most financial cycles have in common, and that includes the cycle in real estate. But the real estate cycle incorporates another ingredient that the others generally don't share: the long lead times required for real estate development to take place.

In the credit market, for instance, good news and rosy psychology will lead to increased lending as soon as investment bankers can line up prospective borrowers and print prospectuses. Thus lenders' increased ardor translates almost instantaneously into increased demand for securities, lower demanded yields, lower lending standards, and increased levels of lending and security issuance.

But in the market for physical real estate — the world of so-called "bricks and mortar"—there can be significant delays. Before a new building can come to market, adding to the supply of space (and thus putting downward pressure on prices for space if demand does not increase apace), economic feasibility studies have to be performed; a site has be found and purchased; the building has to be designed; environmental impact studies have to be performed; permission to build has to be secured from authorities, and sometimes zoning modifications; financing has to be obtained; and construction has to be completed. This process can run to several years, and in the case of a major project it can exceed a decade. But market conditions can change very significantly in the interim.

I'll use a description of the cycle in real estate development from "Ditto" (January 2013) to illustrate. As I said there, "it's usually clear, simple and regularly recurring":

- Bad times cause both the level of building activity to be low and the availability of capital for building to be constrained.
- In a while the times become less bad, and eventually even good.
- Better economic times cause the demand for premises to rise.
- With few buildings having been started during the soft period and now coming on stream, this additional demand for space causes the supply/demand picture to tighten and thus rents and sale prices to rise.
- This improves the economics of real estate ownership, reawakening developers' eagerness to build.
- The better times and improved economics also make providers of capital more optimistic. Their improved state of mind causes financing to become more readily available.
- Cheaper, easier financing raises the pro forma returns on potential projects, adding to their attractiveness and increasing developers' desire to pursue them.

- Higher projected returns, more-optimistic developers and more-generous providers of capital combine for a ramp-up in building starts.
- The first completed projects encounter strong pent-up demand. They lease up or sell out quickly, giving their developers good returns.
- Those good returns — plus each day's increasingly positive headlines — cause still more buildings to be planned, financed and green-lighted.
- Cranes fill the sky (and additional cranes are ordered from the factory, but that's a different cycle).
- It takes years for the buildings started later to reach completion. In the interim, the first ones to open eat into the unmet demand.
- The period between the start of planning and the opening of a building is often long enough for the economy to transition from boom to bust. Projects started in good times often open in bad times, meaning their space adds to vacancies, putting downward pressure on rents and sale prices. Unfilled space hangs over the market.
- Bad times cause the level of building activity to be low and the availability of capital for building to be constrained.

Note that as in the case of many of the other cycles discussed here, each step leads to the next. In particular, the step at the bottom of the list is actually the one that kicks off the next iteration. This is a good example of the way in which cycles are self-perpetuating.

∽

In lending, since the time lags inherent in the process are brief, the economic and business conditions in force at the time that the will to lend arises and the loan is conceived generally are still in force when the loan is funded. And if conditions change materially in the relatively brief interim, the lender may be able to pull his commitment under a "material adverse change" provision in the contract. Thus there's relatively little risk in general lending resulting from the gap between idea and action.

But given the many years that can pass between a building's conception and its opening, conditions can change enormously, as just described. This adds an element to real estate development that makes it potentially risky. Developers hope this risk will be offset by the fact that they can utilize extensive external financing (and thus they risk relatively little of their own money and are able to lever up the return on it to a great degree).

When I moved to Los Angeles in 1980, steel skeletons stood along the "Wilshire corridor" in Westwood, where gleaming condominium buildings had been imagined. The developers who had initiated these projects in the 1970s boom were caught out. The positive conditions that had supported the initiation of those projects had turned negative, as the economy turned down and as supply created by quicker builders sopped up what demand there was.

Some of those rusting skeletons remained uncompleted for years. The developer who had dreamed of a high return on a project's $100 million total cost instead lost his $5 million or $10 million of equity (and the banks lost a good part of the construction loans they had extended for those projects). That illustrates the downside of the real estate cycle and the effect of the extensive time lags.

But investors who bought those halted projects (often from lenders that had repossessed them) and completed them often benefitted from:

- the ability to buy them for less than the developers had invested in land, planning, entitling and construction of the framework,
- the reduced cost to complete them at lower prices for labor and materials in a non-boom environment,
- the shorter period remaining between the onset of their involvement and the completion of the building, and
- the possibility that—just as they had been approved in good times and run into bad times—stalled projects purchased in bad times might come onto the market in good times.

The long lead time in real estate development gave rise to this possibility, and my team participated in it. It illustrates the impact of cycles on profit potential. Initiating projects in boom times can be a source of risk. Buying them in weak times can be very profitable. It all depends on what you do and when you do it. Or as they say in golf, "Every putt makes someone happy."

~

There's another aspect of cycles that can be seen clearly in the real estate arena—although it affects cycles in many other areas as well—and that's the fact that people's decisions often fail to take into account what others are doing. Here's an example:

When prosperity is rolling along and wealth and good feelings are rising, there generally will be increases in the demand for homes—resulting in increases in the price of homes—and increases in the availability of mortgage financing to home buyers. Often this causes a housing shortage to develop, as demand for homes increases relative to supply, which adjusts slowly. High home prices combine with eager lenders' financing of homebuilders to encourage the construction of new homes to meet the demand.

A homebuilder might conclude there is unmet demand for 100 homes in his town. Out of an abundance of caution — and because of the limits on his scale and his access to funds — he decides to build just 20 new homes. So far so good.

But what if ten homebuilders all make the same decision? In that case, 200 homes will be built. First, more homes will be built than there's demand for. And second, by the time those homes come on the market, the economy may have cooled; people may not feel as prosperous; and thus demand for homes might be sharply lower. In that case, the 200 new homes may encounter a dearth of demand, meaning they'll go unsold or sell for prices far below those on which the developers had based their decision to build.

Now conditions have reversed. The economy is slow. Access to financing dries up, making it hard for would-be home buyers to obtain mortgages. And there's a sizable inventory of unsold homes. Clearly the smart thing is for the builders to stop building. So they all do so at the same time ... meaning the next time the economy improves, there may not be enough homes to meet the increase in demand. And so forth.

This is a straightforward description of one aspect of a cycle at work. And it isn't hypothetical. At the 2012 Oaktree Conference, my partner Raj Shourie showed one of the most compelling graphs I've ever seen:

This graph presents the record of annual housing starts in the U.S. from 1940 through 2010. The reason it made such an impression on me is that whereas it showed that 2010 housing starts were at the lowest level

U.S. Housing Production

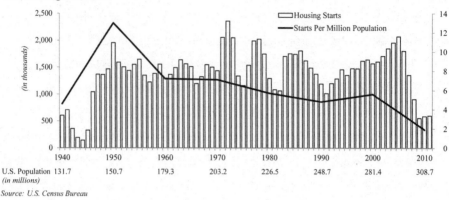

Source: U.S. Census Bureau

since wartime 1945 (and just equal to 1940's slightly less-depressed level), that observation tells only part of the story. It fails to take into account the growth since the '40s in the U.S. population, the source from which long-run increases in demand for housing arise.

Thus, while the number of starts in 2010 was the same as in 1940, the ratio of starts to population — arguably a far more meaningful figure — was only *half* the highly depressed 1940 level. The explanation is that practically no one had resumed building homes following the sub-prime mortgage crisis, housing bust, and Global Financial Crisis of 2007–08. The key inference to draw from this observation was that the supply of new homes in the years immediately following clearly would be insufficient to meet a pickup in demand for homes.

Of course, "conventional wisdom" at the time held that there could never be a pickup in demand for homes. Instead, most people were convinced that the American dream of home ownership was over; demand for homes would remain depressed forever; and thus the overhang of unsold homes would be absorbed only very slowly. They cited the trend among young people—having been burnt by the collapse of the housing and mortgage bubbles—to rent rather than buy, and as usual they extrapolated it rather than question its durability. As in so many of the examples in this book, for most people, psychology-driven extrapolation took the place of an understanding of and belief in cyclicality.

It was clear to me and my Oaktree colleagues, from the graph and from our knowledge of the data behind it, that because the greatest economic crash in almost eighty years had halted additions to the housing supply, home prices could recover strongly if there was any material increase in demand. And, rejecting conventional wisdom, we were convinced that housing demand would prove cyclical as usual, and thus would pick up sometime in the intermediate-term future. This conclusion—supported by other data and analysis—contributed to our decision to invest heavily in non-performing home mortgages and non-performing bank loans secured by land for residential construction, and to purchase North America's largest private homebuilding company. These investments worked out quite well. (It's interesting in this context to note what the *Wall Street Journal* said in a May 12, 2017 article headlined "Generation of Renters Now Buying": "In all [first-time home buyers] have accounted for 42% of buyers this year, up from 38% in 2015 and 31% at the lowest point during the recent housing cycle in 2011." So much for extrapolating widespread abandonment of home ownership.)

This is an example of a case where awareness of the nature of cycles and our position in the current one permitted a profitable inference. And it is a case where a cycle standing at an extreme—this time housing starts at a deep trough—sent a signal calling for a highly profitable action.

The proper course seems clear now, when we look back on the evidence. The reasons behind successful decisions invariably are obvious in hindsight. But in this case, dispassionate analysis of cyclical data permitted the right conclusion to be reached in real time . . . which is when it counts.

~

While I'm on the subject of cycles in real estate, I want to touch — for the first time but not the last — on the way people occasionally conclude that some financial phenomenon has ceased being cyclical, and to that end, I'll discuss one of the greatest cases. When things go well, people tend to think the good times will roll on forever. In fact, not much time has to have elapsed since the last correction before cyclical history is overlooked in its entirety. Thus it's appropriate to again cite John Kenneth Galbraith's observation regarding attitudes toward history:

> There can be few fields of human endeavor in which history counts
> for so little as in the world of finance. Past experience, to the extent
> that it is part of memory at all, is dismissed as the primitive refuge of
> those who do not have the insight to appreciate the incredible won-
> ders of the present.

Much of investing is subject to gross generalizations and sweeping statements — usually stressing the positives, because of humans' tendency toward greed and wishful thinking — and for some reason this seems particularly true in real estate. Over the course of my career I've heard investment in real estate rationalized by easily digested statements like "they're not making any more" (in connection with land), "you can always live in it" (in connection with houses), and "it's a hedge against inflation" (in connection with properties of all types). What people eventually learn is that regardless of the merit behind these statements, they won't protect an investment that was made at too high a price.

In the late 1990s and early 2000s, as I mentioned earlier, a number of elected officials decided that as a step toward benefitting society and increasing access to the American dream, it would be swell if more people owned homes. As a result, government-sponsored mortgage lenders got the message that home financing should be made more easily available, and they complied. The combination of this message, the resulting increase in mortgage availability, and the sharp decline in interest rates that was taking place at the time had a powerful stimulative effect on potential home buyers.

The flow of money for mortgages was strongly encouraged by another real estate platitude: "mortgage lending is safe." This was based on conviction that a nationwide wave of mortgage defaults couldn't happen. The combination of strong economic growth, generally moderate economic fluctuations, and prudent mortgage lending practices had prevented the occurrence of such a wave in the period since the Great Depression ... long enough for the last such episode to be forgotten, as Galbraith says. But that didn't mean lenders were incapable of lapsing into lending practices so generous and imprudent that a powerful recession could bring on such a wave of defaults.

In the early years of the 21st century, the combination of strong demand for homes and plentiful mortgage money—abetted by optimistic media coverage—caused home prices to rise strongly. Thus we started to hear yet another sweeping generalization concerning real estate: "home prices always go up" (see the section that follows).

I hope by now you've caught on to the fact that the merits of the asset in question matter only so much, and certainly they can't be strong enough to always carry the day. Human emotion inevitably causes the prices of assets — even worthwhile assets — to be transported to levels that are extreme and unsustainable: either vertiginous highs or overly pessimistic lows.

In short, conscientious belief in the inevitability of cycles like I'm urging means that a number of words and phrases must be excluded from the intelligent investor's vocabulary. These include "never," "always," "forever," "can't," "won't," "will" and "has to."

∿

In the years leading up to the sub-prime mortgage crisis of 2007 and Global Financial Crisis of 2007–08, a great deal of bullish behavior (which was later shown to have been reckless) was underlaid by the belief that homes could be depended on to appreciate steadily and not prove cyclical. As part of — or contributing to — the bullish trend, some researchers rendered supportive statements and optimistic projections:

- According to a *New York Times Magazine* article from March 5, 2006 titled "This Very, Very Old House," a vice president of the Federal Reserve Bank of New York had concluded that "the sharp rise in home prices is in line with economic conditions . . . not a skewed vision of reality." It even quoted him as saying, "We sometimes wonder why home prices haven't increased much more, given the tremendous increase in the size of mortgage the average family can finance."
- The article also mentioned "like-minded experts [from Columbia University and the Wharton School] who focus on what they call 'superstar cities,' places so desirable that they not only are not headed for a correction but they also can sustain 'ever-increasing' prices compared with less-sought-after cities." (Of course, willing-

ness to employ terms like "ever-increasing" should serve as an absolute red flag for the alert investor.)

But there was a lot to question regarding the reasonableness of these conclusions:

- the brevity of the data on home prices,
- the fact that statements made about the trend in the price of the *average* home sold in a given year don't necessarily say anything about the price performance of a given home or of all homes standing (e.g., there is no adjustment for physical changes in the average house over time, or in the mix of homes sold that year relative to all homes), and
- likewise, there is no adjustment for the fact that neighborhoods and whole cities go in and out of favor over time, affecting the value of homes. For this reason, statements about homes in a given city or neighborhood wouldn't necessarily be applicable to homes in general.

Thus I found it very interesting when "This Very, Very Old House" was published in 2006. It reported on a study that solved many of these methodological problems by following the price of a single house in Amsterdam: one that Pieter Fransz built in 1625. It had stood since then, virtually unaltered, and had changed hands six times, but its location in the Herengracht canal neighborhood had remained Amsterdam's most desirable throughout. Thus the article provided insight not as to whether the price of the average home had risen, but how the price of a particular home had performed.

In contrast to the long-term optimists on housing quoted earlier, Yale's

Robert Shiller said of the Fransz house and its neighbors, "Looking at
the Herengracht data is very instructive, because you can see 50-year
intervals of growth, then it turns around. That's more realistic than the
superstar-cities argument." The author of the study, Piet Eichholtz, was
described as being "skeptical of those who claim that property values can
continue to increase ad infinitum." He considered the economic argu-
ments for it being "different this time" but said, "you can see similarly
rosy assessments made over and over, which are then quashed by circumstances." Amen.

Here's more from the *Times* article:

> "There is a myth which says that real-estate values go up significantly
> over time, . . ." Eichholtz said, ". . . but the data ended up challenging
> that myth."
>
> That is to say, where everyone from your wise old uncle to the
> broker who sold you your house holds it as gospel that real estate is
> one of the best long-term investments, this longest of long-term indi-
> ces suggests that, on the contrary, it sort of stinks. Between 1628 and
> 1973 (the period of Eichholtz's original study), real property values
> on the Herengracht—adjusted for inflation—went up a mere 0.2
> percent per year, worse than the stingiest bank savings account. As
> Shiller wrote in his analysis of the Herengracht index, "Real home
> prices did roughly double, but took nearly 350 years to do so."
>
> . . . It's only in recent years, Shiller says, that huge increases in re-
> al-estate prices have become the norm and that people have come to
> expect them.
>
> . . . if this description of the past few years [in which "prices just
> went up amazingly"] typifies the brave new world we live in, putting
> it into the perspective of time—rise, fall, rise, fall—leads us back to
> what may be the oldest history lesson of all: it tends to repeat. [em-
> phasis added]

The long-term data on home prices is valuable, but the most important lesson is that, in times of rising asset prices, people turn bullish and commentators provide authoritative support. That's only natural. In fact, rationalization for price appreciation that has taken place (and prediction of still more to come) invariably occurs at highs, not lows. For real help I'd look to commentators who issue sober statements in bullish times, or who argue against negativity when markets are down.

∽

The real estate industry is subject to cyclical ups and downs like all others. But real estate cycles can be amplified by special factors:

- the time lags between conception and readiness for sale,
- the extremely high financial leverage that is typical, and
- the fact that the supply is generally too inflexible to be adjusted as demand fluctuates. (That is, a manufacturer can eliminate a factory shift, lay off workers or reduce production if demand for his product falters. But a landlord, hotelier or real estate developer has a much harder time reducing the premises he has on offer if demand falls short.)

The cycle in real estate illustrates and exemplifies the ways in which cyclical factors lead to and cause each other, as well as the tendency of cycles to go to extremes. It's not for nothing that they often say cynically — in tougher times, when optimistic generalizations can no longer be summoned forth — that "only the third owner makes money." Not the developer who conceived and initiated the project. And not the banker who loaned the money for its construction and then repossessed the project from the developer in the down-cycle. But rather the investor who bought the property from the bank amid distress and then rode the up-cycle.

Of course this is an exaggeration, like all generalizations. But it does serve as a reminder of the relevance of cyclicality to the real estate market, and especially of the way cyclicality can function in the less-good times.

XII

PUTTING IT ALL TOGETHER— THE MARKET CYCLE

===

The first time an inexperienced investor lives through an upward market cycle, the beginnings of the progression may seem logical, as the positives compound in a bull market or bubble. The fact that so much good news and good feeling can end in losses can come as a surprise. It is inescapable that it will seem so to the uninitiated, of course, because if the progressions weren't permitted to go on to extremes on the basis of errors in judgment, markets wouldn't reach bull market tops to collapse from (or bear market bottoms to recover from).

Our job as investors is simple: to deal with the prices of assets, assessing where they stand today and making judgments regarding how they will change in the future. Prices are affected primarily by developments in two areas: fundamentals and psychology.

- Fundamentals, which I've been calling "events," can largely be reduced to earnings, cash flow, and the outlook for the two. They are affected by many things, including trends in the economy, profitability and the availability of capital.

- And psychology — how investors feel about fundamentals and value them — is likewise affected by many things, particularly investors' level of optimism and attitude toward risk.

There are cycles in the elements mentioned above, and several aspects to each cycle. The themes behind the cycles' behavior — and the ways in which they interact and combine — have a repeating, understandable pattern, as we have discussed at length. They all come together — and they combine with idiosyncratic and random influences — to cause the behavior of the securities market.

It's my goal in this chapter to give you a feel for the cyclical ups and downs of the market. Not for the fact that it rises and falls, or how it has done so in the past, or what these movements were in reaction to. But rather the forces — and specifically the non-fundamental, non-economic forces — that cause it to go up and down, often in manic fashion.

If the market were a disciplined calculator of value based exclusively on company fundamentals, the price of a security wouldn't fluctuate much more than the issuer's current earnings and the outlook for earnings in the future. In fact, the price generally should fluctuate less than earnings, since quarter-to-quarter changes in earnings often even out in the long run and, besides, don't necessarily reflect actual changes in the company's long-term potential.

And yet security prices generally fluctuate much more than earnings. The reasons, of course, are largely psychological, emotional and non-fundamental. Thus price changes exaggerate and overstate fundamental changes. Here's the shorthand version as to why:

- Events in the economy and in corporate profits turn increasingly positive.

- Positive events feed investor psychology. Emotion, so-called "animal spirits" and investors' tolerance for risk all rise with those positive events (or sometimes despite negative ones).

- Rising psychology causes investors to be less demanding in terms of risk protection and prospective return.

- The combination of positive events, strengthening psychology and the lowering of investors' return requirements causes asset prices to rise.

- Eventually, however, the process goes into reverse. Events fail to live up to expectations, perhaps because the environment that produces them becomes less hospitable, or perhaps because expectations were unrealistically high.

- Investors eventually prove that psychology can't remain positive forever. Cooler heads conclude that prices have reached levels that are unjustified, or psychology may soften for any of a million possible reasons (or for no apparent reason).

- Prices fall when events are less positive or come to be viewed less positively. Sometimes it happens simply because prices have reached levels that are unstainable, or because of negative developments in the environment.

- Having turned downward, asset prices continue to decline until they fall so low that the stage is set for their recovery.

It's important to understand the way fundamentals and psychology interact, as described above. But it's essential that I repeat something about this process: while the description above is of one that is orderly and sequential, the process is nowhere as neat as this description may make it seem. The sequence in which these things occur is subject to change, as is the very direction of causality.

- Sometimes events cause psychology to strengthen, and sometimes improving psychology has a positive impact on events (for example, bolstering the economy and corporate profits).
- And while it's obvious that improved investor psychology makes asset prices rise, it's just as obvious that rising prices make investors feel wealthier, smarter and more optimistic.

So, in other words, these relationships can work in both directions . . . and even do so simultaneously. And each can cause the other. The speed at which things play out is highly variable from cycle to cycle and over the course of a given cycle. And lastly, cycles don't necessarily progress smoothly; rather, they can be marked by dips, recoveries and feints along the way.

It's for reasons like these that investing can't be described as scientific, and can't be depended on to work the same every time. I keep coming back to Mark Twain's observation that "history doesn't repeat itself, but it does rhyme." The reasons and results are never the same as in the past, but they're usually reminiscent of developments we've seen before.

Regardless of the imprecision of the process, it's clear that past events and expected future events combine with psychology to determine asset prices. Events and psychology also influence the availability of credit, and the availability of credit greatly affects asset prices, just as it feeds back to influence events and psychology.

In sum, these things all come together to create the market cycle. We hear about it every day, most prominently in connection with the ups and downs of the stock market, but also with regard to markets for things like bonds, gold and currencies. This is where many cycles intersect, and it's the subject of this chapter.

∾

Financial theory portrays investors as "economic men": objective, rational optimizers. Thus it suggests that the market they collectively form is what author and investor (and Warren Buffett's teacher) Ben Graham called a "weighing machine": a disciplined assessor of the value of assets.

In stark contrast, however, the truth is that financial facts and figures are only a starting point for market behavior; investor rationality is the exception, not the rule; and the market spends little of its time calmly weighing financial data and setting prices free of emotionality.

Investment fundamentals are rather straightforward. Past events have already taken place and been recorded, and many people have the quantitative skills required to analyze them. Current performance is captured in financial statements, which sometimes present an accurate picture and sometimes require skillful adjustment. And future events are unknown to everyone (although some investors are better able than others to foresee them). Fundamentals aren't the most variable part of investing or the part that intrigues me most. And anyway, I can't write a book telling you how to know more than others about future events. Doing a superior job of that requires elements of foresight, intuition and "second-level thinking" that I doubt can be reduced to paper or taught.

The part of investing that fascinates me — that I find myself thinking of most, and where my Oaktree colleagues and I have made some of our greatest contributions to our clients' welfare — regards the ways in which investors deviate from the assumption of rationality, and the contribution of those ways to the oscillation of cycles.

A large number of elements play parts in this aspect of investment decision making, interfering with the process of arriving at purely economic decisions. They may come under the headings of human nature, psychology or emotion — the distinction isn't straightforward or important for our purposes here — and they absolutely are capable of dominating investor behavior and thus markets. Some but not all vary cyclically, and they all can affect or exacerbate cycles. Here are the most important influences:

- the way investors fluctuate rather than hold firmly to rational thinking and the resulting rational decisions;
- the tendency of investors to hold distorted views of what's going on, engaging in selective perception and skewed interpretation;
- quirks like confirmation bias, which makes people accept evidence that confirms their thesis and reject that which doesn't, and the tendency toward non-linear utility, which causes most people to value a dollar lost more highly than a dollar made (or a dollar of potential profit forgone);
- the gullibility that makes investors swallow tall tales of profit potential in good times, and the excessive skepticism that makes them reject all possibility of gains in bad times;
- the fluctuating nature of investors' risk tolerance and risk aversion, and thus of their demands for compensatory risk premiums;
- the herd behavior that results from pressure to fall into line with

what others are doing, and as a result the difficulty of holding non-conformist positions;

- the extreme discomfort that comes from watching others make money doing something you've rejected;

- thus the tendency of investors who have resisted an asset bubble to ultimately succumb to the pressure, throw in the towel and buy (even though — no, *because* — the asset that is the subject of the bubble has appreciated substantially);

- the corresponding tendency to give up on investments that are unpopular and unsuccessful, no matter how intellectually sound, and

- finally, the fact that investing is all about money, which introduces powerful elements such as greed for more, envy of the money others are making, and fear of loss.

Bulls and Bears

Investors have been characterized for at least a hundred years as either "bulls" (optimists who think stocks will rise and behave aggressively as a result) or "bears" (pessimists who think they'll fall and who thus behave defensively). Consequently, people apply the label of "bull market" to a market that has risen, is rising or will rise (it's quite imprecise) and "bear market" to the opposite.

About 45 years ago — in the early 1970s — I received one of the greatest gifts I was ever given, when an older and wiser investor introduced me to "the three stages of a bull market":

- the first stage, when only a few unusually perceptive people believe things will get better,

- the second stage, when most investors realize that improvement is actually taking place, and
- the third stage, when everyone concludes things will get better forever.

The arrival of this simple truth opened my eyes to the notion of investors' psychological extremes and the impact of those extremes on market cycles. Like many of the great quotations and adages, it captures disproportionate wisdom in a few simple words. It's all about the changeability of attitudes, the pattern they follow over the course of a cycle, and how they contribute to error.

In the first stage, because the possibility of improvement is invisible to most investors and thus unappreciated, security prices incorporate little or no optimism. Often the first stage occurs after prices have been pounded in a crash, and the same downtrend that decimated prices also has wiped out psychology, turning the members of the crowd against the market and causing them to swear off investing forever.

In the last stage, on the other hand, events have gone well for so long — and have been reflected so powerfully in asset prices, further lifting the mood of the market — that investors extrapolate improvement to infinity and bid up prices to reflect their optimism. Trees generally don't grow to the sky, but in this stage investors act as if they will . . . and pay up for the limitless potential they perceive. Few things are as costly as paying for potential that turns out to have been overrated.

It follows from the above that someone who invests in the first stage — when almost no one can see a reason for optimism — buys assets at bargain prices from which substantial appreciation is possible. But someone who buys in the third stage invariably pays a high price for the market's excessive enthusiasm and loses money as a result.

The description of the three stages of the bull market offers a lot of wisdom with great economy. But not long after learning about the three stages, I came across something even better and briefer—essentially the same message in just 14 words: "What the wise man does in the beginning, the fool does in the end."

I consider this the number-one piece of investment wisdom and an incredible distillation of the import of cycles. Again, the early discoverer—who by definition has to be that rare person who sees the future better than others and has the inner strength to buy without validation from the crowd—garners undiscovered potential at a bargain price. But every investment trend eventually is overdone and bid up too far, so that the buyer in the end pays up for potential that is overrated. He ends up with capital punishment, not capital appreciation.

"What the wise man does in the beginning, the fool does in the end" tells you 80% of what you have to know about market cycles and their impact. Warren Buffett has said much the same thing even more concisely: "First the innovator, then the imitator, then the idiot."

Of course, cycles work in both directions, and the depths of the Global Financial Crisis gave me an opportunity to invert the old saying and describe the three stages of a bear market in "The Tide Goes Out" (March 2008):

- the first stage, when just a few thoughtful investors recognize that, despite the prevailing bullishness, things won't always be rosy,

- the second stage, when most investors recognize that things are deteriorating, and
- the third stage, when everyone's convinced things can only get worse.

I've mentioned capitulation before. It's a fascinating phenomenon, and there's a dependable cycle to it, too. In the first stage of either a bull or bear market, most investors refrain (by definition) from joining in on the thing that only a tiny minority does. This may be because they lack the special insight that underlies that action; the ability to act before the case has been proved, and others have flocked to it (after which it's no longer unappreciated and un-reflected in market prices); or the spine needed to take a different path than the herd and behave as a non-conforming contrarian.

Having missed the opportunity to be early, bold and right, investors may continue to resist as the movement takes hold and gathers steam. Once the fad has resulted in market movement, they still may not join in. With steely discipline, they refuse to buy into the market, asset class or industry group that has been lifted by bullish buyers, or to sell once selling by others has caused prices to fall below intrinsic value. It's not for them to join the trend late.

But most investors do capitulate eventually. They simply run out of the resolve needed to hold out. Once the asset has doubled or tripled in price on the way up — or halved on the way down — many people feel so stupid and wrong, and are so envious of those who've profited from the fad or side-stepped the decline, that they lose the will to resist further. My favorite quote on this subject is from Charles Kindleberger: "There is nothing as disturbing to one's well-being and judgment as to see a friend get rich" (*Manias, Panics, and Crashes: A History of Financial Crises*, 1989).

Market participants are pained by the money that others have made and they've missed out on, and they're afraid the trend (and the pain) will continue further. They conclude that joining the herd will stop the pain, so they surrender. Eventually they buy the asset well into its rise or sell after it has fallen a great deal.

In other words, after failing to do the right thing in stage one, they compound the error by taking that action in stage three, when it has become the wrong thing to do. That's capitulation. It's a highly destructive aspect of investor behavior during cycles, and a great example of psychology-induced error at its worst.

Of course, when the last resister has given up and bought well into the rise — or sold well into the decline — there's no one left to fall in line. No more buyers means the end of the bull market, and vice versa. The last capitulator makes the top or bottom and sets the scene for a cyclical swing in the opposite direction. He is the "fool in the end."

The following account from history shows that even the most brilliant among us can fall prey to capitulation:

> Sir Isaac Newton, who was the Master of the Mint at the time of the "South Sea Bubble," joined many other wealthy Englishmen in investing in the stock [of the South Sea Company]. It rose from £128 in January of 1720 to £1,050 in June. Early in this rise, however, Newton realized the speculative nature of the boom and sold his £7,000 worth of stock. When asked about the direction of the market, he is reported to have replied "I can calculate the motions of the heavenly bodies, but not the madness of the people."
>
> By September 1720, the bubble was punctured and the stock price fell below £200, off 80% from its high three months earlier. It turned out, however, that despite having seen through the bubble earlier, Sir Isaac, like so many investors over the years, couldn't stand the pressure of seeing those around him make vast profits. He bought back

the stock at its high and ended up losing £20,000. Not even one of the world's smartest men was immune to this tangible lesson in gravity! ("bubble.com," January 2000)

Bubbles and Crashes

We've always had rising and falling markets, and we always will. When they continue to a significant extent, they're called bull markets and bear markets. Even further and they're called booms, manias and crazes; busts, crises and panics. The most popular terms today for describing extreme bull and bear markets are "bubble" and "crash."

These latter terms have been around for a long time. The "South Sea Bubble" cited above, a mania for investing in the company that supposedly would pay off the national debt by exploiting a monopoly to trade with South America, caught England by storm in 1720. And the market collapse that kicked off the Great Depression is called the Great Crash of 1929. But it was the "tech bubble," "Internet bubble" and "dot-com bubble" of 1995–2000 — and the housing and mortgage bubbles that ended in 2007, bringing on significant crashes in markets around the world — that brought the word "bubble" into everyday use.

As a result of the foregoing, there's a tendency these days — especially on the part of the media — to call any big market rise a bubble. As of this writing in fall 2017, the S&P 500 index of U.S. stocks has roughly quadrupled (including dividends) from its low in March 2009, and the yield on U.S. high yield bonds has fallen to a piddling 5.8%. Thus I'm often asked whether we're in a new bubble of one kind or another, perhaps implying a crash is imminent. That's why I want to spend some time on my conviction that not every big rise is a bubble. For me, the term "bubble" has special psychological connotations that should be understood and looked out for.

I've lived through bubbles much older than those in tech stocks and housing mentioned on the preceding page. One of the best examples was the 1960s mania for the "Nifty Fifty" stocks — the shares of the highest-quality, fastest-growing companies in America. As far as I'm concerned, there's a common thread that runs through bubbles and was exemplified by the Nifty Fifty: conviction that, as far as the subject asset is concerned, "there's no such thing as a price too high." And of course it follows that no matter what price you pay, you're sure to make money.

There's only one form of intelligent investing, and that's figuring out what something's worth and buying it for that price or less. You can't have intelligent investing in the absence of quantification of value and insistence on an attractive purchase price. Any investment movement that's built around a concept other than the relationship between price and value is irrational.

The idea of "growth stocks" began to be popularized in the early 1960s, based on the goal of participating in the rapidly growing profits of companies benefitting from advances in technology, marketing and management techniques. It gathered steam, and by 1968, when I had a summer job in the investment research department of First National City Bank (the predecessor of Citibank), the Nifty Fifty stocks — the fastest growing and best — had appreciated so much that the bank trust departments that did most of the investing in those days generally lost interest in all other stocks.

Everyone wanted a piece of Xerox, IBM, Kodak, Polaroid, Merck, Lilly, Hewlett-Packard, Texas Instruments, Coca-Cola and Avon. These companies were considered to be so great that nothing bad could ever happen to them. And it was accepted dictum that it absolutely didn't matter what price you paid. If it was a little too high, no matter: the companies' fast-rising earnings would soon grow into it.

The result was predictable. Whenever people are willing to invest regardless of price, they're obviously doing so based on emotion and popularity rather than cold-blooded analysis. So Nifty Fifty stocks that had been selling at 80–90 times earnings in 1968, in the vanguard of a powerful bull market, came down to earth when ardor cooled. Thus many sold at 8–9 times earnings in the much weaker stock market of 1973, meaning investors in "America's best companies" had lost 80–90% of their money. And note that several of the "flawless" companies mentioned have since gone bankrupt or experienced serious brushes with distress.

So much for "no price too high." No asset or company is so good that it can't become overpriced. Certainly that notion must have been banished forever.

But lest you think this lesson truly was learned, let's fast-forward to the late 1990s. Now it was technology stocks that were commanding widespread attention. Just as corporate innovation had sparked the growth stock fad, now gains in telecommunications (cell phones and transmission via optical fiber), media (including the limitless demand for "content" to fill the new entertainment channels), and information technology (especially the Internet) were firing investors' imaginations.

"The Internet will change the world," was the battle cry, followed as usual by "for an e-commerce stock, there's no price too high." Whereas the Nifty Fifty stocks had sold at inflated multiples of their companies' earnings, that wasn't a problem with Internet stocks: these companies had no earnings. Not only was the investing purely conceptual, but so were many of the companies. So instead of p/e ratios, the stocks sold at multiples of revenues (if there were any) or "eyeballs": the number of consumers visiting their websites.

Just as with the Nifty Fifty, there was a grain of truth underlying the investment fad; one is usually required in order for a bubble to get going. But investors slipped the moorings of reason and discipline when they concluded that price didn't matter. They were right; the Internet certainly did change the world, which is unrecognizable today from what it was twenty years ago. But the companies behind the vast majority of the Internet stocks of 1999 and 2000 no longer exist. The Nifty Fifty losses of 80–90% are enviable; these companies' investors lost 100%.

The bottom line is clear: I think "price doesn't matter" is a necessary component — and a hallmark — of a bubble. Likewise, in bubbles, investors often conclude that you can make money by borrowing money to buy into the mania. No matter what the interest rate is on your loan, the asset is sure to appreciate at a rate above that. Clearly this is another example of the suspension of analytical disbelief.

"No price too high" is the ultimate ingredient in a bubble, and thus a foolproof sign of a market gone too far. There is no safe way to participate in a bubble, only danger. It should be noted, however, that "overpriced" is far from synonymous with "going down tomorrow." Many fads roll on well past the time when they first reach bubble territory. Several prominent investors threw in the towel in early 2000 because their resistance to the tech bubble had proved so painful. Some saw clients withdraw a large part of their capital, some became dispirited and quit the business, and others gave up and bought into the bubble . . . just in time to see it collapse, compounding their error.

∾

The following progression serves to sum up regarding the upswing of the market cycle. It shows how cycles in economics, profits, psychology, risk aversion and media behavior combine to move market prices well beyond intrinsic value, and how one development contributes to the next.

- The economy is growing, and the economic reports are positive.
- Corporate earnings are rising and beating expectations.
- The media carry only good news.
- Securities markets strengthen.
- Investors grow increasingly confident and optimistic.
- Risk is perceived as being scarce and benign.
- Investors think of risk-bearing as a sure route to profit.
- Greed motivates behavior.
- Demand for investment opportunities exceeds supply.
- Asset prices rise beyond intrinsic value.
- Capital markets are wide open, making it easy to raise money or roll over debt.
- Defaults are few.
- Skepticism is low and faith is high, meaning risky deals can be done.
- No one can imagine things going wrong. No favorable development seems improbable.
- Everyone assumes things will get better forever.
- Investors ignore the possibility of loss and worry only about missing opportunities,
- No one can think of a reason to sell, and no one is forced to sell.
- Buyers outnumber sellers.
- Investors would be happy to buy if the market dips.
- Prices reach new highs.

- Media celebrate this exciting event.
- Investors become euphoric and carefree.
- Security holders marvel at their own intelligence; perhaps they buy more.
- Those who've remained on the sidelines feel remorse; thus they capitulate and buy.
- Prospective returns are low (or negative).
- Risk is high.
- Investors should forget about missing opportunity and worry only about losing money.
- This is the time for caution!

The most important thing to note is that maximum psychology, maximum availability of credit, maximum price, minimum potential return and maximum risk all are reached at the same time, and usually these extremes coincide with the last paroxysm of buying.

Likewise, the following progression outlines what happens in a market downswing.

- The economy is slowing; reports are negative.
- Corporate earnings are flat or declining, and falling short of projections.
- Media report only bad news.
- Securities markets weaken.
- Investors become worried and depressed.
- Risk is seen as being everywhere.
- Investors see risk-bearing as nothing but a way to lose money.
- Fear dominates investor psychology.

- Demand for securities falls short of supply.
- Asset prices fall below intrinsic value.
- Capital markets slam shut, making it hard to issue securities or refinance debt.
- Defaults soar.
- Skepticism is high and faith is low, meaning only safe deals can be done, or maybe none at all.
- No one considers improvement possible. No outcome seems too negative to happen.
- Everyone assumes things will get worse forever.
- Investors ignore the possibility of missing opportunity and worry only about losing money.
- No one can think of a reason to buy.
- Sellers outnumber buyers.
- "Don't try to catch a falling knife" takes the place of "buy the dips."
- Prices reach new lows.
- The media fixate on this depressing trend.
- Investors become depressed and panicked.
- Security holders feel dumb and disillusioned. They realize they didn't really understand the reasons behind the investments they made.
- Those who abstained from buying (or who sold) feel validated and are celebrated for their brilliance.
- Those who held give up and sell at depressed prices, adding further to the downward spiral.
- Implied prospective returns are sky-high.
- Risk is low.

- Investors should forget about the risk of losing money and worry only about missing opportunity.
- This is the time to be aggressive!

In the reverse of the "top" that results from the upswing of the market cycle, now we see that the nadir of psychology, a total inability to access credit, minimum price, maximum potential return and minimum risk all coincide at the bottom, when the last optimist throws in the towel.

The progressions outlined here are simplistic. In fact, they can seem like cartoonish depictions of the road to failure. But they are not imaginary or exaggerated. It is absolutely logical that each event will bring on the next one in both directions . . . until an illogical extreme is reached and the house of cards collapses.

The events don't always occur in the same order, and not all of them are necessarily present in every market cycle. But these behaviors are real, and they certainly are elements that rhyme in the markets from decade to decade.

The first time an inexperienced investor lives through an upward market cycle, the beginnings of the progression may seem logical, as the positives compound in a bull market or bubble. The fact that so much good news and good feeling can end in losses can come as a surprise. It is inescapable that it will seem so to the uninitiated, of course, because if the progressions weren't permitted to go on to extremes on the basis of errors in judgment, markets wouldn't reach bull market tops to collapse from (or bear market bottoms to recover from).

∾

On pages 19–21, I discussed the relationship between where we stand in cycles and what that implies for prospective returns. Now, to close this chapter, I want to further illustrate that connection.

In the last few weeks — while on the verge of submitting my final draft of this book — I hit upon a way to show the relationship I have in mind: Let's assume first that the market cycle is at its. midpoint. That usually implies economic growth is on-trend, profits are normal, valuation metrics are reasonable in the context of history, asset prices are in line with intrinsic value, and emotions aren't extreme. Given all the above, the outlook for returns, too, is "normal," meaning the probability distribution governing future returns looks like the one on page 19.

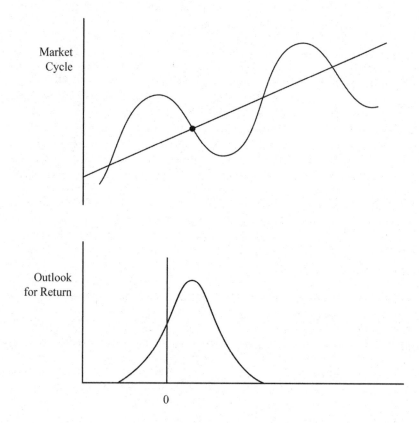

But what happens if the market is, instead, at a cyclical high? Regardless of what's going on in terms of fundamentals, that means valuations are stretched, prices far exceed intrinsic value, and a high level of optimism is baked in. At such a point, the outlook for returns is sub-par and biased toward the negative, as shown by the new distribution below.

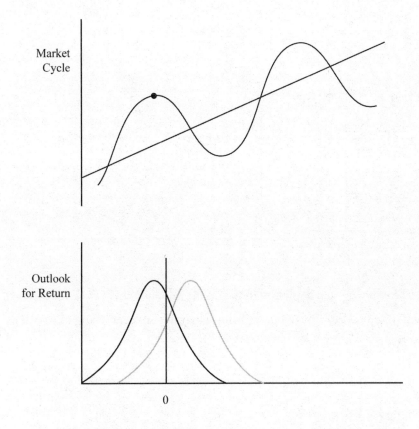

And how about at a cyclical low? Now, thanks to depressed investor psychology, valuation metrics are at historically low levels that suggest the presence of bargains, and thus asset prices are well below intrinsic value. Now the distribution regarding future returns is shifted well to the right, implying unusually high potential for profit.

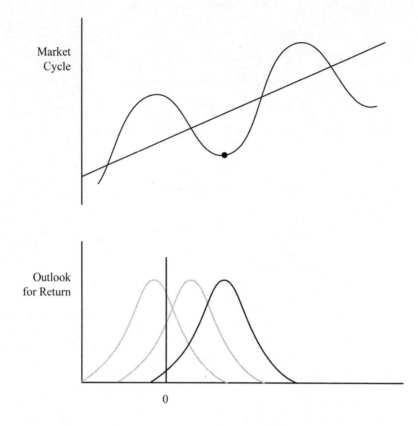

This conceptual depiction indicates the relationship between cycle level and potential for return. It's far from scientific, but everything I know tells me it's right.

XIII

HOW TO COPE WITH
MARKET CYCLES

═══════

What's the key in all of this? To know where the pendulum of psychology and the cycle in valuation stand in their swings. To refuse to buy—and perhaps to sell—when too-positive psychology and the willingness to assign too-high valuations cause prices to soar to peak levels. And to buy when downcast psychology and the desertion of valuation standards on the downside cause panicky investors to create bargains by selling, despite the low prices that result.

The investor's goal is to position capital so as to benefit from future developments. He wants to have more invested when the market rises than when it falls, and to own more of the things that rise more or fall less, and less of the others. The objective is clear. The question is how to accomplish this.

The first step is to decide how you will deal with the future. Some people believe in economic and market forecasting, and in taking the actions that such forecasts demand. Thus they invest more aggressively when forecasts call for favorable events, and vice versa.

As I've made clear, I don't believe in forecasting. Very few people can know enough about what the future holds for it to add to their returns, and the record of most forecasters — in terms of both predicting events better than others and having better investment performance than others as a result — is quite lackluster. A few people become famous in each period for singular, spectacular successes, but usually their next correct forecast doesn't come for many years.

In the absence of the ability to see the future, how can we position our portfolios for what lies ahead? I think much of the answer lies in understanding where the market stands in its cycle and what that implies for its future movements. As I wrote in *The Most Important Thing*, "we may never know where we're going, but we'd better have a good idea where we are."

To do that requires an understanding of the basic nature of cycles in general: what gives rise to their movements, what causes them to progress toward peaks and troughs, and what causes them to retreat from those extremes? We've touched on the key elements that concern us:

- the tendency of basic themes to repeat and of history to rhyme,
- the tendency of things to rise and fall, especially those determined by human nature,
- the way each development in a cycle has implications for the next,
- the way the various cycles interact and influence each other,
- the role of psychology in pushing cyclical phenomena beyond rational levels,
- thus the tendency of cycles to go to extremes,

- their tendency to move from extremes back toward a midpoint, and
- the regularity with which that movement continues past the midpoint, toward the opposite extreme.

These are the generalities that affect cycles of all kinds. In addition, we have to bear in mind the specific elements that influence the market cycle:

- the economic and profit cycles that shape the investment environment,
- the tendency of psychology to overreact to developments in the environment,
- the way risk is considered non-existent and benign at some times, and then enormous, inescapable and lethal at others, and
- the way market prices reflect only positives and overstate them at one point, and then reflect only negatives and ignore all the positives at another.

These are the fundamentals — the basics regarding cycles in general and the specific ways they work in the markets — that we must perceive, attend to and obey. We must use the insights we garner to assess where the market is positioned, what that implies for its future movements, and what we should do as a result.

∿

Equipped with a deep understanding of the above, we turn to the task of figuring out where we stand in the cycle.

What's the key in all of this? To know where the pendulum of psychology and the cycle in valuation stand in their swings. To refuse to buy — and perhaps to sell — when too-positive psychology and the willingness to assign too-high valuations cause prices to soar to peak levels. And to buy when downcast psychology and the desertion of valuation standards on the downside cause panicky investors to create bargains by selling despite the low prices that prevail. As Sir John Templeton put it, "To buy when others are despondently selling and sell when others are greedily buying requires the greatest fortitude and pays the greatest reward."

The upward movement of prices from fair value to excess usually is related to the presence of some combination of important elements:

- generally good news,
- complacency regarding events,
- uniformly upbeat treatment by the media,
- the unquestioning acceptance of optimistic accounts,
- a decline in skepticism,
- a dearth of risk aversion,
- a wide-open credit market, and
- a positive general mood.

Conversely, the collapse of prices from fair value to bargain levels is usually marked by some or all of the following:

- generally bad news,
- rising alarm regarding events,
- highly negative media accounts,
- the wholesale acceptance of scare stories,
- a strong rise in skepticism,
- a significant increase in risk aversion,

- a credit market that has slammed shut, and
- a mood of general depression.

The question is how we can tell where the market stands in its cycle. Importantly, the elements that contribute to the market's rise manifest themselves via valuation metrics — p/e ratios on stocks, yields on bonds, capitalization ratios on real estate, and cash flow multiples on buyouts — that are elevated relative to historic norms. All of these things are precursors of low prospective returns. The reverse is true when a market collapse takes asset prices to bargain valuations. These things can be observed and quantified.

In addition, our understanding of cycle positioning can be greatly aided by an awareness of how investors are behaving. To respond to market cycles and understand their message, one realization is more important than all others: the risk in investing doesn't come primarily from the economy, the companies, the securities, the stock certificates or the exchange buildings. It comes from the behavior of the market participants. So do most of the opportunities for exceptional returns.

When investors act in a prudent manner, reflect risk aversion, apply skepticism and restrain their positive emotions, security prices tend to be reasonable relative to underlying value, making the market a safe and sane place. On the other hand, when investors become euphoric, their over-enthusiastic buying lifts prices to dangerous levels. And when they're despondent, their panicked selling takes prices to bargain lows.

Warren Buffett tells us, "The less prudence with which others conduct their affairs, the greater the prudence with which we should conduct our own affairs." When others are euphoric, we should be terrified. And when others are terrified, we should turn aggressive.

It's not what you buy that determines your results, it's what you pay for it. And what you pay — the security's price and its relationship to intrinsic value — is determined by investor psychology and the resulting behavior. The key to being able to behave in a way that's appropriate given the market climate lies significantly in assessing psychology and the behavior of others. You have to know whether the market is red-hot and thus over-priced, or frigid and thus a bargain.

In "It Is What It Is" (March 2006) — and also in *The Most Important Thing* — I included what I called a guide to market assessment. I can't think of a reason not to include it again here, or of a better substitute. Please note that these points are non-scientific, non-quantitative and non-quantifiable, and even somewhat jocular. But they should give you a sense for the things to watch out for:

Economy:	Vibrant	Sluggish
Outlook:	Positive	Negative
Lenders:	Eager	Reticent
Capital markets:	Loose	Tight
Capital:	Plentiful	Scarce
Terms:	Easy	Restrictive
Interest rates:	Low	High
Yield Spreads:	Narrow	Wide
Investors:	Optimistic	Pessimistic
	Sanguine	Distressed
	Eager to buy	Uninterested in buying

Asset owners:	Happy to hold	Rushing for the exits
Sellers:	Few	Many
Markets:	Crowded	Starved for attention
Funds:	Hard to gain entry	Open to anyone
	New ones daily	Only the best can raise money
	General Partners hold the cards on terms	Limited Partners have bargaining power
Recent performance:	Strong	Weak
Asset prices:	High	Low
Prospective returns:	Low	High
Risk:	High	Low
Popular qualities:	Aggressiveness	Caution and discipline
	Broad reach	Selectivity
The right qualities:	Caution and discipline	Aggressiveness
	Selectivity	Broad reach
Available mistakes:	Buying too much	Buying too little
	Paying up	Walking away
	Taking too much risk	Taking too little risk

As I said in introducing the guide, "for each pair, check off the one you think is most descriptive of the current market. And if you find that most of your checkmarks are in the left-hand column, hold on to your wallet."

These sorts of markers can tell us where we stand in the cycle and what that's likely to imply for the future. Thus they help in what I call "taking the temperature of the market." Here's how I described the process in *The Most Important Thing:*

> If we are alert and perceptive, we can gauge the behavior of those around us and from that judge what we should do.
>
> The essential ingredient here is *inference,* one of my favorite words. Everyone sees what happens each day, as reported in the media. But how many people make an effort to understand what those everyday events say about the psyches of market participants, the investment climate, and thus what should be done in response?
>
> Simply put, we must strive to understand the implications of what's going on around us. When others are recklessly confident and buying aggressively, we should be highly cautious; when others are frightened into inaction or panicked selling, we should become aggressive.
>
> So look around, and ask yourself: Are investors optimistic or pessimistic? Do the media talking heads say the markets should be piled into or avoided? Are novel investment schemes readily accepted or dismissed out of hand? Are securities offerings and fund openings being treated as opportunities to get rich or possible pitfalls? Has the credit cycle rendered capital readily available or impossible to obtain? Are price/earnings ratios high or low in the context of history, and are yield spreads tight or generous?
>
> All of these factors are important, and yet none of them entails forecasting. We can make excellent investment decisions on the basis of present observations, with no need to make guesses about the future.
>
> The key is to take note of things like these and let them tell you what to do. While the markets don't cry out for action along these lines every day, they do at the extremes, when their pronouncements are highly important.

At any time, lots of things are happening in the world, the economy and the investment environment. No one can study, parse, understand and incorporate all of them into investment decisions. And no one need try. At any rate, different events occur in each cycle, and in a different sequence, and with different results.

My point here is that not all the details are important. Rather, the key is to (a) figure out which are the important ones, (b) make inferences about what's going on from the important ones (and then perhaps consider as many of the less-important ones as we can), and (c) conclude from those inferences what are the one or two things that most characterize the investment environment and what action they call for. In other words, being attuned to cyclical developments and their significance.

In particular, however, you can't have the extremes of market cycles without a departure of valuation metrics from their norms. Valuations are the result — and thus symptomatic or indicative — of investor psychology.

The psychological and emotional elements I've listed have their primary impact by convincing investors that past valuation standards have become irrelevant and can be departed from. When investors are flying high and making money, they find it easy to come up with convenient reasons why assets should be untethered from the constraints of valuation norms. The explanation usually begins with, "it's different this time." Watch out for this ominous sign of the willing suspension of disbelief. Likewise, when asset prices collapse in a crash, it's usually because of an assumption that none of the things that supported value in the past can be trusted to work in the future.

So the key to understanding where we stand in the cycle depends on two forms of assessment:

- The first is totally quantitative: gauging valuations. This is an appropriate starting point, for if valuations aren't out of line with his-

tory, the market cycle is unlikely to be highly extended in either
direction.

• And the second is essentially qualitative: awareness of what's going on around us, and in particular of investor behavior. Importantly, it's possible to be disciplined even in observing these largely
   non-quantitative phenomena.

The key questions can be boiled down to two: how are things priced,
and how are investors around us behaving? Assessing these two elements
—consistently and in a disciplined manner—can be very helpful. The answers will give us a sense for where we stand in the cycle.

In closing on this subject, I want to repeat something I've been harping
on: even the best of temperature-taking can't tell us will happen next . . .
just the tendencies.

Since market cycles vary from one to the next in terms of the amplitude,
pace and duration of their fluctuations, they're not regular enough to enable us to be sure what'll happen next on the basis of what has gone before.
Thus, from a given point in the cycle, the market is capable of moving in
any direction: up, flat or down.

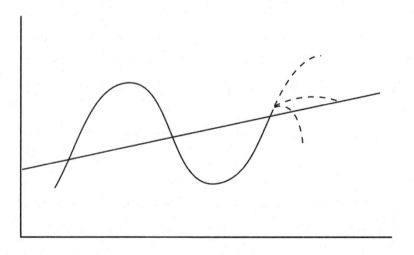

But that doesn't mean all three are equally likely. Where we stand influences the tendencies or probabilities, even if it does not determine future developments with certainty. All other things being equal, when the market is high in its cycle, a downward correction is more likely than continued gains, and vice versa. It doesn't have to work out that way, of course, but that's the safer bet. Assessing our cycle position doesn't tell us what will happen next, just what's more and less likely. But that's a lot.

∾

The best way to teach the recognition of cyclical excesses is through examples of how it can be done at the extremes, where it matters most. Thus over the following pages I'm going to review the formation of two recent bubbles and the crash that followed the second of them. Even the two bubbles were different, but each of these three market events illustrates the importance of assessing the market's temperature.

First, let's review the meteoric rise of stocks in the late 1990s and early 2000, and especially the formation of the Internet bubble. What should the alert investor have noted during that time?

- In the decade of the 1990s, the U.S. economy enjoyed the longest peacetime expansion in its history.
- In December 1996, when the S&P 500 index of equities stood at 721, Fed Chairman Alan Greenspan asked, "How do we know when irrational exuberance has unduly escalated asset values?" But he was never heard from again on this subject, even as the S&P more than doubled to a high of 1527 in 2000.
- In 1994, Prof. Jeremy Siegel of the Wharton School published his book *Stocks for the Long Run*, in which he pointed out that there

had never been a long period of time in which stocks had failed to outperform bonds, cash and inflation.

- Whereas researchers at the University of Chicago had earlier concluded that the normal return on U.S. equities was in the vicinity of 9% per year, in the 1990s the average return on the S&P was nearly 20%.

- The better stocks performed, the more capital investors allocated to them. This was especially true of technology stocks, which were the clear market leaders.

- More tech stocks were added to equity indices like the S&P 500 — meaning index and quasi-index investors had to buy more of them — which made them go up — which attracted still more capital to them. This was a classic "virtuous circle," and no one could imagine it ending.

- The absence of earnings at most "new-economy" companies eliminated any requirement that their stocks should sell at reasonable price/earnings ratios.

- In the latter stages of the bubble, the prices of some dot-com stocks increased several hundred percent on the day of their initial public offerings. To be willing to buy the new stocks at their inflated post-IPO prices, buyers who thought about it would have to have concluded that either (a) the companies' founders had been happy to sell the stocks at a fraction of their true value or (b) the founders knew less about the stocks' value than the buyers did. Both of these conclusions were highly tenuous.

- In order to share in this miracle — and to avoid the pain of watching as others profited — investors took part in IPOs of companies that had no earnings (and in some cases no revenues) and about whose business models they knew little or nothing.

- The year 1999 saw the publication of *Dow 36,000,* a book whose authors, James Glassman and Kevin Hassett, argued that because stocks were so low in risk (see Siegel on page 217), they needn't offer as large a risk premium as they historically had. That meant their prices should immediately rise to levels from which they would offer appropriately reduced prospective returns. Thus the Dow Jones Industrial Average deserved to more than triple from just over 10,000 at the time.

- The p/e ratio on the S&P 500 — fueled by rampaging growth and technology stocks — reached a high of 33 during the tech-stock boom, fully double the post-war norm and the highest valuation in the index's history up to that point in time.

So what ingredients actually were present?

- good economic news,
- favorable articles and books,
- carefree, risk-oblivious behavior on the part of investors,
- unusually strong investment returns,
- extremely high valuations relative to history,
- widespread willingness to pay prices that could not be justified analytically, and
- belief in a perpetual motion machine that would never stop.

This last point is particularly important. Every bubble starts with a grain of truth, as I noted earlier. But the import and profit potential of that truth are overestimated in bubbles; disbelief is suspended; and it is widely accepted that the gains can roll on forever.

Certainly an objective temperature-taker could have known the pieces were in place for a substantial bubble that was likely to fall to earth. Here are some of phenomena as I described them in "bubble.com" (January 2000):

- Webvan Group, which started in business in 1999, had sales of $3.8 million and a $350,000 profit in the September quarter. The stock market currently values it at $7.3 billion.

- On December 9, VA Linux went public at 30 and soared 698% that day to $239, for a market value of $9.5 billion, half that of Apple. To that date, the company's 1999 sales were $17.7 million and it had lost $14.5 million (versus Apple's profit of $600 million in the most recent twelve months).

- Because the price/earnings ratios of Internet companies are so outlandish — usually negative — one may be forced to look to the price/sales ratio in order to speak about valuation. Red Hat, for example, sells at about 1,000 times its annualized revenues in the August 1999 quarter.

- Among non-Internet tech companies, Yahoo! is worth $119 billion, more than General Motors and Ford together. At the current stock price of $432, its p/e ratio on 1999 estimated earnings is just over 1,000.

Under these unusual circumstances, the *Wall Street Journal* wrote on December 10, 1999 that "stock valuations take on an unusually large importance in gauging a business's performance." In other words — in the absence of other signs — people must look to the share price for an indication of how the company is doing. Isn't that backwards? In the old days, investors figured out how the business was doing and then set the share price to reflect it.

In this valuation parameter vacuum, a "lottery ticket mentality" seems to govern the purchase decision. The model for investments in the tech and dot-com companies isn't the likelihood of a 20% or 30% annual return based on projected earnings and p/e ratios, but a shot at a 1,000% gain based on a concept. The pitch may be, "We're looking for first-round financing for a company valued at $30 million that we think can IPO in two years at $2 billion." Or maybe it's "The IPO will be priced at $20. It may end the day at $100 and be at $200 in six months."

Would you play? Could you stand the risk of saying no and being wrong? The pressure to buy can be immense.

There have always been ideas, stocks and IPOs that produced great profits. Yet the pressure to participate wasn't as great as it is today, because in the past the winners made millions, not billions, and it took years, not months. The upside in the deals that've worked so far has been 100-to-1 (give or take a zero). With that kind of potential, (a) the upside becomes irresistible and (b) it doesn't take a very high probability of success to justify the investment. I have said in the past that while the market is usually driven by fear and greed, sometimes the biggest motivator is the fear of missing out. Never was that as true as today. This only intensifies the pressure to join in and crawl further out on that limb of risk.

The bottom line is that in an extreme bubble like this one, the rational investor doesn't have to make fine distinctions. All you have to be able to do is identify nutty behavior when you see it. To me — as an observer viewing it in detached fashion from the sidelines, rather than someone with skin in the tech-investing game — the events of the tech/Internet craze had the appearance of a Hans Christian Andersen tale. Those who participated in it so wanted it to roll on that no one would step forward to say the emperor had no clothes. Developments like those just described were signs of the mass hysteria that is part of every bubble.

Those who were enriched by the performance of equities in the

1990s — and especially by the tech and Internet stocks — took it to fore-tell a new era of prosperity and wealth creation, and they responded to the returns they had enjoyed by ratcheting up their expectations for future returns. (As Charlie Munger quotes the ancient Greek statesman and or-ator Demosthenes, "For what each man wishes, that he also believes to be true.") But cooler heads concluded that euphoria-driven buying in the 1990s had overpaid for value and borrowed from future performance, with highly negative implications. It just took a couple of years for them to be proved right.

The eventual result in 2000–02 was (a) the first three-year decline of the stock market since 1929–31, with a 49% drop in the S&P 500 from top to bottom (ignoring income), (b) massive declines in tech stocks, and (c) losses of 100% on many Internet and e-commerce stocks.

∾

Usually one would expect that the painful deflating of such a bubble — which had been driven by excesses of optimism and credulousness — would have had serious instructional impact, meaning it would take a decade or two for another such bubble to arise. But that was not to be the case. Because it's so important, I'm going to repeat once more what John Kenneth Galbraith said about the learning of financial lessons:

> Contributing to . . . euphoria are two further factors little noted in our time or in past times. The first is the extreme brevity of the financial memory. In consequence, financial disaster is quickly forgotten. In further consequence, when the same or closely similar circumstances occur again, sometimes in only a few years, they are hailed by a new, often youthful, and always supremely self-confident generation as a brilliantly innovative discovery in the financial and larger economic world.

The events that only a few years later began to lead to the sub-prime mortgage boom — adequately described earlier in this book — provided a great example of the way cyclical excesses are built on error:

- As I wrote on page 119, some U.S. leaders decided that only good could come from increased home ownership.
- The federal agencies charged with issuing mortgages got the message and ramped up the availability of mortgages.
- Declining interest rates made mortgages — and thus home ownership — increasingly affordable.
- Increased home affordability and increased mortgage availability allowed home buying to increase and the demand for homes to swell.
- This increased demand caused the prices of homes to increase substantially. The canard that "home prices only go up" became an accepted truth, feeding back to produce still more demand for homes.
- The further platitude that "there can never be a nationwide wave of mortgage defaults" caused mortgage backed securities to be accepted as prime candidates for investment, particularly by financial institutions.
- Wall Street came forward with a model for securitizing prosaic, reliable home mortgages into tranched collateralized debt obligations — the next high-return, low-risk thing.
- The construction and selling of CDOs and other mortgage backed securities (MBS) added greatly to bank profits.
- With relaxed regulations allowing banks to employ materially greater leverage, large amounts of capital were available for investment in the equity required for MBS creation.

- The meteoric growth of MBS packaging created rapidly increasing demand for the essential raw material in the process: newly issued mortgages.

- In order to expand the volume of mortgages they issued, lenders hit on novel ways to increase their appeal to borrowers: interest-only mortgages that minimized monthly payments by eliminating the traditional requirement that the principal balance be paid down; adjustable-rate mortgages that allowed borrowers to benefit from the ultra-low interest rates at the short end of the yield curve; and, most importantly, "sub-prime" mortgages (sometimes called "liar loans") that didn't require applicants to document income and employment.

- With sub-prime mortgages being packaged into securities and sold onward, as opposed to being retained as in the past, lenders' emphasis shifted from borrowers' creditworthiness to loan volume. With lenders being paid fees simply for making loans — and able to sell them off immediately and thus retain no risk of default — there was no reason for them to worry about the creditworthiness of their borrowers. Clearly this gave them perverse incentives. (Incentives like these — which allow participants to engage in pro-risk behavior without having to worry about the consequences — were described in the Global Financial Crisis as creating "moral hazard," a term that came into widespread use. While it's heard less often these days, the concept survives, and it remains dangerous.)

- The key to the purported success of sub-prime mortgage backed securities lay in "financial engineering" performed by "quants" and Ph.D.'s, many of them in their first jobs. They modeled risk based on the flawed assumption that mortgage defaults would remain uncorrelated and benign as in the past.

- The creation of large amounts of sub-prime MBS meant there was a lot of business for the rating agencies whose imprimatur was essential. But these profitable assignments would go to the agency that provided the highest rating. This led to ratings shopping and created further perverse incentives, this time supporting widespread ratings inflation.

- These trends caused the rating agencies to issue many thousands of triple-A ratings to mortgage backed securities (as compared to the *four* U.S. companies enjoying triple-A ratings at the time). Rating agency personnel clearly lacked the ability to fully understand the complex MBS they were assessing.

- Banks and other financial institutions bought huge amounts of MBS, abetted by "risk-management" techniques such as Value at Risk that relied heavily on the short, benign history and overly generous ratings, and thus vastly understated the risk buyers were assuming.

- All of the above occurred in and was facilitated by risk-oblivious attitudes characterized by risk-is-gone rhetoric (see page 120).

So what was at the root of the formation of this bubble? According to "Now It's All Bad?" (September 2007):

> . . . a standard combination that proved perfectly incendiary:
>
> - underlying greed,
> - good returns in the up-leg of the cycle,
> - euphoria and complacency,
> - a free-and-easy credit market,
> - Wall Street's inventiveness and salesmanship, and
> - investors' naiveté.

The resulting developments that fed the upswing are clear:

- a huge decrease in risk aversion, and thus the disappearance of skepticism,
- the acceptance of sweeping positive generalizations regarding homes and mortgages,
- excessive faith in new tools like financial engineering and risk management, and
- widespread blindness to the impact of improper incentives on participants in the process.

In addition to short memories, psychological excesses and logical lapses, the bubble that arose in mortgage backed securities was abetted by two additional factors:

- Because this new bubble arose in mortgage-land — a part of the financial markets completely separate from that which had been visited by the tech and Internet bubble — the fixed income investors and financial institutions it appealed to were ones who hadn't been affected firsthand by the other, and hadn't learned from it.
- The terrible recent performance of equities had so discouraged equity investors — and interest rates brought low by the dovish Fed had so diminished the yields available on fixed income investments — that investors gave up on obtaining strong returns from stocks and bonds. That rendered them highly susceptible to the promise of a new source of return without risk: mortgage backed securities.

This is a good time for a valuable aside. Falling for the sure thing — the asset that will provide return without risk, or what I call the "silver bullet" (dating back to *The Lone Ranger*, a 1950s TV Western about a lawman whose gunshots never missed) — is one of investors' greatest recurring failings. It exemplifies "what every man wishes," as Demosthenes said, but it makes no sense. If there were a silver bullet:

- Why would the purveyor offer it to you rather than buying it up himself?
- And wouldn't everyone else buy it and drive up its price to the point where it's no longer a sure thing?

I've seen dozens of silver bullets touted over the course of my 48-year career. Not one has proved out. No investment strategy or tactic will ever deliver a high return without risk, especially to buyers lacking a high level of investing skill. Outstanding investment results can only come from exceptional skill (or perhaps in isolated moments from good luck).

As I said earlier, bubbles generally spring from a grain of truth. But they're all taken too far, and their eventual puncturing brings the greatest pain in the investment world. Belief in a silver bullet underlies many bubbles. The fact that investors are willing to swallow a promise of return without risk is an infallible indicator that skepticism is in short supply, psychology is overheated, and the subject asset is overestimated and thus probably overpriced. Watch out for it, and resist if you can. By definition, when it comes to bubbles, few people do.

I would sum up the key conclusion this way: The sub-prime mortgage bubble arose from broad acceptance that phenomena would work that had never before been seen in action. The analysis of investment vehicles should entail (a) the application of skepticism and conservative assumptions and (b) examination over a long history that includes some trying times. These things were clearly missing.

In fact, most bubbles, if not all, are characterized by the unquestioning acceptance of things that have never held true in the past; of valuations that are dramatically out of line with historic norms; and/or of investment techniques and tools that haven't been tested.

～

The sub-prime mortgage bubble demonstrated an extremely important principle in action that I haven't touched upon before now. The financial and investment environment—and the performance of investment techniques and instruments—is not immutable. Rather, as I've said many times with regard to cycles, these things are affected by the involvement of people.

There is no such thing as a market that is separate from—and unaffected by—the people who make it up. The behavior of the people in the market changes the market. When their attitudes and behavior change, the market will change.

In the case at hand:

- market forces changed the participants' motivations, as just described,
- these changed motivations changed their behavior, and
- their changed behavior clearly determined the results.

An essential progression was at work, as is clear to see:

- History was taken as saying there couldn't be a nationwide wave of mortgage defaults.
- Acceptance of this benign history caused vast sums to be invested in mortgage backed securities.
- It permitted the securities to be structured aggressively.
- It also caused rating agencies to extrapolate the benign experience and grant high ratings.
- Most importantly, the strong demand for mortgage backed securities created a need for the raw material — mortgage loans — and led to an eagerness to issue them that caused lending standards to deteriorate.
- These developments, taken together, virtually guaranteed that there *would* be a nationwide wave of mortgage defaults.

As I mentioned earlier, because of the impact of careless lending practices — the import of which went largely unnoticed and unremarked at the time — the default experience on mortgages issued from the late 1990s through 2007 turned out to be much worse than it historically had been; worse than the security structurers and rating agencies had thought possible; and worse than buyers' models had said it would be. Ignoring this possibility made a significant contribution to the creation of the sub-prime mortgage bubble. Its occurrence caused the resulting crisis.

The key is to understand that the behavior of investors can alter the market, changing the results that investors can expect the market to deliver. This reflects George Soros's theory of reflexivity:

In situations that have thinking participants, the participants' . . . distorted views can influence the situation to which they relate because false views lead to inappropriate actions. ("Soros: General Theory of Reflexivity," *Financial Times,* October 26, 2009)

People trying to understand how things work in the economic and financial worlds should take this lesson very much to heart.

~

All it takes for the perpetual motion machine to grind to a halt is the failure of one or two assumptions and the operation of some general rules:

- Interest rates can go up as well as down.
- Platitudes can fail to hold.
- Improper incentives can lead to destructive behavior.
- Attempts to quantify risk in advance — particularly as to novel financial products for which there is no history — will often be unavailing.
- The "worst case" can indeed be exceeded on the downside.

The error in all these things is always clear in hindsight. But the risky practices with regard to mortgages and mortgage backed securities — which became so prominent and important — were taking place in an obscure corner of the financial world. Thus they were invisible to chief investment officers, portfolio strategists, equity investors, alternative investment managers, traditional bond buyers, and seemingly even mortgage investors.

We at Oaktree were fortunate in the years in which the mortgage bubble arose — leading up to the Global Financial Crisis — to understand that the credit cycle was becoming extended in the upward direction, and thus that the markets were increasingly precarious. This led us to sell assets;

replace large, liquidating distressed debt funds with smaller ones; increase our level of risk-consciousness and conservatism; and raise a stand-by fund several times our largest ever in order to take advantage of the distressed debt opportunities we felt might materialize.

What was the basis on which we did this? In retrospect it was easy . . . although it never seems as easy in real time. All you really had to do in 2005–07 was make the following general observations:

- the Fed had reduced the base rate of interest to very low levels in order to ward off the depressing effects of the tech bubble's bursting, as well as concern over Y2K;
- because of the low yields available on Treasurys and high grade bonds, as well as the disenchantment with equities that had resulted from their three-year decline in 2000–02, investors were eager to put money into alternative instruments;
- investors had shrugged off the pain of the collapse of the tech bubble in 2000 and the telecom meltdown and corporate scandals of 2001–02;
- thus little risk aversion was present (especially in areas other than equities, which remained out of favor), rendering investors generally eager for investments in exotic, structured and synthetic instruments; and
- as a result of all the above, the markets were wide open for the issuance of low-quality debt, poorly structured instruments and untested alternatives.

These were our observations, and it was the last that most called our attention to the negative trends that were afoot. It felt like there wasn't a day on which either Bruce Karsh or I didn't visit each other's office to complain about a newly issued security, saying, "It shouldn't be possible to issue a piece of junk like this. The fact that it is means there's something wrong with the market." Those risky deals told us fear, skepticism and risk aversion were insufficient, and greed, gullibility and risk tolerance were in the ascendency. The implications of this combination are never good.

All the points noted here were obvious and not subject to debate. All that mattered is whether you made these observations and drew the appropriate conclusions. You didn't have to fully understand what was wrong with sub-prime mortgages or deconstruct mortgage backed securities and highly structured collateralized debt obligations. *We certainly didn't.*

And, by the way, in those years when the mortgage bubble was building, stocks weren't doing well or selling at lofty multiples, and the economy wasn't booming (and thus necessarily heading for a recession). But if you made the observations just listed, you likely would have concluded, as we did, that it was time to reduce the quantum of risk in your portfolio. That's really all it took.

And here are the results of the bursting of the mortgage bubble and the associated contagion, as shown in the performance of some of the standard investment indices in 2008, the year it all came apart. Clearly it was a year in which it was enormously important to have reduced risk.

Standard & Poor's 500 Stocks	(37.0)%
Dow Jones Industrial Average	(31.9)
NASDAQ Composite	(40.0)
MSCI Europe, Australasia, Far East Stocks	(45.1)
Citigroup High Yield Market Index	(25.9)
Merrill Lynch Global High Yield European Issuer Index (in Euro)	(32.6)
Credit Suisse Leveraged Loan Index	(28.8)
Credit Suisse Western European Loan Index (in Euro)	(30.2)

~

Finally in discussing how to detect and respond to market cycle extremes, I want to return once more to the widespread panic that followed the bankruptcy filing by Lehman Brothers in September 2008.

Although the sub-prime mortgage crisis originated in a small corner of the financial and investment world, the impact was soon felt widely, particularly by the financial institutions that had underestimated the risk in mortgage backed securities and thus invested too heavily in them. As a result of the threat to these essential institutions, the impact metastasized to the stock and bond markets in all countries — and then to economies all around the world — in the form of the Global Financial Crisis.

Thus, as I described earlier, money market funds and commercial paper had to be guaranteed by the U.S. government. A number of prominent banks and financial institutions failed or had to be bailed out/rescued/absorbed. No one knew how far the carnage would spread. The equity and debt markets collapsed. Now the generalizing was on the negative side: "the financial system could totally melt down" in a vicious circle without end.

Since the generalizations were on the downside, the error-making machine went into reverse. No greed, only fear. No optimism, only pessimism. No risk tolerance, only risk aversion. No ability to see positives, only negatives. No willingness to interpret things positively, only negatively. No ability to imagine good outcomes, only bad. Thus we reached the day on which I had the discussion mentioned back on pages 131–132, in which the pension fund head was unable or unwilling to accept that any assumption regarding possible defaults could be conservative enough.

What was the essential observation? Here's what I wrote in "The Limits to Negativism" (October 2008):

Contrarianism—doing the opposite of what others do, or "leaning against the wind"—is essential for investment success. But as the credit crisis reached a peak last week, people succumbed to the wind rather than resisting. I found very few who were optimistic; most were pessimistic to some degree. Some became genuinely depressed —even a few great investors I know. Increasingly negative tales of the coming meltdown were exchanged via email. No one applied skepticism, or said "that horror story's unlikely to be true." Pessimism fed on itself. People's only concern was bullet-proofing their portfolios to get through the coming collapse, or raising enough cash to meet redemptions. The one thing they weren't doing last week was making aggressive bids for securities. So prices fell and fell, several points at a time—the old expression is "gapped down."

The key—as usual—was to become skeptical of what "everyone" was saying and doing. One might have said, "Sure, the negative story may turn out to be true, but certainly it's priced into the market. So there's little to be gained from betting on it. On the other hand, if it turns out not to be true, the appreciation from today's depressed levels will be enormous. I buy!" The negative story may have looked compelling, but it's the positive story—which few believed—that held, and still holds, the greater potential for profit.

At this market cycle extreme, all the news truly was negative . . . and certainly not imaginary. The only questions I received were "How far will it go?" and "What will be the effects?" Given that asset prices reflected nothing but abject pessimism regarding these things—I'd say near-suicidal thinking—the key to profiting lay in recognizing that even in the face of uniformly bad news and a very poor outlook, pessimism can be overdone, and thus assets can become too cheap.

It was the excessiveness of the prevailing pessimism that led me to write "The Limits to Negativism" at the credit market's low ebb in October 2008. In it I pointed out, as mentioned in the chapter on attitudes toward risk, that the superior investor's essential skepticism "calls for pessimism when optimism is excessive. But it also calls for optimism when pessimism is excessive." That variety of skepticism was totally lacking in the market's darkest days, of course.

Shortly after Lehman's bankruptcy filing on September 15, 2008, Bruce Karsh and I reached the conclusion that (a) no one could know how far the financial institution meltdown would go, but (b) negativity was certainly rampant and very possibly excessive, and assets looked terribly cheap. Thinking strategically, we decided that if the financial world ended —which no one could rule out—it wouldn't matter whether we'd bought or not. But if the world didn't end and we hadn't bought, we would have failed to do our job.

So we bought debt aggressively. Oaktree invested more than a half a billion dollars a week over the fifteen weeks from September 15 through the end of the year. Some days we thought we were going too fast, and some days too slow; that probably meant we had it about right. The world didn't end; the vicious cycle of financial institution implosion stopped with Lehman Brothers; the capital markets reopened; the financial institutions came back to life; debt was again able to be refinanced; bankruptcies turned out to be very few relative to history; and the assets we bought appreciated substantially. In short, paying heed to the cycle was rewarded.

∿

While we're reviewing the climate in late 2008, this is an appropriate time for a discussion of investor behavior on the way to, and at, market bottoms.

First, what is a bottom? It's the point when the lowest prices of the cycle are reached. Thus a bottom can be viewed as the day the last panicked holder sells, or the last day on which sellers predominate relative to buyers. For whatever reason, it's the last day prices go down, and thus the day they reach their nadir. (Of course these definitions are highly exaggerated. The expression "a bottom" — like "a top" — describes a period of time, not a day. Thus the phrase "the last day" is mostly a figure of speech.) From the bottom, prices rise, since there are no holders left to capitulate and sell, or because the buyers now want to buy more strongly than the sellers want to sell.

The question I want to touch on here is, "When should one begin to buy?" I made reference in earlier chapters to "falling knives," which constitute a very important concept. When a market is cascading downward, investors can often be heard to say, "We're not going to try to catch a falling knife." In other words, "The trend is downward and there's no way to know when it'll stop, so why should we buy before we're sure the bottom has been reached?"

What I think they're really saying is, "We're scared — in particular of buying before the decline has stopped, and thus of looking bad — so we're going to wait until the bottom has been reached, the dust has settled, and the uncertainty has been resolved." But hopefully by now I've made it abundantly clear that when the dust has settled and investors' nerves have steadied, the bargains will be gone.

At Oaktree, we strongly reject the idea of waiting for the bottom to start buying.

- First, there's absolutely no way to know when the bottom has been reached. There's no neon sign that lights up. The bottom can be recognized only after it has been passed, since it is defined as the day before the recovery begins. By definition, this can be identified only after the fact.
- And second, it's usually during market slides that you can buy the largest quantities of the thing you want, from sellers

who are throwing in the towel and while the non-knife-catch-ers are hugging the sidelines. But once the slide has culminated in a bottom, by definition there are few sellers left to sell, and during the ensuing rally it's buyers who predominate. Thus the selling dries up and would-be buyers face growing competi-tion.

We began to buy distressed debt immediately after Lehman filed for bankruptcy protection in mid-September 2008 as described on page 235, and we continued through year-end, as prices went lower and lower. By the first quarter of 2009, other investors had collected themselves, caught on to the values that were available, and gathered some capital for investment. But with the motivated sellers done selling and buying having begun, it was too late for them to buy in size without pushing up prices.

Like so many other things in the investment world that might be tried on the basis of certitude and precision, waiting for the bottom to start buying is a great example of folly. So if targeting the bottom is wrong, when should you buy? The answer's simple: when price is below in-trinsic value. What if the price continues downward? Buy more, as now it's probably an even greater bargain. All you need for ultimate success in this regard is (a) an estimate of intrinsic value, (b) the emotional for-titude to persevere, and (c) eventually to have your estimate of value proved correct.

∿

Here's how the prominent investment indices did the following year. The returns that were available in 2009 show the importance of having recog-nized a cycle at a negative extreme and having bought in (or at least held on through) the accompanying chaos.

Standard & Poor's 500 Stocks	26.5%
Dow Jones Industrial Average	22.7
NASDAQ Composite	45.4
MSCI Europe, Australasia, Far East Stocks (in US$)	27.8
Citigroup High Yield Market Index	55.2
BofA Merrill Lynch Global High Yield European Issuer Index	83.0
Credit Suisse Leveraged Loan Index	44.9
Credit Suisse Western European Loan Index (in Euro)	47.2

It's time for another aside: If you look at the last two tables — those showing big losses in 2008 and big gains in 2009 — it's easy to conclude that the two years together were something of a non-event. For example, if you put $100 into the Credit Suisse Leveraged Loan Index on the first day of 2008, you would have lost 29% over the course of the year and had only $71 left at the end. But then you would have gained 45% in 2009 and ended up with $103 at the conclusion of the two-year period, for a net gain of $3. The two-year results in the asset classes listed above ranged from moderate net losses to moderate net gains.

It matters enormously, however, what you did in between. Yes, holding on would have enabled you to recoup most or all of your losses and end up well, with results as described above. But if you lost your nerve and sold at the trough — or if, having bought with borrowed money, you received a margin call you couldn't meet and saw your positions sold out from under you — you experienced the decline but not the recovery, and your net result in this "non-event" two-year period was disastrous.

For this reason, it's important to note that exiting the market after a decline — and thus failing to participate in a cyclical rebound — is truly the cardinal sin in investing. Experiencing a mark-to-market loss in the downward phase of a cycle isn't fatal in and of itself, as long as you hold through the beneficial upward part as well. It's converting that downward fluctuation into a permanent loss by selling out at the bottom that's really terrible.

Thus understanding cycles and having the emotional and financial wherewithal needed to live through them is an essential ingredient in investment success.

∾

Before I declare victory in the Global Financial Crisis and move on, I want to state firmly that the success my colleagues and I enjoyed in profiting from this cycle wasn't inevitable. That's because — reflecting Elroy Dimson's theme — the good outcome we got wasn't the only outcome that could have materialized. I'm convinced that if Hank Paulson, Tim Geithner and Ben Bernanke hadn't acted when they did, or if they had acted differently, or if their actions hadn't been as successful as they were, a financial meltdown and replay of the Great Depression absolutely could have occurred. In that case our actions wouldn't have been cause for celebration.

I fear that people may look back at the decline of 2008 and the recovery that followed and conclude that declines can always be depended on to be recouped promptly and easily, and thus there's nothing to worry about from down-cycles. But I think those are the wrong lessons from the Crisis, since the outcome that actually occurred was so much better than some of the "alternative histories" (as Nassim Nicholas Taleb calls them) that could have occurred instead. And if those incorrect lessons are the ones that are learned, as I believe they may have been, then they're likely to bring on behavior that increases the amplitude of another dramatic boom/bust cycle someday, maybe one with more serious and long-lasting ramifications for investors and for all of society.

But things did break for us in the recovery from the Crisis, and for all "long" investors. Certainly we positioned our clients' portfolios correctly for the future that materialized, and a lot of it was because of our feeling for the way in which psychological and market cycles operate. Given the inability to predict the future, that's the best anyone can do.

~

Bubbles and crashes have a pattern all their own: a logic — or illogic — the essence of which rhymes from one instance to the next. The three episodes reviewed here show the oscillation of the cycle at its most extreme, and hopefully they provide an indication of how cycles can be recognized and dealt with.

I want to make a few last, essential points.

- First, every element in the progressions I've described was clear to see at the time, providing investors could keep their emotions and distorted perception from getting in the way.
- Second, drawing the essential inferences — and thus taking the appropriate actions — didn't require any forecasting at all. The descriptions of the actual progressions are compelling, with no guesses needed regarding the future. The events and resulting cyclical excesses dictated profitable behavior.
- Finally, however, while I say the events were self-evident and the implications obvious, I want to state definitively that nothing was easy at the time. Even the best and least emotional among us are subjected to the same inputs and stimuli as everyone else. We were never sure, but we did the right thing nevertheless. And while the errors leading up to the Global Financial Crisis were easily recognizable, the timing of their correcting was absolutely beyond predicting. The best investors can do is act in light of what they see in the environment. But they must bear in mind what John Maynard

Keynes is reputed to have said: "The market can remain irrational longer than you can remain solvent."

∾

To close on the subject of dealing with cyclical events, I want to provide one more example, from 1991. Leveraged buyouts had boomed in the 1980s, thanks to the ability of buyers of companies to access significant amounts of debt capital, often ranging up to 95% of the total purchase price. This led to many of the subject companies being saddled with debt they wouldn't be able to service in the recession that followed; to large numbers of defaults and bankruptcies; and thus to high yield bonds' first crisis. These developments came to a head just after we formed our Funds II and IIb for distressed debt. Here's how I assessed the environment in a letter to their investors on January 23, 1991:

> In general, the market prices of distressed company debt declined during 1990. Some of this was driven by fundamentals, as the market value of all assets weakened along with the economy, and some was due to "technical conditions," meaning the supply of this sort of debt ballooned and buyers were discouraged and withdrew.
>
> The worsening economic and psychological climate gives us the opportunity to pick and choose among a large number of prospective investments at bargain prices. The environment is dreary, as much of what one buys is soon quoted lower, and there is no ebullience.
>
> These are exactly the conditions under which we want to be working. When buyers are enjoying themselves, and when they are exchanging "high fives" because everything they buy goes higher the next day and makes them feel smart, the "pain index" is too low and buyers are emboldened.
>
> Today's conditions tell me we are more likely to be getting bargains than if we were having fun. There are few competing bidders to drive up the prices of the things we want to buy. Each purchase

price is more likely to turn out to have been a "low" than a "high." In short, this is a good time to be putting money to work in a contrarian investment area such as ours.

We cannot presume to begin investing on the day the economy and market hit bottom. Our greatest hope is that the low point will occur sometime during the period when we are actively investing a fund, and that we will buy on the way to, during, and after that moment.

This is a good example of taking the temperature of the market in real time . . . not just because it was me who took it, and not just because it turned out to be right (the distressed debt funds we were investing at that time had some of the highest returns we've ever achieved). Rather, it was good because it detected and pushed back against the depressing emotional influences that were keeping others from buying. It shows we knew the "dreary" conditions and mark-to-market losses that were driving buyers away were more likely to have favorable rather than unfavorable implications for subsequent returns, and that declining prices are good for buyers, not bad.

Understanding what things really mean — rather than how they make investors feel — is the first step toward doing the things that are right for the times.

∾

Having allowed this chapter to reach great length, I'm going to end with a general discussion of how to think about positioning a portfolio as the market moves through its cycle.

I think it's helpful to take an organized approach to what I call the "twin risks." What I'm talking about here is the fact that investors have to deal daily with two possible sources of error. The first is obvious: the risk of losing money. The second is a bit more subtle: the risk of missing opportunity.

Investors can eliminate either one, but doing so will expose them entirely to the other. So most people balance the two.

What should an investor's normal stance be regarding the two risks: evenly balanced, or favoring one or the other? The answer depends mostly on one's goals, circumstances, personality and ability to withstand risk (and on the same things with regard to one's clients, if any).

And separate and apart from his normal posture, should the investor alter the balance from time to time? And if so, how? I think investors should try to appropriately adjust their stance if they (a) feel they have the requisite insight and (b) are willing to expend effort and bear the risk of being wrong. They should do this based on where the market is in its cycle. In short, when the market is high in its cycle, they should emphasize limiting the potential for losing money, and when the market is low in its cycle, they should emphasize reducing the risk of missing opportunity.

How? Try to travel into the future and look back. In 2023, do you think you're more likely to say, "Back in 2018, I wish I'd been more aggressive" or "Back in 2018, I wish I'd been more defensive"? And is there anything today about which you'd be likely to say, "In 2018, I missed the chance of a lifetime to buy xyz"? What you think you might say a few years down the road can help you figure out what you should do today.

The above decisions relate directly to the choice between aggressiveness and defensiveness. When an investor wants to reduce his chance of losing money, he should invest more defensively. More worried about missing opportunity? In that case, increased aggressiveness is called for. Varying one's stance should be done in response to where the market stands in its cycle and, again, this can be approached in terms of how the market is valued and how other investors are behaving—the two elements in assessing the market mentioned earlier.

When most investors are behaving aggressively, that's a good signal that the market is a risky place, since little risk aversion is being applied. And investors' aggressiveness is likely to have resulted directly in elevated asset prices. In both ways, as I mentioned on page 211, the aggressiveness of others makes the market risky for us.

A good way to think about this decision is to consider which attributes are right for the current market environment. In late 2008/early 2009, an investor needed only two things to make a lot of money: money to invest and the nerve to invest it. If he had those two things, he made a lot of money in the years that followed. In retrospect, what he didn't need was caution, conservativism, risk control, discipline, selectivity and patience; the more of those things he had, the less money he made.

Does that mean "money and nerve" is always a surefire formula for investment success? Absolutely not. If an investor had money and nerve in early 2007, he bore the full brunt of the Global Financial Crisis. That's when he needed caution, conservativism, risk control, discipline, selectivity and patience. Moreover, even in late 2008/early 2009, intelligent investors couldn't completely abandon caution and discipline, because there was no way for them to know that the recovery from the GFC would be so quick and the aftermath so relatively painless for investors. At Oaktree, we invested a lot, but we emphasized the senior debt of high-quality companies, not the junior debt and weaker issuers in which, as it turned out, we would have made even more money.

Among the many factors that make investing interesting is the fact that there's no tactic or approach that always works. The only way to try to be correctly positioned as the cycle moves is to make well-reasoned judgments and adjust the attributes employed. But it's not easy.

One way people tend to respond to the challenges these days is to ask, "What inning are we in?" Ever since the financial meltdown in late 2008,

I've encountered this question on a regular basis. What people really mean by it is, "Where do we stand in the cycle?" In the fourth quarter of 2008 they wondered, "How much of the pain has been felt already, and how much more lies ahead?" More recently they've been inquiring primarily about the credit cycle: how much longer will it continue on the upswing — making it easier to borrow — and when will credit availability begin to tighten?

I consider these questions in the light of my sense for how far things have gone, and I answer in the form the questioners want: second inning (just getting started), fifth inning (game half over), or eighth inning (nearing the end). But recently I've become more conscious of the limitation of this approach: unlike a normal baseball game, we have no way to know how long a particular cycle will go on. There is no regulation length. A normal baseball game will last nine innings, but an economic or market cycle could go seven, nine, twelve or fourteen. These things are not knowable.

None of these approaches offers a foolproof technique for deciding how to position portfolios. There'll all just ways to think systematically about something that isn't subject to easy answers. But hopefully they suggest a route that's superior to deciding on the basis of emotion, guesswork or just following the herd.

How you deal with cycles is one of the most important things in investing. Cycles will happen to you. What you do in response is key.

XIV

CYCLE POSITIONING

Successfully positioning a portfolio for the market movements that lie ahead is dependent on what you do (turning aggressive or defensive) and when you do it (based on a superior understanding of what cycles imply for future market moves).

I once knew a man who was congenitally optimistic and aggressive — perhaps because he'd had the good sense to be born rich and had led a charmed life. He never exhibited self-doubt or seemed to question the accuracy of his forecasts or the likelihood that his stratagems would succeed. He was aggressive as long as I knew him, in what turned out to be a great time for aggressiveness. That experience inspired me to coin a phrase to describe the forces at work:

> There are three ingredients for success — aggressiveness, timing and skill — and if you have enough aggressiveness at the right time, you don't need that much skill.

∾

In February 2017, I found myself working on the final chapters of this book while on vacation in India. One day I visited one of the world's great sights—Jaipur's Amer Fort—and attempted to capture a small fraction of its beauty in photos. While reviewing my photos afterwards, I had the good luck to stumble on some I had taken a few months earlier in another exotic location: China.

In the course of that visit, a Beijing-based client had asked me a series of provocative questions, and in answering them I made some scribbles, as I often do, on a whiteboard. Answers came to me that day that hadn't crossed my mind before. Recognizing that, I took photos of the board with my iPhone before leaving. (What an innovation: twenty years ago I would never have had a camera at a presentation.) Three months later, while reviewing my photographic handiwork at the Amer Fort, I came across those photos from China and thought back to those ideas for the first time. They'll provide much of the grist for this chapter.

Now I found myself in bed in India, after a night's sleep cut short by the 10½-hour time difference from New York. For some reason, a connection dawned between the above saying about success, my photos from Beijing, and the question of how to deal with cycles. In short, I had a thought about how to parse the main components of investment skill.

(Note that I say "a connection dawned" rather than "I made a connection." I consciously choose the passive form here, because I often do feel passive, in that ideas "come to me," rather than feeling I develop them through an effortful, intentional process. That's how many of my insights arise, usually aided by the reduction of a thought to a graphic representation like those I made in China. That's just how my mind works.)

Back when I first arrived at the explanation of success stated above, by the word "timing" I had meant "lucky timing." After all, what could be better than being aggressive at a fortuitous time? But lying in bed in India, I noted that good timing doesn't have to be exclusively the result of luck. Rather, good timing in investing can come from diligently assessing where we are in a cycle and then doing the right thing as a result. The study of cycles is really about how to position your portfolio for the possible outcomes that lie ahead. That, in one sentence, is what this book is about.

~

I'd like to return to that simple sentence and apply a little more thought regarding the formula for investment success. I conclude that it should be considered in terms of six main components, or rather three pairings:

- **Cycle positioning** — the process of deciding on the risk posture of your portfolio in response to your judgments regarding the principal cycles
- **Asset selection** — the process of deciding which markets, market niches and specific securities or assets to overweight and underweight

Positioning and selection are the two main tools in portfolio management. It may be an over-simplification, but I think everything investors do falls under one or the other of these headings.

- **Aggressiveness** — the assumption of increased risk: risking more of your capital; holding lower-quality assets; making investments that are more reliant on favorable macro outcomes; and/or employing financial leverage or high-beta (market-sensitive) assets and strategies
- **Defensiveness** — the reduction of risk: investing less capital and holding cash instead; emphasizing safer assets; buying things than can do relatively well even in the absence of prosperity; and/or shunning leverage and beta

The choice between aggressiveness and defensiveness is the principal dimension in which investors position portfolios in response to where they think they stand in the cycles and what that implies for future market developments.

- **Skill** — the ability to make these decisions correctly on balance (although certainly not in every case) through a repeatable intellectual process and on the basis of reasonable assumptions regarding the future. Nowadays this has come to be known by its academic name: "alpha"
- **Luck** — what happens on the many occasions when skill and reasonable assumptions prove to be of no avail — that is, when randomness has more effect on events than do rational processes, whether resulting in "lucky breaks" or "tough luck"

Skill and luck are the prime elements that determine the success of portfolio management decisions. Without skill on an investor's part, decisions shouldn't be expected to produce success. In fact, there's something called negative skill, and for people who are saddled with it, flipping a coin or abstaining from decisions would lead to better results. And luck is the wildcard; it can make good decisions fail and bad ones succeed, but mostly in the short run. In the long run, it's reasonable to expect skill to win out.

Part of my Indian awakening — stemming from my ruminations in China — concerned the dichotomy between selection and positioning, and the way that skill influences the outcome of those two pursuits.

A market will do what it will do. Some of the outcome will be the result of economic events and corporate profitability; some will be determined by investor psychology and the resulting behavior; and some will be determined by randomness or luck. We may have some ideas about what the future will bring in terms of market performance, they may be based on sound or defective reasoning, and they may prove to be right or wrong. But let's take the market's future performance—whatever it will be, whether knowable or not—as the starting point for our discussion here. Let's express the usual expectation for a market's behavior as a probability distribution:

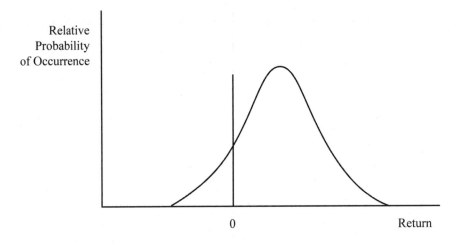

This is the starting point or baseline—the canvas, if you will—for an investor's actions. The question is whether he has the skill required to improve on the market's performance through active decision making, or whether he should give up on doing so and instead invest passively, settling for market performance.

I mentioned above the two main ways in which an investor can add to returns: cycle positioning and asset selection. I'll start by going into great depth regarding the first.

As I also said, I believe cycle positioning primarily consists of choosing between aggressiveness and defensiveness: increasing and decreasing exposure to market movements.

Let's say you conclude you're in a propitious environment:

- the economic and profit cycle are on the rise and/or likely to meet or exceed people's expectations,
- investor psychology and attitudes toward risk are depressed (or at least sober) rather than feverish, and thus
- asset prices are moderate to low relative to intrinsic value.

In such a case, aggressiveness is called for. So you increase your commitments and add to your portfolio's risk posture and "beta" (market sensitivity). The dotted line in the graphic below shows the outlook for your performance. You have increased your potential for gains if the market does well *and* for losses if it does poorly.

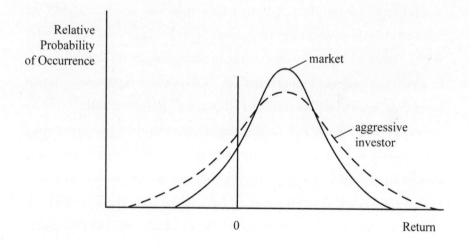

If your judgments are validated by a market rise, your aggressively positioned portfolio, with its enhanced market sensitivity, will rise even more, making you an outperformer, as shown in the following graphic:

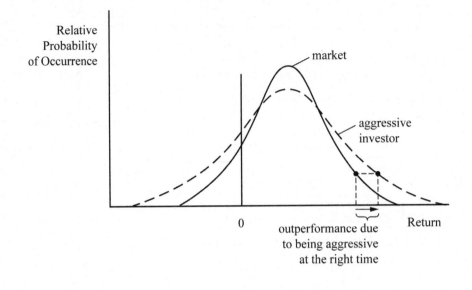

The recipe for success here consists of (a) thoughtful analysis of where the market stands in its cycle, (b) a resulting increase in aggressiveness, and (c) being proved right. These things can be summed up as "skill" or "alpha" at cycle positioning. Of course, "c"—being proved right—isn't fully a matter within anyone's control, in particular because of the degree to which it is subject to randomness. So being proved right won't happen every time, even to skillful investors who reason things out well.

On the other hand, your analysis might tell you the cycle positioning is poor—the economy is tiring, psychology is excessively optimistic, and thus so are asset prices—meaning you should tend toward defensiveness. In that case, you should take some capital off the table and otherwise cut your risk with a portfolio described by the graphic at the top of the next page.

Now you've cut your beta and prepared for bad times. If you're right about the cycle, the market's performance will be drawn from the left-hand side of the probability distribution, and your defensive positioning will make you an outperformer in that market, losing less, again as shown by

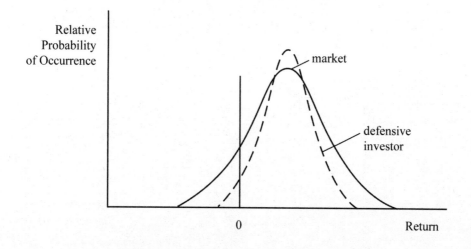

the dotted line in the graph below. Your portfolio, being defensive, is less exposed to market movements and thus right for a weak market:

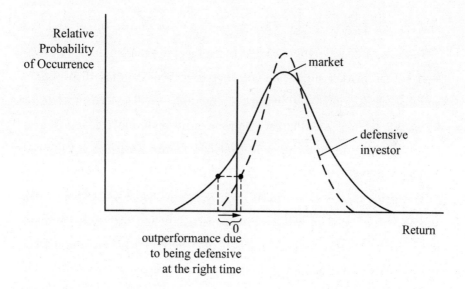

Of course not everyone has a superior understanding of cycles; thus not all efforts at positioning are successful. Suppose an investor who lacks skill regarding positioning decides to turn defensive and cuts his market exposure as shown. If the market surprises on the upside, he turns out to be wrong and his investments underperform:

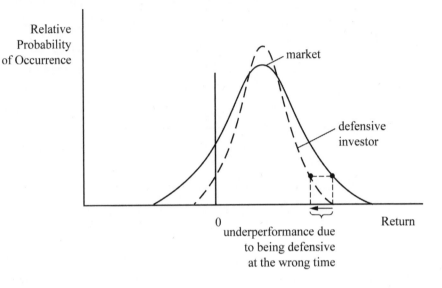

In the first chapter I introduced the subject of "tendencies." The out-look for the market should be considered via a probability distribution, and that distribution — if constructed accurately — will give you a sense for its likely tendency. The market's movement through the cycle repositions the distribution and thus influences its likely future tendency, as I showed on pages 204–206.

When the market is low in its cycle, gains are more likely than usual, and losses are less likely. The reverse is true when the market is high in its cycle. Positioning moves, based on where you believe the market stands in its cycle, amount to trying to better prepare your portfolio for the events that lie ahead. While you can always be unlucky regarding the relationship between what logically should happen and what actually does happen, good positioning decisions can increase the chance that the market's tendency — and thus the chance for outperformance — will be on your side.

In 1977, New York City experienced a wave of lovers' lane murders perpetrated by a serial killer labeled "the Son of Sam." In 2014, I read the obituary of Timothy Dowd, the detective who caught him. I loved the part where it quoted him as saying it was his job "to prepare to be lucky." Given my view of the future as indeterminate and subject to considerable randomness, I think that's a great way to think about it. While it may sound like I'm advocating being passive and leaving things to chance, the truth is that superior investors have favorably skewed distributions of outcomes, but not batting averages of 1.000. They still need favorable outcomes: they need the right tickets to be drawn from the bowl.

One of the best ways to enjoy the skewed distribution of outcomes that marks superior investors is to get the market's tendency on your side. The outcome will never be under your control, but if you invest when the market's tendency is biased toward favorable, you'll have the wind at your back, and if the tendency is biased toward unfavorable, the reverse will be true. Skillful analysis of cycles can give you a better-than-average understanding of the market's likely tendency and thus enable you to improve your chances of properly positioning your portfolio for what lies ahead.

∽

What follows is completely unrelated to the subject of cycles, so if that's all you're interested in, you needn't read it. But I want to complete the discussion of the actions investors can take to improve performance by covering the other component of portfolio management: asset selection.

Asset selection consists of identifying markets, market sectors and individual assets that will do better or worse than the rest, and over- and underweighting them in portfolios. The higher an asset's price is relative to its intrinsic value, the less well it should be expected to do (all other things being equal), and vice versa. The key prerequisite for superior performance in this regard is above-average insight into the asset's intrinsic value, the likely future changes in that value, and the relationship between its intrinsic value and its current market price.

All investors who follow a given asset have (or should have) opinions regarding its intrinsic value. The market price of the asset reflects the consensus of those opinions, meaning investors collectively have set the price. That's where buyers and sellers agree to transact. The buyers buy because they think it's a smart investment at the current price, and the sellers sell because they think it's fully priced or overpriced there. What do we know about the accuracy of those views?

- **Theoretical** — The efficient market hypothesis states that all available information is incorporated into prices "efficiently," so that the prices of assets are fair and investors can't "beat the market" by choosing among them.
- **Logical** — What we're talking about is the ability to make those judgments better than the average investor and thus achieve above-average performance. Yet the one thing we know for sure is that, on average, all investors are average. Thus logic tells us they can't all make above-average judgments.
- **Empirical** — Performance studies show that very few investors are consistently more right than others about those judgments. Most investors do worse than the markets, especially after the subtraction of transaction costs, management fees and expenses. That's the reason for the rising popularity of passive index investing.

That's not to say no one beats the market. Lots of people do so every year, but usually no more than would be the case under an assumption of randomness. A few do it more consistently than randomness would suggest, and some of those become famous. The essential ingredient — superior insight into intrinsic value — is what gives them that ability. I call it "second-level thinking": the ability to think differently from the consensus and better.

I'm not going to go any further regarding intrinsic value, the relationship of price to value, or second-level thinking, since they're all covered at length in *The Most Important Thing*. But the bottom line is that the superior investor — who's capable of second-level thinking — is able to pick more outperforming assets than underperformers, and thus to invest more in the former and less in the latter. The recipe for superior asset selection is that simple.

And what is the hallmark of that superiority? Asymmetrical results.

The investor who has no skill at selection has the same ratio of winners to losers as the market. Thus he does well when the market does well, and poorly when it does poorly:

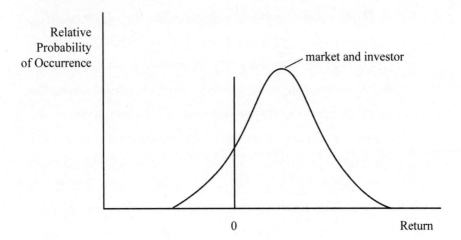

An investor with negative skill at selection picks proportionally more losers than winners and thus does worse than the market, both when it goes up and when it goes down, as shown below. In other words, his probability distribution is shifted to the left of the market's:

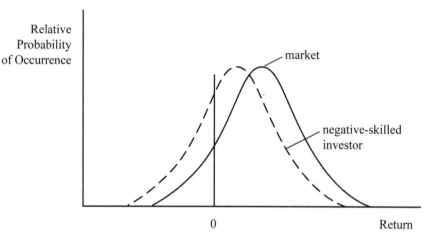

But the skillful selector has a better ratio of winners to losers than the market; he is able to invest more in his winners than his losers; and his winners are more successful than his losers are unsuccessful.

- The holdings of a habitually aggressive investor who is capable of superior selection will go up more than the market when the market goes up and may go down more than the market when it goes down. But his margin of superiority on the upside will exceed his degree of inferiority on the downside, as it comes from his ability to select assets that deliver upside potential without entailing commensurate downside risk. As a result he'll do better than the market when it goes up, but not as badly when the market goes down as his aggressiveness would suggest. That's an example of the asymmetry that marks the superior investor:

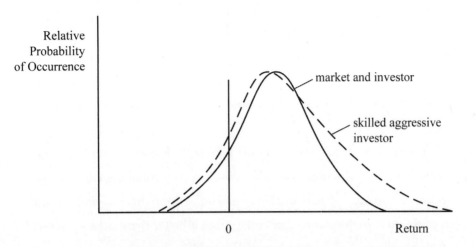

Likewise, the habitually defensive investor with superior selection skill will do better than the market when it goes down, but his skill at selection will keep him from underperforming in rising markets to the full extent that his defensiveness alone would suggest. His skill at asset selection enables him to find defensive assets that have upside participation that is disproportionate to their downside risk. It gives him an asymmetrical distribution as well:

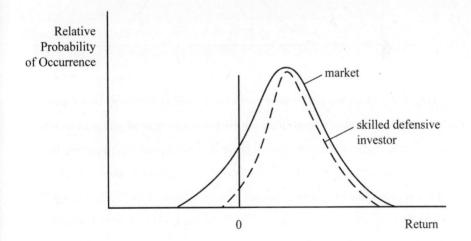

Both of the investors with superior selection skill — the aggressive one and the defensive one — exhibit asymmetry relative to the market. That is, they both have performance distributions that are biased favorably. Both have upside potential that is disproportional to their downside risk (although in different ways). That's how alpha in asset selection manifests itself.

Finally, the investor who is neither habitually aggressive nor habitually defensive — but who possesses skill at both cycle positioning and asset selection — correctly adjusts market exposure at the right time *and* has the asymmetrical performance that comes from a better-than-average ratio of winners to losers. This is the best of all worlds:

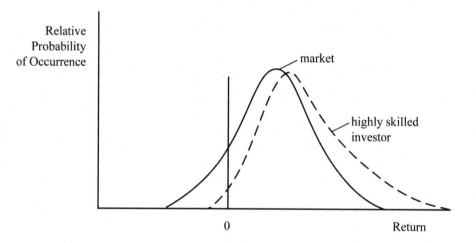

Almost anyone can make money when the market rises and lose money when it falls, and almost anyone can have the same ratio of winners to losers as the market overall. It takes superior skill to improve in those regards and to produce the asymmetry that marks the superior investor.

Please note that in this discussion I have separated skill at cycle positioning from skill at asset selection. This bifurcation is somewhat artificial. I do it to describe the two elements that influence performance, but many great investors have both, and most of the rest have neither. Investors who are capable of both have a better sense for the market's likely tendency *and* can put together portfolios that are better suited for the market environment that likely lies ahead in terms of the ratio of winners to losers. That's what makes them great . . . and rare.

∾

My epiphany in India taught me that successfully positioning a portfolio for the market movements that lie ahead is dependent on what you do (turning aggressive or defensive) and when you do it (based on a superior understanding of what cycles imply for future market moves). It's the goal of this book to help in those regards.

XV

LIMITS ON COPING

In my opinion it's entirely reasonable to try to improve long-term investment results by altering positions on the basis of an understanding of the market cycle. But it's essential that you also understand the limitations, as well as the skills that are required and how difficult it is.

I undertook to write this book to give myself an opportunity to set down what I know about cycles, and because I enjoy writing, but mainly — as I said above — to help the reader deal with the market's ups and downs.

In the preceding pages, I have covered many of the considerations that bear on the process of understanding cycles, as well as the vagaries that properly restrain the confidence anyone should have regarding his ability to do so. My goal here is to repeat these considerations and sum up.

Investing, as I've said, consists of positioning capital so as to benefit from future events. I also said we never know what the future holds, and thus where we're going. But we should do all we can to know where we stand, since the current position of the cycle has powerful implications for how we should cope with its possible future.

Where we stand in cycles has a profound influence on the future tendencies: on what is likely to happen, and perhaps even when. As I discussed in chapter I and illustrated in the last chapter, our cycle positioning shifts the probability distribution governing the future.

Many things can happen. We know we face uncertainty and risk. All we can know about the future — at best — is what the probabilities are. Knowing the probabilities can help us be more right than others on average. But it's essential to remember that knowing the probabilities is far from the same as knowing precisely what's going to happen.

We generally have no choice but to be content with knowing the probabilities. But the sample in terms of each outcome (e.g., each year's GDP growth or each stock's gain next year) will often be limited to one observation — one experience — meaning many things can happen but only one will. There won't be enough observations to allow us to assume that the future reality will be the one the probabilities say is most likely . . . and certainly not that the most likely thing will happen any time soon.

For example, let's take the correction of a euphoria-driven bubble. Theoretically, it doesn't have to happen ever. But the realities of cycles say that (a) it will happen eventually and (b) the more time that passes without it happening — and the longer the cycle continues to move upward — the more likely (and usually the more imminent) the expected correction becomes.

Of course, the more time that passes before this logical event occurs — and the further that the cycle swings in the upward direction — the more people will conclude that the rules of cycles have been somehow suspended and that the called-for correction will *never* happen. This can lead to the kind of buying we saw in 2000, and eventually to an extremely painful outcome.

We have to safeguard our portfolios (and our investment management businesses) against the danger stemming from the fact that the thing that's most likely to happen—which our understanding of cycles can tell us— may not happen until long after it first becomes likely. And we have to steel ourselves emotionally so as to be able to live through the potentially long time lag between reaching a well-reasoned conclusion and having it turn out to be correct.

∾

How about a review of history? In the mid-1990s, the galloping market and rocketing tech sector presented an opportunity for conservative investors to conclude that stocks were highly overvalued. The reasoning might have been solid—based on an effective interpretation of the relevant data —and the case for caution may have been strong. However, it would have taken years for the market to prove those investors right, and as one of the most important investment adages says, "Being too far ahead of your time is indistinguishable from being wrong." The fact that their conclusions were well-founded would have done the investors only limited good; before the correction of 2000–02 finally set in, they might have lost much of the capital under their management.

However, the keen intellect that had led those investors to their conclusions, combined with sufficient conviction, should have allowed them to stick to their guns. Hopefully they would have remained cautious rather than capitulate and buy in higher. If so, they would have been proved right a few years later and recovered their reputations and their assets. But the interim they lived through certainly would have been painful.

Fast-forward to the current decade and the chance for more of the same. Cautious investors have been provided another chance to conclude that U.S. stocks are overheated, reduce holdings, and thus miss out on more strong gains. Clients might have bailed again, and cautious firms' assets could have shrunk (in a rising market).

Is caution appropriate again? Will it be proved appropriate by future events? Will a correction come soon enough for cautious investors to enjoy the benefits of being right? Will they be viewed as perma-bears who luckily are validated every once in a while by downturns? Or as brilliant tacticians who are right in principle but so far thwarted by the undependability of cause and effect in the investment world? These questions are largely un-answerable. But the most important thing is for the reader to note this key lesson: positioning for cycles isn't easy.

≈

In my opinion it's entirely reasonable to try to improve long-term invest-ment results by altering positions on the basis of an understanding of the market cycle. But it's essential that you also understand the limitations, as well as the skills that are required and how difficult it is.

Importantly, I want to call attention to the obvious fact that—rather than the everyday ups and downs of the market—the clear examples I've provided in chapter XII all concerned "once-in-a-lifetime" cy-clical extremes (which these days seem to happen about once a dec-ade). First, the extremes of bubble and crash—and, in particular, the process through which they arise—most clearly illustrate the cycle in action and how to respond to it. And second, it's when dealing with pronounced extremes that we should expect the highest likelihood of success.

Here's how I think about the impact of market movements on the in-vestment environment we work in. It's admittedly a simplistic vision, and it suggests a world that is discernable and much more regular than the real one. But it has worked for me for decades as a general framework, and it beats the heck out of trying to understand the world as a series of irregular, random zigs and zags:

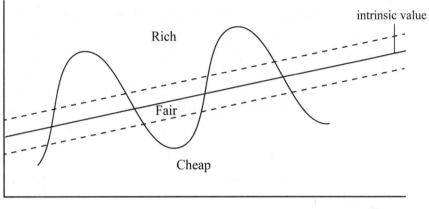

Between the extremes of "rich" and "cheap"—when the cycle is in the middle ground of "fair"—the state of the relationship between price and value is, by definition, nowhere as clear-cut as at the extremes. As a result:

- It's hard to make frequent distinctions and hard to do so correctly.
- Thus distinctions in the middle ground aren't as potentially profitable as at the extremes, and those distinctions can't be expected to work out as dependably.

Detecting and exploiting the extremes is really the best we can hope for. And I believe it can be done dependably—if you're analytical, insightful, experienced (or well-versed in history) and unemotional. That means, however, that you shouldn't expect to reach profitable conclusions daily, monthly or even yearly.

We can't create great opportunities to time the market through our understanding of cycles. Rather, the market will decide when we'll have them.

Remember, when there's nothing clever to do, the mistake lies in trying to be clever.

The reasonableness of the effort at cycle timing depends simply on what you expect of it. If you frequently try to discern where we are in the cycle in the sense of "what's going to happen tomorrow?" or "what's in store for us next month?" you're unlikely to find success. I describe such an effort as "trying to be cute." No one can make fine distinctions like those often enough or consistently right enough to add materially to investment results. And no one knows when the market developments that efforts at cycle positioning label "probable" will materialize.

On the other hand, positioning portfolios for the major cycles has been a big contributor to Oaktree's success. My colleagues and I became aggressive in 1990–93, 2002 and 2008, and we turned cautious and pulled in our horns in 1994–95 and 2005–06, and to some extent in the last few years. We have tried to use the cycle to our advantage and to add value for our clients, and I'd say we got the positioning largely right on those occasions. Also, there weren't any major opportunities to do so that we missed.

So thus far our major cycle calls have all proved correct. The word "all" makes it sound like this is a battle that's consistently winnable. But my personal "all" consists of four or five times in 48 years. By making my calls only at the greatest cyclical extremes, I've maximized my chances of being right. No one — and certainly not I — can succeed regularly, other than perhaps at extremes.

So please note — as I always try to remind people — that it's not easy, and I don't want to give the impression that readers should expect to find it easy or be disappointed when they don't. As I said in "On the Couch" (January 2016):

I want to make it abundantly clear that when I call for caution
in 2006–07, or active buying in late 2008, or renewed caution in
2012, or a somewhat more aggressive stance here in early 2016, I
do it with considerable uncertainty. My conclusions are the result
of my reasoning, applied with the benefit of my experience (and
collaboration with my Oaktree colleagues), but I never consider
them 100% likely to be correct, or even 80%. I think they're right,
of course, but I always make my recommendations with trepida-
tion.

I read the same newspapers as everyone else. I see the same economic data. I'm buffeted by the same market movements. The same
factors appeal to my emotions. Maybe I'm a little more confident in
my reasoning, and certainly I have more experience than most. But
the key is that—for whatever reason—I'm able to stand up to my
emotions and follow my conclusions. None of my conclusions can
be documented or proved. If they could be, most intelligent people would reach the same conclusions, with the same degree of
confidence. I tell you this only to communicate my feeling that no
one should fear he's not up to the task just because he's unsure
of his conclusions. These aren't things about which certainty is
attainable.

Peter Bernstein contributed some useful wisdom on this subject. I'll
conclude this chapter with his thoughts:

> After 28 years at this post, and 22 years before this in money manage-
> ment, I can sum up whatever wisdom I have accumulated this way:
> The trick is not to be the hottest stock-picker, the winningest fore-
> caster, or the developer of the neatest model; such victories are tran-
> sient. The trick is to survive! Performing that trick requires a strong
> stomach for being wrong because we are all going to be wrong more
> often then we expect. The future is not ours to know. But it helps to
> know that being wrong is inevitable and normal, not some terrible

tragedy, not some awful failing in reasoning, not even bad luck in most instances. Being wrong comes with the franchise of an activity whose outcome depends on an unknown future . . . (Jeff Saut, "Being Wrong and Still Making Money," Seeking Alpha, March 13, 2017, emphasis added)

XVI

THE CYCLE IN SUCCESS

The important lesson is that — especially in an interconnected, informed world — everything that produces unusual profitability will attract incremental capital until it becomes overcrowded and fully institutionalized, at which point its prospective risk-adjusted return will move toward the mean (or worse).

And, correspondingly, things that perform poorly for a while eventually will become so cheap — due to their relative depreciation and the lack of investor interest — that they'll be primed to outperform. Cycles like these hold the key to success in investing, not trees that everyone is assuming will grow to the sky.

Hopefully you're now equipped for the task of recognizing, assessing and responding to cycles. That can contribute substantially to your investment success. But as Peter Bernstein said, even the best investors won't be successful all the time. Understanding that is an important part of being able to live with the effort. Success, like the other things mentioned in this book, comes and goes.

In fact, over the course of my career, I've detected a cycle in success. To a large degree, the ebb and flow of success — like the other cycles I've described — stems from the role played by human nature. And, once again, each development in the cycle leads to the next. I've long held the conviction I mentioned back on page 34 — and it's been strongly reinforced over my 29 years of involvement with distressed debt and distressed companies — that "success carries within itself the seeds of failure, and failure the seeds of success."

Peter Kaufman, Charlie Munger's biographer and the CEO of Glenair, an exceptional producer of aerospace components, describes the workings of dialectical materialism as follows: "As any system grows toward its maximum or peak efficiency, it will develop the very internal contradictions and weaknesses that bring about its eventual decay and demise" (his essay #49: "The Perpetual See-Saw," 2010). This captures the process that guarantees that success will prove cyclical.

The Role of Human Nature

Another way I put it is that "success isn't good for most people." In short, success can change people, and usually not for the better. Success makes people think they're smart. That's fine as far as it goes, but there can also be negative ramifications. Success also tends to make people richer, and that can lead to a reduction in their level of motivation.

In investing there's a complex relationship between humility and confidence. Since the greatest bargains are usually found among things that are undiscovered or disrespected, to be successful an investor has to have enough confidence in his judgment to adopt what David Swensen, the hugely successful head of Yale's high-performing endowment, describes as "uncomfortably idiosyncratic portfolios, which frequently appear downright imprudent in the eyes of conventional wisdom" (*Pioneering Portfolio Management*, 2000). By definition, pronounced bargain prices are most likely to be found among things that conventional wisdom dismisses, that make most investors uncomfortable, and whose merits are hard to comprehend. Investing in them requires considerable inner strength.

When one of those positions initially fails to rise as the investor expects — or perhaps goes in the opposite direction — the investor has to have enough confidence to hold on to his position or even add to it. He can't take a price decline as a sure "sell" signal; in other words, it can't be his default position that the market knows more than he does.

But, on the other hand, the investor also has to know his limitations and not assume he's infallible. He has to understand that no one knows for sure what the macro future holds. While he's likely to have opinions regarding the future course of economies, markets and interest rates, he should acknowledge that they're not necessarily correct. And, counter to the above, he mustn't always assume that he's right and the market's wrong — and thus hold or add without limitation and without rechecking his facts and his reasoning. That's hubris.

As successes accrue, it's common for people to conclude that they're smart. And after making a lot of money in a strongly rising market, they decide they've got investing mastered. Their faith increases in their own opinions and instinct. Their investing comes to reflect less self-doubt, meaning they think less about the possibility of being wrong and worry less about the risk of loss. This can cause them to no longer insist on the full margin of safety that gave rise to their earlier successes. This is the reason for one of the oldest and most important investment adages: "don't confuse brains with a bull market."

The plain truth is, there's little of value to be learned from success. People who are successful run the risk of overlooking the fact that they were lucky, or that they had help from others. In investing, success teaches people that making money is easy, and that they don't have to worry about risk — two particularly dangerous lessons.

They may conclude that the small opportunity that gave them their big winner is infinitely scalable, which most are not. And many people — including investors who became famous for having had a single success — conclude that they can branch out into any number of other fields: that the intelligence that produced that first epic success must be broadly applicable.

Factors like these make investment success hard to replicate, meaning it can prove cyclical rather than serial. In fact, rather than imply that another is coming, one success may in and of itself make a second one less probable. I'll quote Henry Kaufman, formerly Salomon Brothers' chief economist: "There are two kinds of people who lose a lot of money: those who know nothing and those who know everything" ("Archimedes on Wall Street," *Forbes,* October 19, 1998).

It's not for nothing that there are famous jinxes, such as showing up on the cover of *Sports Illustrated* or *Forbes* magazine. A cover appearance can be the result of a singular accomplishment that may have resulted from a lucky break, a unique, non-replicable opportunity, or the bearing of imprudent risk. Or the good outcomes that land people on a magazine cover — including the successful investors lauded by *Forbes* — may cause them to become more confident and cocksure, and less disciplined and hardworking . . . not much of a formula for success.

The Role of Popularity

One of the principal ways in which success carries the seeds of investment failure is through increased popularity. I wrote just before that bargains are most often found among those things that are hard to comprehend, uncomfortable and easily dismissed by the crowd. Short-term investment performance is largely a popularity contest, and most bargains exist for the simple reason that they haven't yet been taken up by the herd and become popular. On the contrary, assets that have performed well are usually the ones that have gained in popularity because of their obvious merit and thus have become high-priced.

Let's think about investment strategies. It's essential to grasp that nothing will work forever: no approach, rule or process can outperform all the time. First, most securities and approaches are right for certain environments and parts of the cycle, and wrong for others. And second, past success will in itself render future success less likely.

In the 1960s, when the idea of investing in stocks was first gaining popularity among Americans, the emphasis was on industry leaders and so-called "blue-chip" securities. Small-capitalization stocks were largely overlooked at first, but eventually they were noticed and bought. This caused them to do better than large-caps. When people noticed small-cap stocks' superior returns in this "catch-up" phase, their buying produced further gains for them . . . until it caused them to be fully priced relative to large-caps. At that point, interest rotated to large-caps, which then regained the lead.

Likewise, growth and tech stocks did far better than more-mundane value stocks in the late 1990s. This divergence reached a maximum in 1999, with growth stocks outperforming value stocks that year by almost 25 percentage points. But growth stocks' dramatic outperformance rendered them overpriced, and when the stock market corrected in 2000–02, they lost far more than value stocks, which previously had languished cheap.

In other words, "outperformance" is just another word for one thing appreciating relative to another. And, clearly, that can't go on forever. Regardless of how great its merits may be, "a" is unlikely to be infinitely more valuable than "b." That means if "a" keeps appreciating relative to "b," there has to be a point at which it will become overvalued relative to "b." And just when the last person gives up on "b" because it's been performing so poorly and jumps to "a," it will be time for "b" (now compellingly cheap relative to "a") to outperform.

Strong forces create a tendency for strategies, investors or investment management firms that succeed for a while to cease doing so. I wrote just above that most ideas aren't infinitely scalable. One essential truth about investing is that, generally speaking, good results will bring more money to "hot" money managers and strategies, and if allowed to grow unchecked, more money will bring bad performance.

In the mid-2000s, convertible arbitrage rapidly gained in popularity. Investors without a view on the prospects for a given stock were willing to buy bonds convertible into it, as long as they were able to short the underlying shares in an appropriate "hedge ratio" (see my memo "A Case in Point," June 2005). Convertible arbitrageurs reported outstanding risk-adjusted returns in all kinds of market environments . . . until so much money and so many competitors were attracted to the strategy that no one could find positions as attractively priced as those of the past.

The important lesson is that—especially in an interconnected, informed world—everything that produces unusual profitability will attract incremental capital until it becomes overcrowded and fully institutionalized, at which point its prospective risk-adjusted return will move toward the mean (or worse).

And, correspondingly, things that perform poorly for a while eventually will become so cheap—due to their relative depreciation and the lack of

investor interest — that they'll be primed to outperform. Cycles like these
hold the key to success in investing, not trees that everyone is assuming will
grow to the sky.

It's all a matter of ebb and flow. In investing, things work until they
don't. Or as Ajit Jain of Berkshire Hathaway told me about investing the
other day, "it's easy until it isn't."

- Cheap small-caps outperform until they reach the point where
  they're no longer cheap.
- Trend-following or momentum investing — staying with the winners — works for a while. But eventually rotation and buying the
  laggards takes over as the winning strategy.
- "Buying the dips" lets investors take advantage of momentary
  weakness, up until the time when a major problem surfaces (or
  the market simply no longer recovers), causing price declines to be
  followed by further price declines, not quick rebounds.
- Risky assets outperform — coming from valuations where they
  were excessively penalized for their riskiness — until they're
  priced more like safe assets. Then they underperform until they
  once again offer adequate risk premiums.

The bottom line is clear: nothing works forever. But it's essential to recognize that when everyone becomes convinced that something will keep
working forever, that's the very time when it'll become certain not to. I say,
"In investing, everything that's important is counter-intuitive, and everything that's obvious to everyone is wrong."

Perhaps the greatest example of the influence of popularity (in reverse)
was seen in 1979, and few investors who were around at the time have
forgotten it. On August 13 of that year, after almost a decade of painfully

poor performance on the part of stocks, *Business Week* magazine published a cover story entitled "The Death of Equities." Its conclusion — that stocks were done for — was based on the opposite of everything recommended in this book.

The article cited a litany of reasons why the poor performance of stocks would continue unabated:

- Seven million people had given up on investing in stocks.
- Many other forms of investment had done better.
- Pension funds were turning to "hard assets" like gold.
- Inflation had sapped corporations' ability to increase profits.

It went on:

> Even institutions that have so far remained in the financial markets are pouring money into short-term investments and such "alternate equity" investments as mortgage-backed paper, foreign securities, venture capital, leases, guaranteed insurance contracts, indexed bonds, stock options, and futures.

And here was its conclusion:

> Today, the old attitude of buying solid stocks as a cornerstone for one's life savings and retirement has simply disappeared. Says a young U.S. executive: "Have you been to an American stockholders' meeting lately? They're all old fogies. The stock market is just not where the action's at."

In short, what "The Death of Equities" said was that stocks had become so unpopular that they would never do well again. It takes a highly simplistic first-level thinker to conclude that poor past performance has led to unpopularity today, which implies poor performance tomorrow. Rather, the insightful second-level thinker says poor past performance has led to unpopularity today, *which implies low prices today,* which in turn implies *good* performance tomorrow.

"The Death of Equities" was published just a few years before — and in essence laid out the entire case for — the 1982 kickoff of the greatest bull market in history. At the time it was published, the S&P 500 stood at 107, and in March of 2000 it reached 1527. That's a price gain of more than 14 times, or 13.7% per year for almost 21 years (and those figures ignore dividends, which took the total gain to more than 28 times and the annualized total return to 17.6%). The lesson is simple: investors should be leery of popular assets. Rather, it's unpopularity that is the buyer's friend.

The Role of Companies

Companies, too, are subject to ups and downs in terms of success, also based on a series of cause-and-effect events. One of the most pronounced such processes I've witnessed took place at Xerox.

The office-copying giant — the first to make it possible to avoid the "wet" process of photostatting, which required that documents be sent out to a photo lab to be duplicated — was one of the first companies I visited as a rookie office-equipment analyst in the late 1960s. At that time, Xerox had a monopoly on "dry" copying and appeared to be in full command of its destiny. My senior analyst and I used to meet with Xerox's "analyst contact," and for each copier model in the product line he would help us triangulate on the company's projections in terms of the number of machines it would have in the field in the coming year and the annual rental revenue per machine.

Because of Xerox's dominant market position, it was largely able to make those projections come true. It could charge monopolistic prices that enabled it to fine-tune the size of its rental fleet and that gave it very high profit margins. It also insisted on a rental-only model, refusing to sell or lease its machines and lose control of them. What a perpetual motion machine!

But Xerox management may have ignored the possibility that those high margins would prove unsustainable. In 1975, Xerox resolved an anti-trust complaint over control of the copier market by entering into a consent decree requiring it to make its powerful portfolio of patents available for licensing. Competitors began to produce and sell their own copiers. They were able to undercut Xerox's prices and displace part of its rental population. This reduced Xerox's U.S. market share in copiers from nearly 100% to the low teens, and it ate significantly into Xerox's profits. As the incumbent, Xerox had trouble responding to the price competition, as this would cannibalize its existing business. The competitors did so in an early example of what's now called disruption.

In 1968, thanks to its monopolistic position, strong growth and high profitability, Xerox was a leader of the Nifty Fifty I described earlier — companies that were considered so strong and so fast growing that "nothing bad could happen" and "no stock price was too high." But trees rarely grow to the sky, and success is rarely unending.

Because Xerox's behavior had invited competition that it was unprepared to respond to — and for other reasons as well — by the early years of the 21st century it was experiencing serious difficulty.

Companies, like people, have the potential to respond to success with behavior that dooms that very success. Thus companies can:

- get complacent and become "fat and happy,"
- become bureaucratic and slow-moving,
- fail to take action to defend their positions,

- cease to be innovative and non-conforming, and join the crowd of mediocrity, and/or
- conclude that they can do pretty much anything, and thus venture into areas beyond their competence.

In these ways and more, success truly carries the seeds of failure. But the good news — as I said earlier — is that failure also carries the seeds of success.

- Once under attack, companies can regain their motivation and sense of purpose.
- They can shed bureaucratic fat and get serious about meeting competition and making money.
- And in the ultimate form of unsuccess, they can go through bankruptcy, slim down, and shed losing business lines, unprofitable locations, onerous contracts and burdensome debt. (Of course, however, the owners of companies that go into bankruptcy usually lose their entire positions.)

Thus Jahan Janjigian wrote about Xerox in 2002:

> [In 2000,] a new management team implemented a number of restructuring initiatives aimed at returning the company to profitability. These included aggressive cost cuts and the elimination of 13,600 positions. Xerox also sold off its Chinese and Hong Kong operations, as well as 50% of Fuji Xerox to Fuji Photo Film. Furthermore, Xerox allowed GE Capital to take over the financing of receivables, for which it already has received $2.7 billion. And Xerox has exited the struggling small-office and home-office business.

In April, Xerox agreed to pay $10 million to settle the SEC's two-year investigation. It later restated all of its past financial results as required under the agreement. Additionally, the company was successful in working with creditors in renegotiating its debt obligations to more manageable terms. Perhaps most important, the company's products are now more competitive in terms of price and quality.

Due to the success of these efforts, Xerox returned to profitability sooner than expected. . . . Given significant operational improvements, we think Xerox makes for a compelling buy at current levels. ("Xerox Back from the Brink," *Forbes Growth Investor,* October 2002)

Because companies don't last as long as economies and markets do, the long-term cycle in company success may not take as long either. But over their lifetimes, companies' gains can lead to losses, and losses can lay the groundwork for gains. There is a cycle in business success.

The Role of Timing

Among the factors that can contribute greatly to an individual's or a company's success is timing. Among other things, it helps to get involved in things at an above-average time. That's what put Xerox on the map in the 1960s, and it helped me out as well.

In August 1978, shortly after shifting from running Citibank's equity research department to managing bond portfolios, I got the phone call that changed my life. "There's a guy named Milken in California," my boss said, "and he's involved in something called high yield bonds. A client wants a portfolio of those bonds. Can you figure out what that means?"

It was just in 1977 or 1978 that high yield bond investing had its institutional inception. That's when Michael Milken achieved his first success in convincing investors that it's okay for below-investment grade companies to issue bonds — and for institutions to buy them — if the interest rate is high enough to compensate for the risk. The high yield universe consisted of less than $3 billion of bonds at the time I first got involved. The vast majority of investing organizations had a rule against buying bonds rated below investment grade, which were commonly called "junk bonds." And Moody's categorically rejected B-rated bonds, saying they "fail to possess the characteristics of a desirable investment."

How could these unpopular bonds *not* have been underrated bargains? How could early participation *not* have been a boon?

And then, a decade later, Bruce Karsh brought his legal skills and strategic insight to my team, complementing Sheldon Stone's expertise in credit, and we organized one of the first distressed debt funds from a major financial institution. What could be more risky and thus more unseemly than investing in the debt of companies in bankruptcy or considered destined for it? To what idea could people be more averse? In other words, where else could as much money be made so safely?

In both these instances and more, I've been lucky to come across asset classes when they were still undiscovered, uncrowded and thus bargain-priced. There's little that can make investing as easy as having a market largely to oneself. It beats the heck out of trying to wring decent returns from a market that everybody has discovered, figured out, taken to and crowded into. The latter is far from a formula for success. The latecomer to a now-crowded field isn't "the wise man in the beginning"; rather, he's more far likely to be "the fool in the end." Those of us who've been lucky enough to be early rather than late know — or certainly should know — that our success wasn't all our doing. The times have to cooperate.

And that brings me to a great observation from Henry Phipps, the less-celebrated partner of Andrew Carnegie and Henry Clay Frick, two of the 19th century's greatest businessmen. In 1899, Phipps wrote as follows:

> Good times like the present, make bad times; a law sure as the swing of the pendulum. We have experience to know these elementary truths. Have we the sense to put them into practice? (George Harvey, *Henry Clay Frick: The Man*, 2002)

As with people—whose successes may constitute isolated instances rather than indicators of great things to come as they might be wont to believe—the times may not remain conducive to continued success. Good times can encourage investment decisions that depend on the perpetuation of such times in order to succeed. But those good times can lead instead to bad times that test the decisions in ways they can't withstand.

Not only are good times followed sooner or later by bad times, but—as with so many other examples of cycles—good times often *produce* bad times. Good times can lead to unwise debt issuance (as we saw in the discussion of the distressed debt cycle) or to overbuilding (as we saw in the discussion of the real estate cycle).

Likewise as Ruchir Sharma, chief global strategist at Morgan Stanley Investment Management, wrote in his book *The Rise and Fall of Nations* regarding the effect of fresh new reformers, "Reform leads to growth and good times, and good times encourage an arrogance and complacency that leads to a new crisis."

Phipps pointed out that history shows these trends clearly. The key question is whether we are astute and unemotional enough to know that good times don't necessarily lead to further good times, and thus that success truly can be cyclical.

Let's return to Charlie Munger's quote from Demosthenes: "For that which a man wishes, that he will believe." In other words, wishful thinking often takes hold. This can cause investors to believe that good times will be followed by more good times. But that ignores the cyclical nature of things, and especially of success.

XVII

THE FUTURE OF CYCLES

The tendency of people to go to excess will never end. And thus, since those excesses eventually have to correct, neither will the occurrence of cycles. Economies and markets have never moved in a straight line in the past, and neither will they do so in the future. And that means investors with the ability to understand cycles will find opportunities for profit.

Thus far I've covered a lot of the past and a bit of the present. Now, as I conclude, I want to turn to the future.

Over the course of my career, I've witnessed numerous occasions on which pundits said the occurrence of one type of cycle or another had come to an end. Whether because of economic vitality, financial innovation, astute corporate management, or the supposed omniscience of central bankers and heads of Treasury, they observed that the fluctuations of either the economic cycle or the cycle in profits would be seen no more.

I spent some time on this subject in "Will It Be Different This Time?" (November 1996). First I described a newspaper article that had appeared a few days earlier:

It recounted the case currently being made for this remaining a continuous, recession-free economic expansion. As its lead paragraph says:

> From boardrooms to living rooms and from government offices to trading floors, a new consensus is emerging: The big, bad business cycle has been tamed.

The current expansion, at 67 months, has already far exceeded the post-war average. Nevertheless, 51 of the 53 "top economists" surveyed by Blue Chip newsletter (my favorite experts and the subject of my July 1996 memo, "The Value of Predictions II") predict growth next year of 1.5% or more. And the University of Michigan survey finds that among consumers, more expect five more good years than expect bad times to emerge.

The Chairman of Sears states "There is no natural law that says we have to have a recession." According to Amoco's Chairman, "I don't see any reason to believe [the recovery] can't go on until the turn of the century." Sara Lee's CEO says "I don't know what could happen to make a cyclical downturn." ("The Business Cycle is Tamed, Many Say, Alarming Others," *Wall Street Journal,* November 15, 1996)

Clearly these statements, made in 1996, did not truly mark the end of cycles. Rather, there was a modest recession in 2001 and then, just a few years later, the Great Recession of 2008–09, the most powerful cyclical event ever experienced by most people alive today.

I went on in "Will It Be Different This Time?" to quote a number of similar assertions from other respected leaders:

> "There will be no interruption of our present prosperity."
> "I cannot help but raise a dissenting voice to the statements that . . . prosperity in this country must necessarily diminish and recede in the future."

"We are only at the beginning of a period that will go down in history as the golden age."

"The fundamental business of the country ... is on a sound and prosperous basis."

In assessing the reasonableness of these statements, it's important to note that they were made, respectively, by the president of the Pierce-Arrow Motor Car Company, the president of the New York Stock Exchange, the president of the Bush Terminal Company, and the president of the United States. The positions of the first and third should serve as a giveaway that these statements came in the distant past, even without your knowing that the president in question was Herbert Hoover. The timing of these statements in 1928 and 1929 — on the doorstep of the Great Depression that plagued the world for more than a decade — was less than auspicious. So much, I thought, for prosperity without slowdowns, and for the end of cyclicality.

But then, in the 2000s, the expectation of "permanent prosperity" reared its head again. While not specifically arguing that there would be no more cycles, a lot of investors, bankers and members of the media certainly embraced the belief that risk was gone — essentially the same thing.

In his autobiography, *Stress Test,* former Treasury secretary Tim Geithner describes the climate when he arrived at the Fed in 2003:

> Economists were starting to debate whether America's long stretch of stability constituted a new normal, a Great Moderation, a quasi-permanent era of resilience to shocks. There was growing confidence that derivatives and other financial innovations designed to hedge and distribute risk — along with better monetary policy to respond to downturns and better technology to smooth out inventory cycles — had made devastating crises a thing of the past.

The fact that this purportedly permanent prosperity was given a name like "the Great Moderation" suggests it had entered the popular consciousness. And thus it met my requirement for the riskiest possible environment: one in which there's widespread belief that there's no risk. On page 120, I described the media accounts to that effect that enumerated the forces that had caused risk's elimination: Fed omniscience, unremitting demand for securities from cash-flow-rich nations, and the latest inventions from Wall Street.

Not only were all these "cycles are over" proclamations wrong, but it's very much worth noting that each of them coincided with — and certainly contributed to — the upward march to a cyclical high. And that the events that followed those highs would be unusually painful: the Great Depression of 1929–39, a three-year stock market decline in 2000–02 (the first such decline since 1929) and the Global Financial Crisis of 2007–08.

In "Will It Be Different This Time?" I went on from recalling the Pollyanna statements just cited to drawing what I think are the essential conclusions on this subject:

> Of course, what these observations signaled wasn't that cycles wouldn't repeat, but rather that the onlookers had grown too confident. Cycles in economies, companies and markets will continue to occur at least as long as people are involved in making the key decisions — which I believe means forever.
>
> … There is a right time to argue that things will be better, and that's when the market is on its backside and everyone else is selling things at giveaway prices. It's dangerous when the market's at record levels to reach for a positive rationalization that has never held true in the past. But it's been done before, and it'll be done again.

"It's different this time" are four of the most dangerous words in the business world — especially when applied, as is often the case, to something that has reached what in prior times would have been called an extreme.

When people say "it's different" in this case, what they often mean is that the rules and processes that produced cycles in the past have been suspended. But the cyclical behavior of the financial past did not result from the operation of physical or scientific rules. In science, cause and effect enjoy a dependable and repeatable relationship, so that it's possible to say with confidence, "if a, then b." But while there are some principles that operate in the world of finance and business, the resulting truth is very different from that in science.

The reason for this — as I've harped on repeatedly — is the involvement of people. People's decisions have great influence on economic, business and market cycles. In fact, economies, business and markets consist of nothing but transactions between people. And people don't make their decisions scientifically.

Some take history, facts and data into account, and some approach their decisions as "economic men." But even the most unemotional and stoic among them are subject to human influences and the loss of objectivity.

Richard Feynman, the noted physicist, wrote, "Imagine how much harder physics would be if electrons had feelings!" That is, if electrons had feelings, they couldn't be counted on to always do what science expects of them, so the rules of physics would work only some of the time.

The point is that people *do* have feelings, and as such they aren't bound by inviolable laws. They'll always bring emotions and foibles to their economic and investing decisions. As a result, they'll become euphoric at the wrong time and despondent at the wrong time — exaggerating the upside potential when things are going well and the downside

risk when things are going poorly — and thus they'll take trends to cyclical extremes.

A few paragraphs from *The Most Important Thing* provide a good foundation for a recap of the main points regarding cycles' persistence:

> The basic reason for the cyclicality in our world is the involvement
> of humans. Mechanical things can go in a straight line. Time moves
> ahead continuously. So can a machine when it's adequately powered.
> But processes in fields like history and economics involve people, and
> when people are involved, the results are variable and cyclical. The
> main reason for this, I think, is that people are emotional and incon-
> sistent, not steady and clinical.
>
> Objective factors do play a part in cycles, of course — factors such
> a quantitative relationships, world events, environmental changes,
> technological developments and corporate decisions. But it's the ap-
> plication of psychology to these things that causes investors to over-
> react or underreact, and thus determines the amplitude of the cyclical
> fluctuations.
>
> When people feel good about the way things are going and op-
> timistic about the future, their behavior is strongly impacted. They
> spend more and save less. They borrow to increase their enjoyment
> or their profit potential, even though doing so makes their financial
> position more precarious (of course, concepts like precariousness are
> forgotten in optimistic times). And they become willing to pay more
> for current value or a piece of the future.

Investors tend to look at the processes that are afoot, attribute mechanical dependability to them, rely on that dependability, and extrapolate the
processes. What they overlook is the role of emotions: greed on the upswing and fear on the downswing.

Emotions operate on cycles two ways: they magnify the forces that lead
to extremes that eventually require correction, and they cause market par-

ticipants to overlook the cyclicality of cyclical things at just those moments when recognition of excesses is most essential and most potentially profitable: stage three of the bull and bear markets described on pages 191–192 and 193–194.

The following passage from *The Most Important Thing* may serve to wrap up regarding the outlook for cycles' recurrence:

> Cycles will never stop occurring. If there were such a thing as a completely efficient market, and if people really made decisions in a calculating and unemotional manner, perhaps cycles (or at least their extremes) would be banished. But that'll never be the case.
>
> Economies will wax and wane as consumers spend more or less, responding emotionally to economic factors or exogenous events, geopolitical or naturally occurring. Companies will anticipate a rosy future during the up cycle and thus over-expand facilities and inventories; these will become burdensome when the economy turns down. Providers of capital will be too generous when the economy's doing well, abetting over-expansion with cheap money, and then they'll pull the reins too tight when things cease to look as good. Investors will overvalue companies when they're doing well and undervalue them when things get difficult. . . .
>
> Ignoring cycles and extrapolating trends is one of the most dangerous things an investor can do. People often act as if companies that are doing well will do well forever, and investments that are outperforming will outperform forever, and vice versa. Instead, it's the opposite that is more likely to be true.

A deep understanding of emotions and the overdoing they lead to is one of key bottom lines of this book. Cyclical deviations from the trendline are produced largely by overdoing and its eventual correction. This is obviously true in the securities markets, which are nothing but a collection of people making decisions (often in a herd-like manner) that they hope will prove profitable. But it is no less true of economies and companies; they may seem like independent, well-oiled machines, but they, too, are nothing but groups of people making decisions, with all that implies.

> The first time rookie investors see this phenomenon occur, it's understandable that they might accept that something that has never happened before — the cessation of cycles — could happen. But the second time or the third time, those investors, now experienced, should realize it's never going to happen, and turn that realization to their advantage.
>
> The next time you're approached with a deal predicated on cycles having ceased to occur, remember that invariably it's a losing bet. (*The Most Important Thing*)

I was 22 years old and a newcomer to investing in 1968, the time of my initial exposure to the Nifty Fifty. People far more experienced than I was held forth regarding the companies' greatness, their boundless potential for growth, the fact that nothing bad could ever happen to them, and thus the absence of any limits on their stock prices. I swallowed those stories; at any rate I don't remember pushing back on the illogicality of their extremeness. Thus I was lucky to learn my first lessons regarding cyclicality, value and risk at an early age and with relatively little bet on the erroneous concepts.

I was a little less naive when I organized Citibank's response to the Arab oil embargo of 1973, when the price of oil went from $20 a barrel to $60 and energy analysts saw few impediments to continued increases. And when the wonders of computers led to the formation of far more disc-drive companies in the 1980s than would turn out to be needed.

But later, with a few decades of experience under my belt, I was able to recognize the excesses of the tech/Internet/e-commerce bubble of the late 1990s, and of the unquestioning capital market behavior that ultimately led to the Global Financial Crisis of 2007–08. This learning process regarding excesses in the markets — and their contribution to cycles — is an indispensable part of every investor's education.

∾

The tendency of people to go to excess will never end. And thus, since those excesses eventually have to correct, neither will the occurrence of cycles. Economies and markets have never moved in a straight line in the past, and neither will they do so in the future. And that means investors with the ability to understand cycles will find opportunities for profit.

XVIII

THE ESSENCE OF CYCLES

I'm going to conclude by pulling together some of the book's paragraphs that I think hold the keys to understanding cycles, their genesis, and how they should be dealt with. I'll alter them only as necessary to allow them to stand alone here, out of context. This won't be a summary of the book, but rather a recap of some of its key observations. (And for those who wish, reading just the bolded sentences will provide a good synopsis of the recap.)

H.M.

Investment success is like the choosing of a lottery winner. Both are determined by one ticket (the outcome) being pulled from a bowlful of tickets (the full range of possible outcomes). In each case, one outcome is chosen from among the many possibilities.

Superior investors are people who have a better sense for what tickets are in the bowl, and thus for whether it's worth participating in the lottery. In other words, while superior investors — like everyone else — don't know exactly what the future holds, they do have an above-average understanding of future tendencies. (page 14)

~

The odds change as our position in the cycles changes. If we don't change our investment stance as these things change, we're being passive regarding cycles; in other words, we're ignoring the chance to tilt the odds in our favor. But if we apply some insight regarding cycles, we can increase our bets and place them on more aggressive investments when the odds are in our favor, and we can take money off the table and increase our defensiveness when the odds are against us. (page 21)

~

In my view, the greatest way to optimize the positioning of a portfolio at a given point in time is through deciding what balance it should strike between aggressiveness and defensiveness. And I believe the aggressiveness/ defensiveness balance should be adjusted over time in response to changes in the state of the investment environment and where a number of elements stand in their cycles.

The key word is "calibrate." The amount you have invested, your allocation of capital among the various possibilities, and the riskiness of the things you own all should be calibrated along a continuum that runs from aggressive to defensive. When we're getting value cheap, we should be aggressive; when we're getting value expensive, we should pull back. Calibrating one's portfolio position is what this book is mostly about. (page 12)

~

In the world investors inhabit, cycles rise and fall, and pendulums swing back and forth. Cycles and pendulum swings come in many forms and relate to a wide variety of phenomena, but the underlying reasons for them —and the patterns they produce—have a lot in common, and they tend to be somewhat consistent over time. Or as Mark Twain is reputed to have said (although there's no evidence he actually said it), "History doesn't repeat itself, but it does rhyme."

Whether Twain said it or not, that sentence sums up a lot of what this book is about. Cycles vary in terms of reasons and details, and timing and extent, but the ups and downs (and the reasons for them) will occur forever, producing changes in the investment environment — and thus in the behavior that's called for.

The fact is that the performance of these things is heavily influenced in the short run by, among other things, the involvement of people, and people are far from steady. Rather they fluctuate from time to time, often because of things we can lump under the broad heading of "psychology." Thus people's behavior varies . . . certainly as the environment varies, but sometimes in the absence of changes in the environment, too. (pages 24–25)

∿

The cycle oscillates around the midpoint. The midpoint of a cycle is generally thought of as the secular trend, norm, mean, average or "happy medium," and generally as being in some sense as "right and proper." The extremes of the cycle, on the other hand, are thought of as aberrations or excesses to be returned from, and generally they are. While the thing that's cycling tends to spend much of the time above or below it, eventual movement back in the direction of the midpoint is usually the rule. The movement from either a high or a low extreme back toward the midpoint is often described as "regression toward the mean," a powerful and very reasonable tendency in most walks of life. But it can also be seen that the cyclical pattern generally consists as much of movement from the reasonable midpoint toward a potentially imprudent extreme as it does going from an extreme back toward the midpoint.

The rational midpoint generally exerts a kind of magnetic pull, bringing the thing that's cycling back from an extreme in the direction of "normal." But it usually doesn't stay at normal for long, as the influences responsible for the swing toward the midpoint invariably continue in force and thus cause the swing back from an extreme to proceed through the midpoint and then carry further, toward the opposite extreme.

It's important to recognize and accept the dependability of this pattern. The details vary, but the underlying dynamics are usually similar. (pages 27–28)

∿

The themes that provide warning signals in every boom/bust are the general ones: that excessive optimism is a dangerous thing; that risk aversion is an essential ingredient for the market to be safe; and that overly generous capital markets ultimately lead to unwise financing, and thus to danger for participants. In short, the details are unimportant and can be irrelevant. But the themes are essential, and they absolutely do tend to recur. Understanding that tendency — and being able to spot the recurrences — is one of the most important elements in dealing with cycles. (page 36)

∿

Cycles have more potential to wreak havoc the further they progress from the midpoint — i.e., the greater the aberrations or excesses. If the swing toward one extreme goes further, the swing back is likely to be more violent, and more damage is likely to be done, as actions encouraged by the cycle's operation at an extreme prove unsuitable for life elsewhere in the cycle.

In other words, the potential for havoc increases as the movement away from the midpoint increases: as economies and companies do "too well" and stock prices go "too high." Advances are followed by mere corrections, and bull markets by bear markets. But booms and bubbles are followed by much more harmful busts, crashes and panics. (pages 28–29)

≈

Most people think of cycles as series of events that follow each other in a usual sequence: upswings are followed by downswings, and then eventually by new upswings. But to have a full understanding of cycles, that's not enough. The events in the life of a cycle shouldn't be viewed merely as each being followed by the next, but—much more importantly—as each *causing* the next. (page 30)

≈

The things I call cycles do not stem completely—or sometimes at all—from the operation of mechanical, scientific or physical processes. They would be much more dependable and predictable if they did—but much less potentially profitable. (This is because the greatest profits come from seeing things better than others do, and if cycles were totally dependable and predictable, there would be no such thing as superiority in seeing them.) Sometimes there is an underlying principle (and sometimes not), but much variation is attributable to the role of humans in creating cycles. The involvement of humans in this process enables their emotion- and psychology-induced tendencies to influence cyclical phenomena. Chance or randomness also plays a big part in some cycles, and human behavior contributes to their existence, too. Humans are a big part of the reason these cycles exist, but also—along with randomness—for their inconsistency and thus their undependability.

The effort to explain life through the recognition of patterns—and thus to come up with winning formulas—is complicated, in large part, because we live in a world that is beset by randomness and in which people don't behave the same from one instance to the next, even when they intend to. The realization that past events were largely affected by these things — and thus that future events aren't fully predictable — is unpleasant, as it makes life less subject to anticipation, rule-making and rendering safe. Thus people search for explanations that would make events understandable . . . often to an extent beyond that which is appropriate. This is as true in investing as it is in other aspects of life. (pages 41–42)

∿

Why is the pendulum of psychology important? In essence, the too-strong upward and downward swings of the cycles I'm covering in this book largely result from — and represent — psychological excesses in action.

In business, financial and market cycles, most excesses on the upside — and the inevitable reactions to the downside, which also tend to overshoot — are the result of exaggerated swings of the pendulum of psychology. Thus understanding and being alert to excessive swings is an entry-level requirement for avoiding harm from cyclical extremes, and hopefully for profiting from them.

The norms in terms of growth and appreciation are in some sense "right" and "healthy." And if the participants built their behavior around those norms — instead of occasionally building up hopes for more and thus setting the stage for eventual moves toward less — the world would be a steadier, less-tempestuous, and less-error-prone place. But that's not the nature of things. (pages 85–86)

∿

It all seems so obvious: investors rarely maintain objective, rational, neutral and stable positions. First they exhibit high levels of optimism, greed, risk tolerance and credulousness, and their resulting behavior causes asset prices to rise, potential returns to fall, and risk to increase. But then, for some reason — perhaps the arrival of a tipping point — they switch to pessimism, fear, risk aversion and skepticism, and this causes asset prices to fall, prospective returns to rise, and risk to decrease. Notably, each group of phenomena tends to happen in unison, and the swing from one to the other often goes far beyond what reason might call for.

That's one of the crazy things: in the real world, things generally fluctuate between "pretty good" and "not so hot." But in the world of investing, perception often swings from "flawless" to "hopeless." The pendulum careens from one extreme to the other, spending almost no time at "the happy medium" and rather little in the range of reasonableness. First there's denial, and then there's capitulation. (page 96)

∾

At the greatest extremes of the pendulum's swing, a process can take on the appearance of a virtuous circle or a vicious circle. When events are predominantly positive and psychology is rosy, negative developments tend to be overlooked, everything is interpreted favorably, and things are often thought to be incapable of taking a turn for the worse. On the other hand, when things have been going badly for months or years and psychology is highly negative, it's the potential for improvement that can be forgotten.

The superior investor — who resists external influences, remains emotionally balanced and acts rationally — perceives both positive and negative events, weighs events objectively, and analyzes them dispassionately. But the truth is that sometimes euphoria and optimism cause most investors to view things more positively than is warranted, and sometimes depression and pessimism make them see only bad and interpret events with a negative cast. Refusing to do so is one of the keys to successful investing.

Usually, when either set of polar extremes is in the ascendancy, that fact is readily observable, and thus the implications for investors should be obvious to objective observers. But of course, the swing of the market pendulum to one extreme or the other occurs for the simple reason that the psyches of most market participants are moving in the same direction in a herd-like fashion. (pages 98–99)

≈

My view that risk is the main moving piece in investing makes me conclude that at any given point in time, the way investors collectively are viewing risk and behaving with regard to it is of overwhelming importance in shaping the investment environment in which we find ourselves. And the state of the environment is key in determining how we should behave with regard to risk at that point. Assessing where attitudes toward risk stand in their cycle is perhaps the most important topic covered in this book. (page 103)

≈

Good times cause people to become more optimistic, jettison their caution, and settle for skimpy risk premiums on risky investments. Further, since they are less pessimistic and less alarmed, they tend to lose interest in the safer end of the risk/return continuum. This combination of elements makes the prices of risky assets rise relative to safer assets. Thus it shouldn't come as a surprise that more unwise investments are made in good times than in bad. People are more inclined to make risky investments in good times even though the higher prices often mean the prospective risk premiums offered are skimpier than they were in more risk-conscious times. And when negative events occur, the lack of adequate risk premiums and margin for error shows the investments to have been unwise.

It follows from the above that risk is high when investors feel risk is low.

And risk compensation is at a minimum just when risk is at a maximum (meaning risk compensation is most needed). So much for the rational investor!

For me, the bottom line of all of this is that the greatest source of investment risk is the belief that there is no risk. Widespread risk tolerance — or a high degree of investor comfort with risk — is the greatest harbinger of subsequent market declines. But this is rarely perceived at the time when perceiving it — and turning cautious — is most important. (pages 111–113)

∾

Just as the inadequacy of investors' risk aversion allows them to push prices up and buy at the top — egged on by the vision of easy money in a world in which they can't discern any risk — in less positive times they push prices down and sell at the bottom. Their unpleasant experience convinces them — contrary to what they had thought when everything was going well — that investing is a risky field in which they shouldn't engage. And, as a consequence, their risk aversion goes all the way from inadequate to excessive.

They become worrywarts. Just as risk tolerance had positioned them to become buyers of overpriced assets at the highs, now their screaming risk aversion makes them sellers — certainly not buyers — at the bottom. (pages 114–115)

∾

During panics, people spend 100% of their time making sure there can be no losses . . . at just the time that they should be worrying instead about missing out on great opportunities.

In times of extreme negativism, exaggerated risk aversion is likely to cause prices to already be as low as they can go; further losses to be highly unlikely; and thus the risk of loss to be minimal. Thus, the safest time to buy usually comes when everyone is convinced there's no hope. (page 132)

∾

As risk attitudes swing from high to low, so do opportunities for profit or loss. When everything's going well and asset prices are soaring, investors tend to view the future as rosy, risk as their friend, and profit as easily achieved. Everyone feels the same, meaning little risk aversion is incorporated in asset prices, and thus they're precarious. Investors become risk-tolerant just when they should increase their risk aversion.

And when events are down, so are investors. They think of the markets as a place to lose money, risk as something to be avoided at all cost, and losses as depressingly likely. Under the excess of caution that prevails, (a) no one will accept possibilities that incorporate any optimism at all and (b) they likewise cannot countenance the possibility that an assumption could be "too *bad* to be true."

Just as risk tolerance is unlimited at the top, it is non-existent at the bottom. This negativity causes prices to fall to levels from which losses are highly unlikely and gains could be enormous. But the sting of prior declines tends to increase risk aversion and send investors to the sidelines just as prices (and thus risk) are at their lowest. (page 116)

∾

Understanding how investors are thinking about and dealing with risk is perhaps the most important thing to strive for. In short, excessive risk tolerance contributes to the creation of danger, and the swing to excessive risk aversion depresses markets, creating some of the greatest buying opportunities.

The fluctuation — or inconstancy — in attitudes toward risk is both the result of some cycles and the cause or exacerbator of others. And it will always go on, since it seems to be hard-wired into most people's psyches to become more optimistic and risk-tolerant when things are going well, and then more worried and risk-averse when things turn downward. That means they're most willing to buy when they should be most cautious, and most reluctant to buy when they should be most aggressive. Superior investors recognize this and strive to behave as contrarians. (pages 134–135)

≈

Changes in the availability of capital or credit constitute one of the most fundamental influences on economies, companies and markets. Even though the credit cycle is less well-known to the man on the street than most of the other cycles discussed in this book, I consider it to be of paramount importance and profound influence.

When the credit window is open, financing is plentiful and easily obtained, and when it's closed, financing is scarce and hard to get. Finally, it's essential to always bear in mind that the window can go from wide open to slammed shut in just an instant. There's a lot more to fully understanding this cycle — including the reasons for these cyclical movements and their impact — but that's the bottom line. (page 138)

≈

Prosperity brings expanded lending, which leads to unwise lending, which produces large losses, which makes lenders stop lending, which ends prosperity, and on and on. (page 143)

≈

Looking for the cause of a market extreme usually requires rewinding the videotape of the credit cycle a few months or years. Most raging bull markets are abetted by an upsurge in the willingness to provide capital, usually imprudently. Likewise, most collapses are preceded by a wholesale refusal to finance certain companies, industries, or the entire gamut of would-be borrowers. (page 147)

≈

The key to dealing with the credit cycle lies in recognizing that it reaches its apex when things have been going well for a while, news has been good, risk aversion is low, and investors are eager. That makes it easy for borrowers to raise money and causes buyers and investors to compete for the opportunity to provide it. The result is cheap financing, low credit standards, weak deals, and the unwise extension of credit. Borrowers hold the cards when the credit window is wide open — not lenders or investors. The implications of all of this should be obvious: proceed with caution.

The exact opposite becomes true at the other extreme of the credit cycle. Its nadir is reached when developments are unpleasant, risk aversion is heightened, and investors are depressed. Under such circumstances, no one wants to provide capital, the credit market freezes up, and proposed offerings go begging. This puts the cards into the hands of providers of capital rather than borrowers.

Because borrowing is difficult and capital is generally unavailable, those who possess it and are willing to part with it can apply rigorous standards, insist on strong loan structures and protective covenants, and demand high prospective returns. It's things like these that provide the margin of safety required for superior investing. When these boxes can be ticked, investors should swing into an aggressive mode.

Superior investing doesn't come from buying high-quality assets, but from buying when the deal is good, the price is low, the potential return is substantial, and the risk is limited. These conditions are much more the case when the credit markets are in the less-euphoric, more-stringent part of their cycle. The slammed-shut phase of the credit cycle probably does more to make bargains available than any other single factor. (pages 159–160)

≈

The merits of the asset in question matter only so much, and certainly they can't be strong enough to always carry the day. Human emotion inevitably causes the prices of assets — even worthwhile assets — to be transported to levels that are extreme and unsustainable: either vertiginous highs or overly pessimistic lows.

In short, conscientious belief in the inevitability of cycles like I'm urging means that a number of words and phrases must be excluded from the intelligent investor's vocabulary. These include "never," "always," "forever," "can't," "won't," "will" and "has to." (pages 179–180)

≈

About 45 years ago — in the early 1970s — I received one of the greatest gifts I was ever given, when an older and wiser investor introduced me to "the three stages of a bull market":

- the first stage, when only a few unusually perceptive people believe things will get better,
- the second stage, when most investors realize that improvement is actually taking place, and
- the third stage, when everyone concludes things will get better forever.

The arrival of this simple truth opened my eyes to the notion of investors' psychological extremes and the impact of those extremes on market cycles. Like many of the great quotations and adages, it captures disproportionate wisdom in a few simple words. It's all about the changeability of attitudes, the pattern they follow over the course of a cycle, and how they contribute to error.

In the first stage, because the possibility of improvement is invisible to most investors and thus unappreciated, security prices incorporate little or no optimism. Often the first stage occurs after prices have been pounded in a crash, and the same downtrend that decimated prices also has wiped out psychology, turning the members of the crowd against the market and causing them to swear off investing forever.

In the last stage, on the other hand, events have gone well for so long — and have been reflected so powerfully in asset prices, further lifting the mood of the market — that investors extrapolate improvement to infinity and bid up prices to reflect their optimism. Trees generally don't grow to the sky, but in this stage investors act as if they will . . . and pay up for the limitless potential they perceive. Few things are as costly as paying for potential that turns out to have been overrated.

It follows from the above that someone who invests in the first stage — when almost no one can see a reason for optimism — buys assets at bargain prices from which substantial appreciation is possible. But someone who buys in the third stage invariably pays a high price for the market's excessive enthusiasm and loses money as a result. (pages 191–193)

∾

The most important thing to note is that maximum psychology, maximum availability of credit, maximum price, minimum potential return and maximum risk all are reached at the same time, and usually these extremes co-incide with the last paroxysm of buying. (page 201)

~

In the reverse of the "top" that results from the upswing of the market cy-cle, we see that the nadir of psychology, a total inability to access credit, minimum price, maximum potential return and minimum risk all coincide at the bottom, when the last optimist throws in the towel. (page 203)

Since the generalizations at the lows of the financial crisis of 2007–08 were on the downside, the error-making machine went into reverse. No greed, only fear. No optimism, only pessimism. No risk tolerance, only risk aversion. No ability to see positives, only negatives. No willingness to in-terpret things positively, only negatively. No ability to imagine good out-comes, only bad. (page 233)

~

What is a bottom? It's the point when the lowest prices of the cycle are reached. Thus a bottom can be viewed as the day the last panicked holder sells, or the last day on which sellers predominate relative to buyers. From the bottom, prices rise, since there are no holders left to capitulate and sell, or because the buyers now want to buy more strongly than the sellers want to sell.

When a market is cascading downward, investors can often be heard to say, "We're not going to try to catch a falling knife." In other words, "The trend is downward and there's no way to know when it'll stop, so why should we buy before we're sure the bottom has been reached?" What I think they're really saying is, "We're scared — in particular of buying before the decline has stopped, and thus of looking bad — so we're going to wait until the bottom has been reached, the dust has settled, and the uncertainty has been resolved." But hopefully by now I've made it abundantly clear that when the dust has settled and investors' nerves have steadied, the bargains will be gone.

It's usually during market slides that you can buy the largest quantities of the thing you want, from sellers who are throwing in the towel and while the non-knife-catchers are hugging the sidelines. Once the slide has culminated in a bottom, by definition there are few sellers left to sell, and during the ensuing rally it's buyers who predominate. Thus the selling dries up and would-be buyers face growing competition. (pages 235–237)

∿

Exiting the market after a decline — and thus failing to participate in a cyclical rebound — is truly the cardinal sin in investing. Experiencing a mark-to-market loss in the downward phase of a cycle isn't fatal in and of itself, as long as you hold through the beneficial upward part as well. It's converting that downward fluctuation into a permanent loss by selling out at the bottom that's really terrible.

Thus understanding cycles and having the emotional and financial wherewithal needed to live through them is an essential ingredient in investment success. (pages 238–239)

∿

If the market were a disciplined calculator of value based exclusively on company fundamentals, the price of a security wouldn't fluctuate much more than the issuer's current earnings and the outlook for earnings in the future. In fact, the price generally should fluctuate less than earnings, since quarter-to-quarter changes in earnings often even out in the long run and, besides, don't necessarily reflect actual changes in the company's long-term potential.

And yet security prices generally fluctuate much more than earnings. The reasons, of course, are largely psychological, emotional and non-fundamental. Thus price changes exaggerate and overstate fundamental changes. (page 186)

The truth is that financial facts and figures are only a starting point for market behavior; investor rationality is the exception, not the rule; and the market spends little of its time calmly weighing financial data and setting prices free of emotionality. (page 189)

∾

The investor's goal is to position capital so as to benefit from future developments. He wants to have more invested when the market rises than when it falls, and to own more of the things that rise more or fall less, and less of the others. The objective is clear. The question is how to accomplish this.

In the absence of the ability to see the future, how can we position our portfolios for what lies ahead? I think much of the answer lies in understanding where the market stands in its cycle and what that implies for its future movements. As I wrote in *The Most Important Thing*, "we may never know where we're going, but we'd better have a good idea where we are." (pages 207–208)

∾

What's the key in all of this? To know where the pendulum of psychology and the cycle in valuation stand in their swings. To refuse to buy — and perhaps to sell — when too-positive psychology and the willingness to assign too-high valuations cause prices to soar to peak levels. And to buy when downcast psychology and the desertion of valuation standards on the downside cause panicky investors to create bargains by selling despite the low prices that prevail. As Sir John Templeton put it, "To buy when others are despondently selling and sell when others are greedily buying requires the greatest fortitude and pays the greatest reward." (pages 209–210)

∾

The essential ingredient here is *inference*, one of my favorite words. Everyone sees what happens each day, as reported in the media. But how many people make an effort to understand what those everyday events say about the psyches of market participants, the investment climate, and thus what should be done in response?

Simply put, we must strive to understand the implications of what's going on around us. When others are recklessly confident and buying aggressively, we should be highly cautious; when others are frightened into inaction or panicked selling, we should become aggressive.

Psychological and emotional elements have their primary impact by convincing investors that past valuation standards have become irrelevant and can be departed from. When investors are flying high and making money, they find it easy to come up with convenient reasons why assets should be untethered from the constraints of valuation norms. The explanation usually begins with, "it's different this time." Watch out for this ominous sign of the willing suspension of disbelief. Likewise, when asset prices collapse in a crash, it's usually because of an assumption that none of the things that supported value in the past can be trusted to work in the future. (pages 214–215)

∾

"It's different this time" are four of the most dangerous words in the business world—especially when applied, as is often the case, to something that has reached what in prior times would have been called an extreme.

When people say "it's different" in this case, what they mean is that the rules and processes that produced cycles in the past have been suspended. But the cyclical behavior of the financial past did not result from the operation of physical or scientific rules. In science, cause and effect enjoy a dependable and repeatable relationship, so that it's possible to say with confidence, "if a, then b." But while there are some principles that operate in the world of finance and business, the resulting truth is very different from that in science.

The reason for this — as I've harped on repeatedly — is the involvement of people. People's decisions have great influence on economic, business and market cycles. In fact, economies, business and markets consist of nothing but transactions between people. And people don't make their decisions scientifically.

People have feelings, and as such they aren't bound by inviolable laws. They'll always bring emotions and foibles to their economic and investing decisions. As a result, they'll become euphoric at the wrong time and despondent at the wrong time — exaggerating the upside potential when things are going well and the downside risk when things are going poorly — and thus they'll take trends to cyclical extremes. (pages 288–290)

∽

Cycle positioning is the process of deciding on the risk posture of your portfolio in response to your judgments regarding the principal cycles, and asset selection is the process of deciding which markets, market niches and specific securities or assets to overweight and underweight. These are the two main tools in portfolio management. It may be an over-simplification, but I think everything investors do falls under one or the other of these headings. (page 248)

∽

Cycle positioning primarily consists of choosing between aggressiveness and defensiveness: increasing and decreasing exposure to market movements.

The recipe for success here consists of (a) thoughtful analysis of where the market stands in its cycle, (b) a resulting increase in aggressiveness or defensiveness, and (c) being proved right. These things can be summed up as "skill" or "alpha" at cycle positioning. Of course, "c"—being proved right—isn't a matter fully within anyone's control, in particular because of the degree to which it is subject to randomness. So being proved right won't happen every time, even to skillful investors who reason things out well. (page 252)

∽

When the market is low in its cycle, gains are more likely than usual, and losses are less likely. The reverse is true when the market is high in its cycle. Positioning moves, based on where you believe the market stands in its cycle, amount to trying to better prepare your portfolio for the events that lie ahead. While you can always be unlucky regarding the relationship between what logically should happen and what actually does happen, good positioning decisions can increase the chance that the market's tendency—and thus the chance for outperformance—will be on your side. (pages 254–255)

∽

In my opinion it's entirely reasonable to try to improve long-term investment results by altering positions on the basis of an understanding of the market cycle. But it's essential that you also understand the limitations, as well as the skills that are required and how difficult it is.

Importantly, I want to call attention to the obvious fact that — rather than the everyday ups and downs of the market — the clear examples provided in this book all concern "once-in-a-lifetime" cyclical extremes (which these days seem to happen about once a decade). First, the extremes of bubble and crash — and, in particular, the process through which they arise — most clearly illustrate the cycle in action and how to respond to it. And second, it's when dealing with pronounced extremes that we should expect the highest likelihood of success.

Between the extremes of "rich" and "cheap" — when the cycle is in the middle ground of "fair" — the state of the relationship between price and value is, by definition, nowhere as clear-cut as at the extremes. As a result:

- It's hard to make frequent distinctions and hard to do so correctly.
- Thus distinctions in the middle ground aren't as potentially profitable as at the extremes, and those distinctions can't be expected to work out as dependably.

Detecting and exploiting the extremes is really the best we can hope for. And I believe it can be done dependably — if you're analytical, insightful, experienced (or well-versed in history) and unemotional. That means, however, that you shouldn't expect to reach profitable conclusions daily, monthly or even yearly.

The reasonableness of the effort at cycle timing depends simply on what you expect of it. If you frequently try to discern where we are in the cycle in the sense of "what's going to happen tomorrow?" or "what's in store for us next month?" you're unlikely to find success. I describe such an effort as "trying to be cute." No one can make fine distinctions like those often enough or consistently right enough to add materially to investment results. And no one knows when the market developments that efforts at cycle positioning label "probable" will materialize.

As Peter Bernstein said, "The future is not ours to know. But it helps to know that being wrong is inevitable and normal, not some terrible tragedy, not some awful failing in reasoning, not even bad luck in most instances. Being wrong comes with the franchise of an activity whose outcome depends on an unknown future . . ." (pages 265–269)

~

The tendency of people to go to excess will never end. And thus, since those excesses eventually have to correct, neither will the occurrence of cycles. Economies and markets have never moved in a straight line in the past, and neither will they do so in the future. And that means investors with the ability to understand cycles will find opportunities for profit. (page 293)

INDEX

References in italics refer to figures.

Abbey Mortgage Bank,
  122–24
Alchian, Armen, 43
Altman, Roger, 5

Bank of Ireland, 122, 124
Bernanke, Ben, 239
Bernstein, Peter, 5, 13, 268–69,
  315
bond defaults, two-year rule,
  44–45
Brooks, Jon, 97
bubbles and crashes
  extremes, 265, 297–98,
    314
  Internet bubble, 217–22
  patterns, 240, 263
  South Sea Bubble, 195–96
  tech bubble, 146, 196, 198–99,
    231, 264–65, 292–93
  See also Global Financial Crisis of
    2007–08; sub-prime mortgage
    crisis of 2007
Buffett, Warren, 5, 10, 50, 125–26,
  193, 211

bull and bear markets, 29, 99, 147
  bear market stages, 193–96, 201–3,
    219
  "bubble" and "crash," 196–99
  bull market stages, 191–93,
    200–201, 306–7
  great bull market of 1982, 278
Bush, George W., 151
Business Week, 49

"Can We Measure Risk with a Number?"
  (Bernstein), 13
capital market
  closed, 139–40, 157–58
  conditions, 36, 145–46
  definition of, 137
  effect of close off of credit, 139–40,
    154, 304
capitulation, 34, 194–95, 201, 236, 264,
  300, 308
cartoons, *95, 96*
central banks
  employment stimulation, 70
  forecasting economic cycles,
    70–71

central banks (*cont.*)
  inflation management, 68–70
  See also Federal Reserve Bank
Combs, Todd, 5
credit cycle, 167
  auction for lowest yield, 143–44
  boom bust, 145–48, 159
  credit window, 138, 141–42,
    144–45
  definition of, 137
  excess or easy money, 147–52
  influence of, 138–40
  short-term debt, 139–40
  workings of, 141–42, 147, 157–60,
    304–6
  See also capital market; Global
    Financial Crisis of 2007–08;
    sub-prime mortgage crisis of
    2007
credit default swaps. *See* Global Financial
  Crisis of 2007–08
Crutchley, John- Paul, 124
cycles, 3
  causation and progression, 30–32,
    283, 297–98
  cessation of, 178, 180, 285–88,
    290
  cycle of success, 270–71
  definitions of, 40–41
  elements of, 18–19, 25–27,
    208–10
  excess and corrections, 29, 85–86,
    293, 299, 307–9
  interaction of, 32–33, 167, 186–89,
    199–201
  listening to, 3–5, 309
  major cycles, 267

  midpoint and aberrations, 24–29,
    266, 296–97
  regularity and irregularity, 40–42,
    172, 217, 244–45
  timing and extent, 24, 39, 145, 282,
    295–96
  understanding, 17, *22–24, 118*,
    239, 314–15
  See also credit cycle

"Death of Equities, The," 49, 277–78
Demosthenes, 222, 227, 284
Dimson, Elroy, 13–14, 239
distressed debt investments,
    161–62
  credit crunch and, 164–66
  role of high yield bonds, 163–64
  understanding opportunities, 163,
    166–67, 241–42, 282
Dow 36,000 (Glassman & Hassett),
    219
Dowd, Timothy, 255
Drexel Burnham, 165
Drunkard's Walk, The (Mlodinow),
    42

economic cycles, 46–47, 64–66, 167
  long and short term, 29–30
  repetition and fluctuation, *24–25*,
    97, 135
  short-term, 47, 58, 61
economic forecasts, 61–63, 208
Economics and Portfolio Strategy, 13
Economist, The, 141
Eichholtz, Piet, 182
Einstein, Albert, 36
Ellis, Charlie, 5

emotion/psychology, 3, 31, 34, 37,
    167
    "bubble" and "crash," 196–98
    contrarianism, 133, 135, 142, 234,
        244, 301–4
    credulousness and skepticism,
        90–91, 133, 227
    definition of insanity, 36
    effect on economic cycles, 83–86,
        97–99, 211, 228, 289–92,
        298–299
    emotionalism or objectivity,
        95–96
    euphoria and depression, 89, 94,
        99, 125, 211, 222, 305,
        312
    extremes, 113–16, 265
    fear, effect on consumption, 59
    fear and/or greed, 87–89, 92–93,
        114, 221–22, 233–35,
        303
    humility and confidence,
        271–73
    investment psychology, 40–42,
        93–94, 186–88, 190–91,
        214–15, 244
    optimism and pessimism, 89–90,
        133, 299–301, 302–3
    "silver bullet," 227

falling knives, 8, 156, 202, 235–36
Federal Reserve Bank, 68, 119, 180,
    231
Feynman, Richard, 289
Financial Times, 122, 124
Frank, Barney, 151
Friedman, Milton, 62

fundamentals, 185–87, 189, 209
    valuation metrics, 211
future prediction
    macro prediction, 10
    opinions and likelihood, 15, 102,
        208, 263–65
    qualitative awareness, 214–15
    South Sea Bubble, 195–96

Galbraith, John Kenneth, 5, 34, 63, 125,
    178–79, 222
Geithner, Timothy, 155, 239, 287
Glass-Steagall Act, 120, 128
Global Financial Crisis of 2007–08, 36,
    59, 119–22, 127–32, 147–57, 180,
    233
    bear market stages, 193–94
    effect on real estate market, 177
    lessons from, 239–40
    Treasury guarantee of commercial
        paper, 139–40, 155,
        233
Goldman, William, 43
Goldman Sachs, 155
government
    deficits and national debt,
        71–73
    economic management tools,
        71–73
Graduate School of Business, University
    of Chicago, 103
Graham, Ben, 189
Greenblatt, Joel, 5
Greenspan, Alan, 217
gross domestic product (GDP)
    consumption, 59–60
    definition of, 47

gross domestic product (GDP) (*cont.*)
    recession (negative growth), 48
    See also productivity

high yield bonds, 44, 106, 108, 131–32,
    157, 281–82
history and memory, 34, 42, 178
    Arab oil embargo, 292
    blue chips or small-capitalization,
      274
    brevity of, 222
    convertible arbitrage, 275
    growth and tech stocks, 274
    mortgage defaults, 229
    one house in Amsterdam,
      181–82
    permanent prosperity, 288–89
    poor performance of stocks,
      276–77
    projections of the future, 286–87,
      311–12
History of the Peloponnesian War
    (Thucydides), 37–38
Hoover, Herbert, 287

intrinsic value, 11, 92, 133, 194, 200,
    205
    when to buy, 237
investing
    aggressive or defensive, 248,
      250–53, *259–60*, 295
    asset selection, 248, 255–59
    bargains or popularity, 273–78
    capitulation, *34–35*, 194–95
    cycle positioning, 248, *250*, 252,
      254–55, 312–14

definition of, 101–2, 262
fluctuation in, 186–87
growth stocks, 197–98
long or short securities sales,
    8
market cycle, return, *204–6*
overpayment, 144, 169, 179
philosophy, 4–5, 197, 207
security analysis and value
    investing, 11
skill or luck, 249, *253–54*, 258–59,
    272–73
"weighing machine," 189
See also fundamentals;
    psychology
investment indices, 232t, 238t
"it's different this time," 37, 197–99

Jain, Ajit, 5, 276
Janjigian, Jahan, 280
junk bonds. *See* high yield bonds

Karsh, Bruce, 6, 161, 231, 235,
    282
Kass, Doug, 5
Kaufman, Henry, 273
Kaufman, Peter, 5, 271
Keele, Larry, 6
Keynes, John Maynard, 72, 240–41
Klarman, Seth, 5

Lehman Brothers bankruptcy, 59, 129,
    154–55, *233*, 235, 237
listen, definition, 3–4
Lombardi, Vince, 1
long term trends, *48–51*, 63–64

Long-Term Capital Management, 117,
    146

market assessment
    guide to, 212–14
    qualitative awareness, 216
    valuation, 215, 220
market bottoms
    definition of, 235–37
    identifying, 242, 308–9
market efficiency, 110
Marks, Howard — memos
    "bubble.com," 220
    "Ditto," 171
    "Everyone Knows," 100
    "First Quarter Performance,"
        83
    "Genius Isn't Enough," 146
    "Happy Medium, The," 86–87,
        90–91, 116–17, 147
    "It Is What It Is," 212
    "It's All Good," 84
    "Limits to Negativism, The,"
        128–29, 133, 233–34
    "Long View, The," 29–30, 48
    Most Important Thing, The, 1–2, 5,
        7, 23, 39, 134, 208, 212–14,
        290–92
    "Now It's All Bad?" 26, 225
    "On the Couch," 92–95, 267–68
    "Open and Shut," 137, 155, 157,
        159
    "Race to the Bottom, The," 122,
        143, 145
    "Risk and Return Today," 107
    "Risk Revisited Again," 13

"Tide Goes Out, The," 193
"Will It Be Different This Time?"
    285–86, 288
"You Can't Predict. You Can
    Prepare." 33–34, 138, 141–42,
    147
Masson, Richard, 6
Milken, Michael, 5, 165, 281–82
Misbehaving (Thaler), 93
Mlodinow, Leonard, 42–43
Morgan Stanley, 155
mortgage lending, 122–24, 127–28,
    174–75
    government role, 179
    See also Global Financial Crisis of
        2007–08
Munger, Charlie, 4, 5, 222, 284

New York Times Magazine, 180
Newberg, Bruce, 5
Nifty Fifty, 197–99, 279, 292
"no price too high," 198–99, 215,
    288

Oaktree Capital Management, 2, 6,
    267
    colleagues, 45, 126, 177, 190
    distressed debt investments,
        161
    Global Financial Crisis of 2007–08,
        230, 235–36, 244
    levered funds, 129–32
Oaktree Conference (2012), 175
oscillation and secular trends, 24–25,
    27–29, 31
    cycle symmetry, 35–36, 45

oscillation and secular trends (*cont.*)
    secular stagnation, 57

Paulson, Hank, 239
pendulums
    definition of, 24, 83
    positive and negative elements,
        83–84
    stock market average, 85–86
    See also bull and bear markets;
        cycles
Phipps, Henry, 283
population
    birth rate, 52–54, 59
    demographic movement, 54
    unemployment rate, 54
portfolio
    balancing aggressiveness and defen-
        siveness, 12
    twin risks, 242–43
Prince, Charles, 121
probability distributions, 14–15, *19–21*
productivity, effects on
    aspiration, 54–55
    education, 55
    globalization, 56
    population, 51–52, 57–58
    productive process changes, 53,
        55–58
productivity, post-World War II,
    56–57
profits and sales
    cycles of, 74–77, 137–38
    determining profit, 79–80
    disruption by technology, 80–81
    leverage, financial, 78–79
    leverage, operating, 77–78

    See also companies
pronouns, he or she, 7
psychology. *See* emotion/psychology

randomness, 14, 41–44
real estate cycle
    cessation of, 178
    characteristics of, 169–70
    generalizations, 178–83
    history of one old house,
        181–82
    influences on, 175–76
    Los Angeles, 173–74
    psychology, 170, 177
    special factors, 183–84
    time lags in, 170–74
Rise and Fall of Nations, The
    (Sharma), 283
risk
    attitudes toward, 110–11,
        116–17, 118–19, 134–35,
        167
    aversion, 36, 105–7, 114–15, 119,
        126–32
    capital market line, *108–9,*
        112
    definition of, 13, *102–3*
    lottery comparison, 14
    return and, *104–9,* 112–13
    tolerance, 120–22, 125–26
    See also probability distributions
risk and return, 107–8, 117
Rothschild, Jacob, 5

Schafer, Oscar, 5
Sharma, Ruchir, 283
Shiller, Robert, 182

Short History of Financial Euphoria, A
    (Galbraith) 34, 125
Shourie, Raj, 175
Siegel, Jeremy, 217
Soros, George, 229–30
Stone, Sheldon, 6, 35, 282
Stress Test (Geithner), 155, 287
sub-prime mortgage crisis of 2007, 36,
    59, 149–50, 152, 176, 180, 223–28,
    230–32
superior investors, 14–18, 92, 94, 99,
    107
    asymmetry, 250, *257–58*, 260–61,
        300, 309–10
    bargain conditions, 160, 305–6
    dealing with risk, 102
    outcomes, 255
    second-level thinking, 257–58
    skepticism, 235
    understanding tendencies, 255, 294,
        309
Swensen, David, 271

Taleb, Nassim Nicholas, 5
Tavris, Carol, 93
Templeton, John, 210, 310
tendencies, 12
    insight and odds, 15–17, 21
Thaler, Richard, 93
theory of reflexivity, 229–30
"This Very, Very Old House,"
    180–82
Thucydides, 37–38
Tisch, Jim, 5
Train, Nick, 39
Twain, Mark, 24, 35, 45, 296

Wall Street Journal, 93, 177, 220
wealth effect, 60
Wharton School, University of Pennsyl-
    vania, 103
"What the wise man does in the begin-
    ning…," 193

Xerox, 278–81